PUNJAB AND THE RAJ
1849–1947

Punjab and the Raj
1849–1947

IAN TALBOT

MANOHAR
2026

First published 1988
Reprinted 2020, 2021, 2022, 2023, 2024, 2025, 2026

ISBN 978-81-85054-45-2

Published by
Ajay Kumar Jain *for*
Manohar Publishers & Distributors
4753/23 Ansari Road, Daryaganj
New Delhi 110 002

Printed at
Replika Press Pvt. Ltd.

Contents

Preface

Modern research on South Asian history has centred on particular regions and localities rather than on India in its entirety. New insights have, however, emerged into the mechanism of imperial control, the roots of Muslim separatism and the development of the Indian National Congress. And yet, this recent historical trend has bypassed the region of the Punjab.

Little has been written about how the British maintained control of this strategic area which, from the 1880s onwards, formed the major recruiting centre of the Indian Army. The Punjab Unionist Party has been similarly ignored by historians in spite of the fact that it not only dominated politics in the region from the 1920s until the eve of the British departure, but also achieved all-India importance under Mian Fazl-i-Husain's leadership. The growth of the Muslim League in this region has also received only cursory examination, although Punjab formed the heartland of a future Pakistan State and its population's support was crucial to the success of the League's demand for Pakistan.

This study examines Punjab's history during British rule. This began in 1849 when the British annexed it from the disintegrating Sikh Kingdom of Ranjit Singh's successors and ended in 1947 when they quit India and partitioned the Punjab between the States of India and Pakistan. Its findings will aim not only to shed light on developments within this important Indian region, but also to illuminate the processes of imperial control and nation formation.

I am deeply indebted to the large number of people who have helped and encouraged me during the eight years of preparation of this study. I would first like to thank the staff of the India Office Library, of the newspaper section of the British Library at Colindale, and of the National Archives of India and Pakistan for their kind assistance. My thanks also go to the staff at the Freedom Movement Archives at Karachi University.

Whilst I was in India and Pakistan, a number of people freely gave me their time and assistance. I am particularly grateful to my language assistant in Pakistan, Agha Atta, who helped me with Urdu translation. I also thank the editors of the *Khyber Mail* and *Nawa-e-Waqt* for allowing me to see their files. My thanks go especially to Khalid Shamsul Hasan for his continuing interest in my work and his permission to consult his father's papers. I would also like to thank Professor Mushirul Hasan of Jamia Millia Islamia, Delhi, for reading through the manuscript and making a number of helpful suggestions.

From America I would like to thank David Gilmartin, Emily Hodges and Kathy Ewing for their interest and encouragement. In particular, I owe a great deal to the support and advice which I have received from David Page and Clive Dewey, in whose footsteps as a scholar of Punjabi history, I have been proud to follow. I also owe Lois my thanks for her forbearance and active support. Finally, I thank Francis Robinson for his unceasing encouragement and advice throughout all the stages of the preparation of this work.

Introduction

It is well known that the support of local elites was of crucial importance to colonial control in Asia and Africa. It enabled the European powers to rule vast areas of land and huge populations with only a handful of soldiers and administrators. The major task of colonial administration, which Ronald Robinson terms the source of its true genius, was to identify and win local allies to its side. It was achieved by the liberal distribution of patronage and the direction of commercial and agrarian policies in favour of those groups in native* society whose support was essential in maintaining order. They willingly accepted the role of collaborators[1] because it enhanced their power and influence amongst the networks of their rural clients.

During the later period of colonial rule, the Europeans' early allies, chiefs and religious leaders, were joined by native civil servants and businessmen loyal to the regime which provided their livelihood. The informal ties which bound them to the colonial administration were gradually institutionalized through the creation of loyalist political associations and eventually, political parties. These usually had little organization and mass support, unlike the nationalist parties which had developed under the leadership of the counter-elite of the western educated class. Even so, most nationalist movements, in their early stages,

*The term 'native' is used strictly as a definition of an indigenous entity.

did not have much influence in the rural hinterland of their homeland. Consequently, they needed to reach out from the cities and towns into the countryside in order to win power. They had to either sweep aside the traditional collaborating groups or wean them away from the imperial regime. Neither was easily accomplished. However, for nationalists in South East and South Asia, the Second World War created the conditions in which such a political realignment became possible.

Many historians have sketched the functioning and collapse of indirect imperial rule in these general terms. This study attempts to examine how this system of collaboration actually worked and what led to its eventual collapse in one area, the Punjab province of British India. The importance of local allies for the maintenance of British rule has been carefully examined in other areas of India,[2] but little has been written about this aspect of imperial control in the Punjab, despite the fact that the region provides an important field for this study because of its immense value to British interests and its reputation for political loyalty.

From the time of the 1857 revolt to the Gandhian satyagrahas of the 1930s, the Punjab remained overwhelmingly loyal when other regions were in open rebellion. The region's stability was crucial not only for strategic reasons but because of the fact that the Indian Army had made its home there from the 1880s. This Punjabi-dominated volunteer force served wide imperial interests, underpinning British rule in India and safeguarding British influence throughout the Middle East and parts of South-East Asia. One of this study's major themes will be to describe how the British secured the support of the Punjab's rural population from which the Indian Army drew the bulk of its recruits.

The growing relationship between the colonial regime and the collaborating groups is traced carefully. It was marked initially by informal political alliances, but from 1923 onwards it was institutionalized in the Unionist Party. For over twenty years this loyalist coalition of Muslim, Hindu and Sikh landowners dominated the region's politics. Yet, so little has been written about the Unionist Party.[3] We still need to know, for example, why it was not shouldered aside by the Muslim League and the Congress in the 1930s as were similar parties elsewhere in India. A greater knowledge of its history will not only clarify our picture of Punjabi politics during the closing years of British rule, but will suggest the circumstances in which systems of collaboration succeeded or failed as an underpinning of colonial rule.

The Muslim League finally defeated the Unionist Party in the 1946 Punjab elections. Its victory was crucial to the cause of Muslim separatism, because the Punjab formed the heartland of a future Pakistan state. Jinnah, indeed, called it the 'cornerstone' of Pakistan. If the Punjabi Muslims had not supported the Muslim League, Pakistan could never have been created. No adequate explanation has yet been given for the League's success in the region following its crushing defeat at the Unionists' hands in the 1937 elections.

Most Pakistani historians still explain the Muslim League's development in the Punjab as elsewhere in India in terms of the two-nation theory. This official Muslim League creed since the early 1940s maintained that the Muslims had always formed a separate nation from the Hindus and had only awaited Jinnah's inspiration and leadership to assert this fact. Indian historians, on the other hand, attribute the growth of Muslim separatism and the eventual creation of Pakistan to the divide and rule policies of the British authorities. Mehta and Patwardhan's work, *The Communal Triangle in India*, written in 1941, remains the classic exposition of this theory.[4] It points, in particular, to the British introduction of separate electorates as an intentional policy to foster inter-communal conflict and so prevent the growth of a spirit of national resistance to their rule.

Serious doubts can be raised about both these theories. Muslim society in Punjab's countryside was organized around tribal and kinship networks rather than religion. Tribal customs and laws were followed rather than those laid down in the *sharia*. Some religious practice was syncretic in character. British officials were anxious to limit communal violence rather than to risk encouraging it by dividing and ruling. Indeed, the last Governors of the Punjab, Sir Bertrand Glancy and Sir Evan Jenkins, were constantly attacked by the Muslim League because they upheld the ideal of a united Punjab.

Other explanations of the Muslim League's growth in the Punjab are equally unconvincing. V. G. Kiernan attributes it to the League's denunciation of the 'Hindu usurers ... who were the enemies of the Muslim peasantry'.[5] The Muslim League never in fact adopted this method of winning support for the good reason that attacks on the moneylenders' influence had been the major plank of Unionist Party policy from the early 1920s. Such an approach united all rural religious communities as they suffered equally at the moneylenders' hands.

Penderel Moon sees the Muslim League's development in the Punjab as being largely fortuitous. 'Jinnah would never have had the opportunity to seize the lead and make Pakistan the goal of all Muslims', he declares, 'had it not been for the accident of fate which removed from the scene in 1936 the great Punjabi Muslim, Sir Fazl-i-Husain at the early age of 59.... If he had lived Jinnah would not have been able and would not even have attempted to win over the allegiance of the Punjab Muslims and Pakistan would have remained an 'impractical student's scheme'. But fate decreed otherwise and by removing Sir Fazl-i-Husain gave Jinnah his chance.[6]

The scholar cannot, however, rest content with so fatalistic an explanation of this important historical process. Moreover, the question needs to be answered as to why the Unionist Party continue to dominate Punjabi politics for a decade after Mian Fazl-i-Husain's death.

The suggestion has been made by Peter Hardy that the Muslim League succeeded in the Punjab by making an appeal over the heads of the professional Unionist politicians.[7] This, however, raises more questions than it solves. For instance, how did the League bypass the traditional holders of power within the region? Even more damagingly, how can this suggestion be reconciled with the fact that many of the League's candidates in the 1946 elections were experienced politicians who had only very recently defected from the Unionist Party? David Gilmartin sees the Muslim League's rise to power primarily in terms of its ability to exploit the factional divisions within the Unionist Party.[8] According to him, they arose from the succession struggle which followed the death of the Unionist Premier, Sikander Hayat Khan, in 1942. This analysis does not make it clear, however, whether disunity was a cause or a symptom of the Unionist Party's decline. In order to answer this question we need to know more than Gilmartin tell us about the impact of the Second World War on Punjabi politics.

Paul Brass explains the growth of Muslim separatism in North India in terms of the existence both of an elite which chose to manipulate separatist symbols in order to secure its own power interests and of a socially mobilized community which responded to the sense of communal identification communicated to it.[9] This argument (whether it works in the United Provinces seems doubtful) fails to explain the Muslim League's success in the very different social and economic conditions of rural Punjab. A far more fruitful approach than attempting to link successful political mobilization in traditional societies with levels of social mobilization is to ask whether modern political parties can effectively utilize 'traditional' social and religious networks in order to win support.

This work sets out to answer at least some of the questions raised by the Muslim League's growth in Punjab during the decade which preceded partition. It attempts to explain how the League reached down to the rural voters who, in 1946, held the key to the creation of Pakistan.

Partition failed to prevent horrific communal massacres occurring in the Punjab region when the British departed from India. During August 1947 whole villages were destroyed, families split up, refugees attacked and robbed of all their possessions and their womenfolk abducted and raped. At the most conservative estimate, 200,000 people died in the violence and five million were made homeless. Considerable controversy still surrounds the explanation for this. Official publications of the Pakistan Government blame the Hindu paramilitary organization, the Rashtriya Swayam Sevak Sangh and the Sikhs who are depicted as planning the massacres in order to drive out the Muslim population of East Punjab so that Sikh refugees could settle there.[10] These accusations have been strongly denied in India, where historians have maintained that the violence was sparked off by the Muslim League National Guards' attacks on the Hindus and Sikhs in West Punjab.[11]

The responsibility of the British, and Lord Mountbatten in particular, has also been hotly debated. Leonard Mosley, for example, has severely criticized Mountbatten's decision to bring forward the transfer of power from June 1948 to the 15th of August 1947. He maintains that it resulted in 'surely avoidable blunders (which) cost hundreds of thousands of lives'.[12] This interpretation has recently received support from the Indian writer Y. Krishan.[13] Whilst they criticize the speed with which Mountbatten acted, Penderel Moon conversely praises it for enabling the country and the armed forces to be successfully divided, 'before they could be engulfed in universal strife'.[14]

This study will attempt to shed fresh light on this tragic period in Punjab's history by utilizing evidence which has only recently been made available to scholars. It will reveal that British efforts to maintain law and order were severely handicapped by the loss of the landowner's assistance following the 1946 elections. It will also examine Punjab's impact on constitutional decisions during Mountbatten's climatic Viceroyalty.

The opening chapter describes the Punjab and its people and the entry of the British into the region. Chapter two reveals the province's growing importance to imperial interests and the need, therefore, which the British had for dependable local allies. They ways in which they won the support of the leading landowning groups are described in chapter three. The fourth chapter is concerned with the connections between British rule and the growth of communalism in Punjab towns. It discusses the threat which this posed to the British system of control and

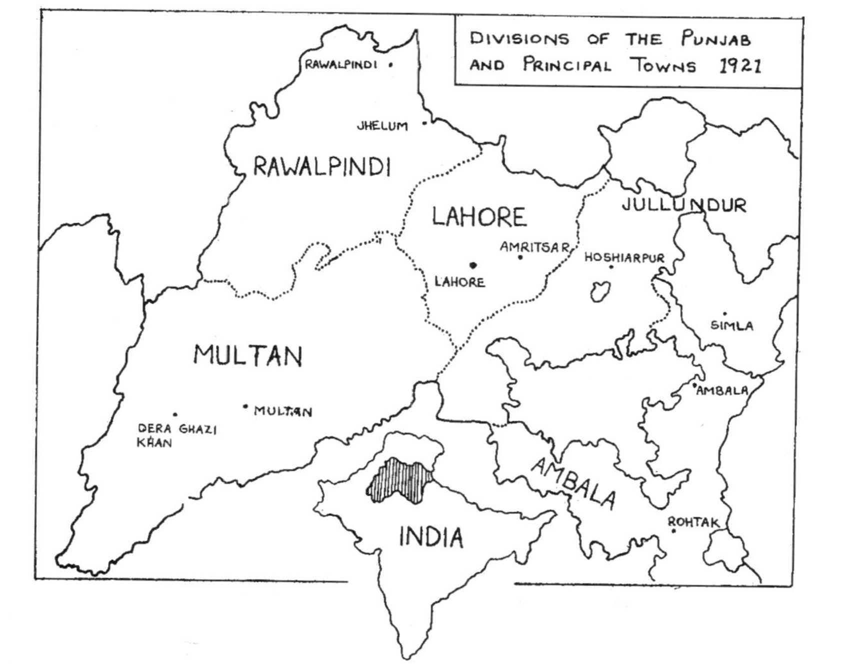

Divisions of the Punjab and Principal Towns 1921

contrasts the urban and rural political traditions which evolved in the region. Chapter five shows how the informal alliances between the colonial administration and the landowners became embodied in the Unionist Party, and reveals why it wielded more political influence than any other party during the years 1919–1937. It concludes with the constitutional and political background to the introduction of Provincial Autonomy within the Punjab. In chapter six the Unionist Party is described at the height of its power and the two succeeding chapters reveal the ways in which the Second World War undermined this. Prominence is especially given to the ways in which the British deserted their allies. The various strategies adopted by the Muslim League to win rural support are also considered in detail. The ninth chapter describes its victory in the 1946 provincial elections which was crucial to the success of its demand for Pakistan. The collapse of the British system of rule in the region and its significance for the timing of the transfer of power is examined in the concluding chapter. The events leading up to the communal holocaust of August 1947 are briefly described.

Notes

1. Historians have used the term 'collaboration' in a non-pejorative sense to describe the relationship between colonial systems of government and their indigenous allies.
2. See eg. F. Robinson, 'Consultation and Control: The United Provinces' Govt. and its allies, 1860–1920', *Modern Asian Studies*, 5, 4 (1971), pp. 313–36; C. Bayly, 'Local Control in Indian Towns: The Case of Allahabad 1880–1920', *ibid*., pp. 289–311.
3. Most of the attention has been directed towards its class composition and reforms. See P. Choudhry, 'Social Basis of Ch. Sir Chhotu Ram's Politics', *The Punjab Past and Present*, Vol. X, Part 1, No. 19 (April 1976).
4. A. Mehta & A. Patwardhan, *The Communal Triangle in India* (Allahabad, 1941).
5. V.G. Kiernan, 'Nationalist Movements and Social Classes' in A.D. Smith (ed.) *Nationalist Movements* (London, 1976), p. 131.
6. P. Moon, 'A Failure of Statesmanship' in T. Wallbank (ed.) *The Partition of India* (Boston, 1966), p. 96.

7. P. Hardy, *The Muslims of British India* (Cambridge, 1972), p. 238.
8. D.P. Gilmartin, 'Tribe, Land and Religion in the Punjab; Muslim Politics and the Making of Pakistan' (Unpublished Ph.D. thesis, Berkeley, 1979), p. 264 & ff.
9. P.R. Brass, *Language, Religion and Politics in North India* (London, 1974), p. 178 & ff. Brass measures social mobilization by rates of literacy and urbanization. In fact, in only 6 of the Punjab's 29 administrative districts did more than a fifth of the Muslims live in towns and in only 2 districts did more than 2 per cent read English. They were thus 'pre-socially mobilised' and according to Brass' theory unavailable for political mobilization.
10. *R.S.S.S. In the Punjab* (Government Printing Press, Lahore, 1948); *Sikhs in Action* (Government Printing Press, Lahore, 1948); *Note on the Sikh Plan* (Government Printing Press, Lahore, 1948).
11. G. Singh Talib, *Muslim League Attacks on Sikhs and Hindus in the Punjab* (Amritsar, 1950).
12. L. Mosley, *The Last Days of the British Raj* (London, 1961), p. 247.
13. Y. Krishan, 'Mountbatten and the Partition of India', *History*, 68, 22 (February 1983).
14. P. Moon, *Divide and Quit* (London, 1961), p. 283.

CHAPTER I

The Punjab and its People

> To us the Punjab loomed grandly as the land of promise; it afforded scope for displaying individuality and perhaps for carving out a considerable career. The very atmosphere of the country nourished a spirit of adventure; the people were known to have in their character the hard grit and high stomach which demand the governing faculty that Englishmen instinctively love to exercise.[1]

From the outset, British rule was more dynamic in the Punjab than elsewhere in India. This resulted both from the province's frontier position and the mature imperial consciousness which the British had developed by the time of its annexation. They came to the Punjab to rule, not trade and were determined to transform Punjabi society in accordance with the dominant early Victorian ideals of utilitarianism and evangelical Christianity.

The British engineered many social and economic changes in the Punjab, the most notable being the development of the Canal Colonies. They also had to adapt their rule to the region's conditions. In particular, they found that they had to base their political control on the support of the leading landowning groups. The new Punjabi society which began to emerge towards the end of the nineteenth century was the result of the interaction between the indigenous population and their British rulers.

This chapter describes Punjabi society and the impact of British rule upon it. It looks in particular at those aspects of the region's geography, economic and social structure which played a part in determining its colonial development.

Geography

Two of Punjab's main geographical features—proximity to the Afghan Frontier and its extensive river system—played an important part in shaping its development under the British. The former was the main factor in the Indian Army's decision to centre its recruiting activities in the province. The latter encouraged the British construction of the world's largest irrigation system in the region. This dramatically transformed Punjab's agricultural life.

The Punjab was a landlocked region in the north-west corner of the Indian subcontinent (Figure 1). Although its political boundaries fluctuated throughout the period which preceded the introduction of British rule, its natural boundaries were clearly defined. These were the Himalayas in the north, the Rajputana Desert in the south, the Upper Ganges Valley in the east and the Indus in the west. The region's name 'Panj-ab' (the land of five rivers) derived from the Beas, Ravi, 'Sutlej, Chenab and Jhelum rivers which flowed through it. Their alluvial deposits created the plains which formed the heartland of the Punjab and bordering them to the north-east and west were the submontane and Himalayan regions.

The Punjab hills were relatively cool in the summer and were often cut off by snow during the winter months. On the plains, the heat before the onset of the monsoon was intense, reaching a peak of 110° F–120° F. Not only did the monsoon rain fall most copiously in the mountainous Kangra and Simla regions but also abundantly watered the submontane areas of Sialkot, Gurdaspur, Hoshiarpur and Ambala. This enabled rich crops of sugar-cane, cotton and wheat to be grown. These densely populated areas had few large landowners.

The central plains of Jullundur, Amritsar, Lahore and Ferozepore also received reasonable amounts of rain. Wells and canals

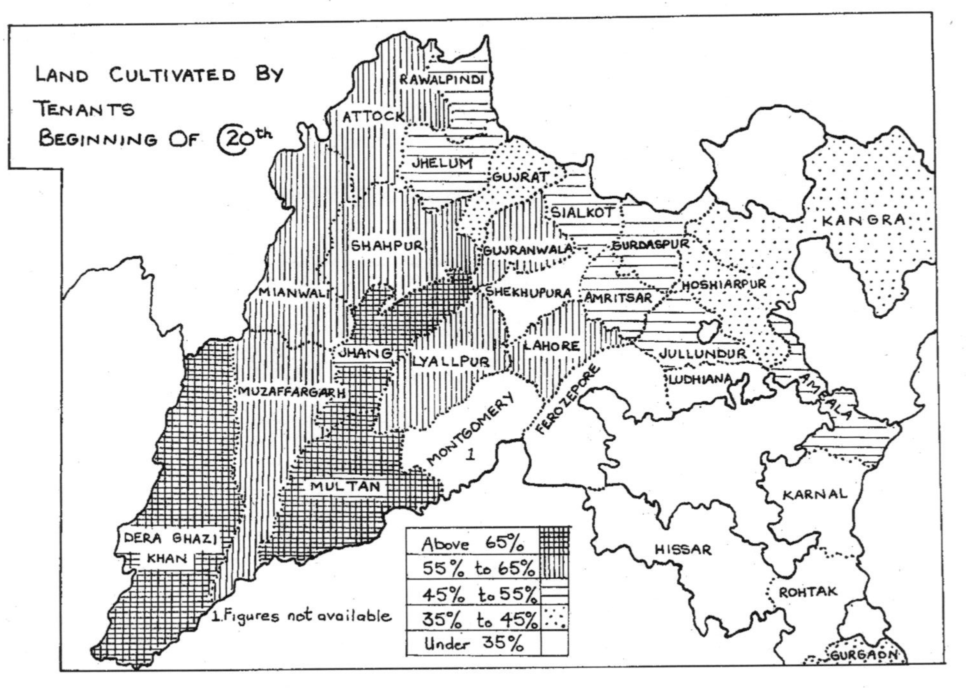

Percentage of Land Cultivated by Tenants in the Punjab
at the Beginning of the Twentieth Century

supplemented this, particularly in the Lahore and Amritsar districts. This region was also heavily populated and cultivated in small parcels of land except in parts of the Lahore and Ferozepur districts. The latter was the driest in this part of the Punjab and consisted mainly of scrub and semi-desert until it was irrigated by the Sirhind Canal which the British opened in 1883.

The areas to the south-east and south-west of the central plains were arid and poor. The former contained the barren 'famine tracts' of Rohtak and Hissar and the latter, the sparsely populated regions of Multan and Jhang. Their soil was sandy and received as little as 5″ of rain a year. Away from the riverine areas, the whole of this south-western region was capable only of supporting a semi-nomadic existence.

Still further west, lying between the Chenab and Sutlej rivers and along the valley of the Indus, were the Mianwali, Muzaffargarh and Dera Ghazi Khan districts. This was the most backward region of the Punjab. Its agriculture was poor, communications were rudimentary and relied heavily on navigation of the Indus. For generations the area had been isolated from the remainder of the Punjab and had consequently developed close ties with Sind. This as reflected in the language and physical characteristics of its scattered population. Most of its cultivated area was in the hands of large landowners.

To the north lay the Shahpur, Jhelum, Rawalpindi and Attock districts. Here, Punjab's plains gave way to the hills and stony moors of the Salt Range. Although the rainfall was adequate, irrigation facilities were poor and the rugged and broken countryside made cultivation difficult. Military service, first in the Mughal armies and later with the Sikh rulers, helped supplement the martial tribesmen's meagre agricultural income.

Punjab's Agrarian Structure

Punjabi society was overwhelmingly rural. Most people lived not in towns but in village settlements whose dwellings were clustered together and surrounded by high mud walls for protection. Political power in the region depended on the control of land. The British, like the Mughals and Sikhs earlier, had to take this important fact into consideration when constructing their administrative machinery. But, unlike their predecessors, they introduced economic changes which led to the growth of a new urban-educated elite whose outlook and interests were at variance with the traditional holders of power. Herein lay the seeds of the development of the two contrasting political traditions—urban and rural—within the British Punjab.

Punjab's rural character resulted from its turbulent history. This had slowed down the rate of economic progress and discouraged the landowners from deserting their estates in order to enjoy a more sophisticated urban life-style. Punjab was the gateway to the rich Gangetic Plain. From the time of Alexander the Great, successive waves of invaders looted and raped their way along the great northern trunk road which ran through it, linking Kabul to Delhi. Most of the region's towns had grown as route centres on or near this highway. Attock, Jhelum and Gujrat, for example, owed their development to their command of strategic river crossings and only slowly outgrew their original garrison character. Only Lahore and to a lesser extent Multan possessed a cultural and political heritage comparable to that of the great North Indian cities of Delhi, Lucknow and Agra.

Lahore first assumed importance at the beginning of the eleventh century when it became the capital of the Ghaznavid empire, though its golden period was during the reigns of Akbar, Jahangir and Shah Jahan. Akbar held court at Lahore from 1584 to 1598 while conducting military operations in Kashmir and Afghanistan. Jahangir also resided in the city from 1622 until shortly before his death five years later. His son Shah Jahan laid out Lahore's famous Shalimar gardens in 1642. At that time, Lahore was reputed to be the equal of the great Persian cities, Shiraz and Isphahan as the 'grand resort of people of all nations' and such luxuries as ice and musk melons were available all the year round.

Multan developed as an important trading centre and manufacturer of silk and carpets. For most of its history, however, it was politically unimportant, the far-flung out-post of the rulers of North India. Between 1220–1227 and 1445–1527 it enjoyed brief spells as the centre of a virtually independent kingdom. Even then, it lacked Lahore's elegance and magnificence because of the harshness of its climate.

From the 1770s onwards, Multan and its surrounding area was continually being overrun by predatory Sikh armies. In 1818, Ranjit Singh's troops stormed the stronghold of Multan fort. This did not however immediately lead to a respite from the anarchy which had plagued the region. It was only when Diwan S. Mal became Governor in 1821 that strong government and peace was restored.

Even cities the size of Lahore, Multan and Amristar, the last of which rose to prominence as the centre of the Sikh religion, retained a rural character before the advent of the British. This arose partly from their close economic links with the surrounding countryside. It also stemmed from the close knit kinship organization adhered to by the main Muslim Arain and Kashmiri urban populations. Traditional rural customs and values lay just beneath the veneer of urban sophistication and culture. But the towns' economic and educational advance during British rule led to an increasing gulf between their religious and social outlook and that of the villages. However, the towns grew only very slowly during the century of British rule. At its close the vast majority of Punjabis still lived in the countryside.

The rural population consisted of five main groups: landlords who owned substantial amounts of land which they let out to tenants to cultivate; peasant cultivators who owned and worked their landholdings; tenants who could often be quite wealthy and own small parcels of land themselves; the village servant class (barbers, potters, washermen etc.) who provided either goods or services to the landowners in return for a share of the crop,[2] and finally, the landless labourers (kisans) who depended on the landowners for employment.

The landholding structure varied considerably between the eastern and western parts of the Punjab.[3] Tenants hardly existed in such eastern districts as Rohtak and Gurgaon where the village structure of communal landholding remained more or less intact.[4] But in western districts such as Attock, well over half the total cultivated area was tilled by occupancy tenants at will who paid either cash rent or *batai*, rent in kind.[5] There were of course local exceptions to this pattern. The Nawab of Mamdot's estate in the East Punjab district of Ferozepore was, for example, over 60,000 acres in extent,[6] whilst in the north-western areas of Gujrat, Rawalpindi and Jhelum most of the land was owned by small peasant proprietors.[7]

The amount of land which the Punjabi landlords possessed was nevertheless much smaller than that of the taluqdars of neighbouring Oudh. Two of the largest landholding families in West Punjab were the Legharis and Kot Ghebas. Their estates in the Dera Ghazi Khan and Attock regions were around 100,000 acres[8] and 60,000 acres (88 square miles) respectively.[9] But they were dwarfed in comparison with the 397 square miles owned by the Mahmudabad taluqdar family in Oudh.[10] The Tiwanas of Shahpur and the Daultanas of Multan were among the most influential landowning families of the Punjab but their Kalra and Luddan estates of around 15,000 and 20,000 acres each were very moderate indeed by Oudh standards. In the Bahraich district of Oudh, for example, 23 taluqdars owned a total of 1,652 villages between them, in total, an area of over a million and a quarter acres.[11] Two-thirds of Rae Bareli district (816,000 acres) was held in 62 great taluqdar estates.[12] The largest taluqdari landholding of all was found in the Kheri district where 44 taluqdars owned nearly 2,000 villages and over 2 million acres.[13]

Although the Oudh taluqdars owned more land than the Punjabi zamindars, they, in fact, wielded less local power than the latter. The size of their estates and the growth of absentee landlordism sapped their power. The traditional portrayal of an Oudh estate as a petty raj in which the tenants passively obeyed their powerful landlord patron was far from the truth. The taluqdars exerted only a nominal control over their scattered estates, real power lying in the hands of the estate manager. He in turn enlisted the collaboration of the village headmen in order to ensure the estate's smooth functioning. 'The estates, far from being simple, or even complex systems of deference, with power concentrated at one point in them were essentially diffuse organisations with no level, even the lowest entirely lacking power.'[14] The single most important factor in weakening the taluqdars' local influence was their withdrawal of traditional patron functions as a result of increasing absentee ownership.

A similar diffusion of landlord power existed in the few large estates of eastern Punjab. The Nawab of Mamdot for example exerted such nominal control over his land in the Ferozepore district that large tracts were taken over by squatters who founded what became known as *mauzah* villages. They were only brought under his control after lengthy litigation in the 1870s.[15] This situation contrasted sharply with that in West Punjab.

The landowners of this region exerted far greater power because of their close links with their landholdings. This was in response both to the area's unsettled social conditions and to the fact that social status derived from the control of land. Land was the major source of an individual's *izzat* (honour). Punjabis still refer to their land today as their *patlaj*, a word which has a meaning similar to *izzat*, that of power, honour, respect. But in the main, the West Punjab landowners' power rested on the fact that they were not only landlords but also tribal chiefs. Their tenants were the lesser members of their tribe. The political leadership of their tribe underpinned their status as landlords. The Sardar of Kot, the head of the Gheba tribe of the Attock district even kept his retinue of mounted followers, whom he had instructed in the use of sword and lance, dressed in scarlet tunics. He was an absolute lord and master of his land, 'his tenants feared him, admired him and even liked him whilst they certainly always obeyed him'.[16]

The Muslim tribal chiefs and landowners of West Punjab enjoyed greater power than the Oudh taluqdars which made them far more valuable allies for the colonial administration. The system of local political control based on the landowners' mediation, which the British developed both in the Punjab and

Oudh, survived much longer in the former than in the latter region.

Punjab's Communal Structure

Muslims made up more than half of Punjab's population, though, there were important regional variations in the communal distribution of its peoples. Whilst West Punjab was overwhelmingly Muslim, in the east the Hindus and large Sikh community together outnumbered the Muslims. The existence of three powerful communities in this turbulent region led to a long history of communal violence. The British regime responded to this by attempting to encourage allegiances based on kinship and tribe which cut across or competed with communal divisions.

1. The Muslims of the Punjab

As early as the eighth century the Arabs extended their power to the extreme south-west of the Punjab, but it was not until after the eleventh century when the Turks under Mahmud of Ghazni invaded the land that Muslim influence became really extensive. Thereafter, although the region remained unstable and power within it changed hands between the rulers of Ghazni, Delhi and Kabul, the Punjab remained under Muslim control for nearly 800 years until Ranjit Singh established his Sikh kingdom in 1799. But the eastern districts never assumed the same character of consolidated Muslim settlement as in the west. They could be likened in some ways to the urban outposts of Muslim rule in the 'Ganges-Jumna heartland of Muslim imperial power'.[17] This pattern of Muslim settlement lasted through the period of British rule. In such western districts as Muzaffargarh, Dera Ghazi Khan, Mianwali, Attock, Rawalpindi and Jhelum, upwards of 80 per cent of the population was Muslim, whereas in the eastern and central districts, Muslims only formed between 15 to 45 per cent of the total inhabitants. Whilst 1 in 6 Muslims dwelt in towns in the east, in the west this proportion fell to 1 in 20.[18]

During the course of their rule, the Muslims came to possess

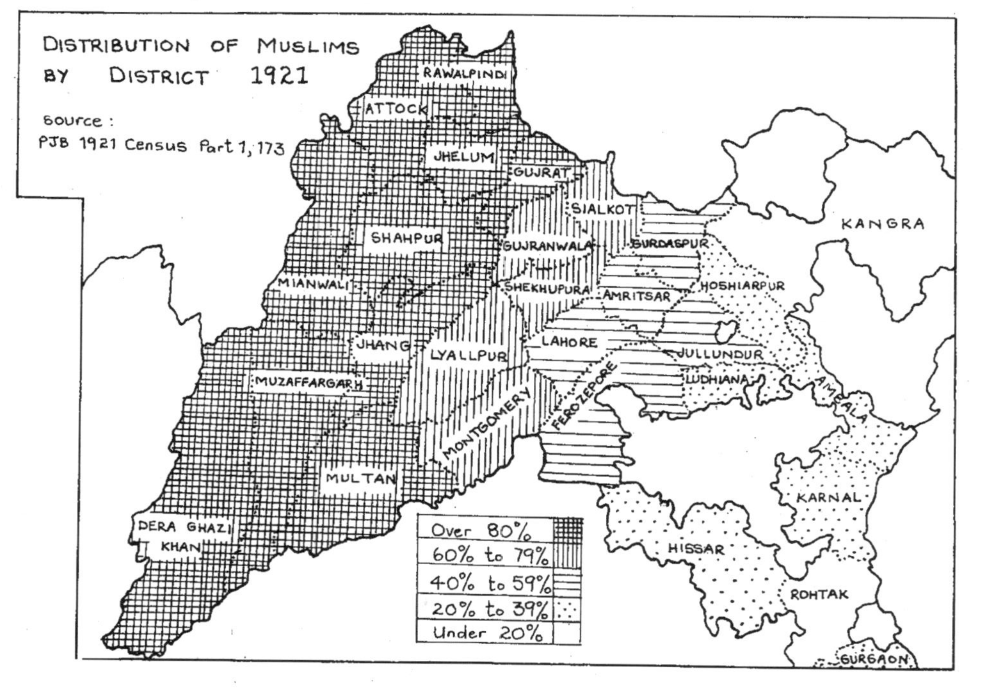
DISTRIBUTION OF MUSLIMS
BY DISTRICT 1921
Source :
PJB 1921 Census Part 1, 173
RAWALPINDI
ATTOCK
JHELUM
GUJRAT
SIALKOT
SHAHPUR
GUJRANWALA
GURDASPUR
KANGRA
MIANWALI
SHEKHUPURA
AMRITSAR
HOSHIARPUR
JHANG
LYALLPUR
LAHORE
JULLUNDUR
LUDHIANA
MUZAFFARGARH
AMBALA
MONTGOMERY
FEROZEPORE
MULTAN
KARNAL
DERA GHAZI KHAN
HISSAR
ROHTAK
GURGAON
Over 80%
60% to 79%
40% to 59%
20% to 39%
Under 20%

most of the land in the Punjab. Ranjit Singh's reign was too short-lived and his position in the western regions too weak to wrest much of this from them. Thus, by the time of British rule, Muslims controlled over 95 per cent of the land in such districts as Gujrat, Jhang, Jhelum and Attock.[19] Even in the eastern districts where the Hindu and Sikh landowning position was much stronger,[20] Muslims still owned substantial amounts of land. In the Gurgaon district they owned over 30 per cent of the land,[21] whilst in Amritsar they possessed over 25 per cent.[22] Muslims owned a far higher percentage of the land in the Punjab than in Bengal, the other leading centre of Muslim population. Whereas a large number of Muslims, particularly in East Bengal, were tenants of the Hindu landlords, in the Punjab this was not so. Its landholding structure made it possible for the rural population to cooperate with each other rather than confront each other on communal lines.

The Muslim Social Structure

Muslim society was organized on a tribal and kinship basis. Tribal political organization was strongest in the north-western areas of the province which had largely escaped the levelling effects of Sikh rule. Even in other regions of the Punjab a strong pattern of tribal ownership of land existed in which tribes had recognized headquarters and areas of land in which they congregated in strength. Some of the smaller tribes, such as the Jodhras, and the Khokkars, were concentrated in just one or two *tehsils*. But the larger tribes like the Rajputs and the Jats were spread throughout the Punjab. Within these large tribal groupings there was a further division into clans consisting of kinship groups (*biradaris*), which were patrilineage groups. The ideal marriage within a *biradari* was the cross-cousin type to a father's brother's daughter. Indeed, an individual's status was judged on his ability to give his daughter in marriage only to members of his own *biradari*. Control of marriage was an important factor in maintaining *biradari* cohesion and as a result, marriages were strictly regulated by the *biradari panchayats* or ruling councils.

The British recognized the social and political importance of the tribal and kinship groups and did all they could to strengthen them. They felt far safer in basing their rule around the cohesion of such local social organizations than around communal allegiances. Significantly, in sharp contrast to the Mughals, the British based their legal system not on Islamic law but on local tribal custom.[23]

Islam in the Punjab

The most striking aspect of Islam in the Punjab was the widespread influence of the *Sufi Pirs*. Sufism was embedded in the life of the countryside. Although the smallest villages had their own mosques, peasants found that its austere formalities offered them little as compared to the *Pir* with his personal touch and the excitement of the various celebrations at the Saint's shrine. The four most important Sufi orders in the Punjab were the Qadiri *silsilah* which had closer links with the urban centres of Islamic orthodoxy than the other orders and was centred in Lahore and Multan; the Naqshbandi order whose political importance was considerable since the Mughal period and whose influence radiated outwards from the home of its leading saint in Sirhind in the neighbouring state of Patiala; the Suhrawardy with its major shrine of Sheikh Bahaud-Din Zakaria in Multan; and finally, the indigenous Chishti order which had its greatest influence in East Punjab. Its most important shrine was that of Baba Farid at Pakpattan. Baba Farid was acknowledged as Punjab's leading Sufi saint.

The Pirs of Punjab possessed great authority in the eyes of Muslim tribesmen. Apart from their spiritual influence they were also large landowners, and were thus ideally placed to play a leading rôle in rural politics. After a period of initial hesitation, the British recognized them as important allies.

The modern-day Pirs' religious influence sprang from the belief that they had inherited *baraka* (charisma) from their ancestors who from the eleventh century onwards had played a major role in the Punjab's conversion to Islam. *Baraka* was also believed to have been transmitted to the tomb (*dargah*) of the saint itself. Religious leadership of the ever-growing number of shrines at these tombs was usually provided by the Pirs who were the original saint's descendants. They were called the shrine's *sajjada nashin* (custodian, literally, 'he who sits on the prayer carpet'). The *sajjada nashin*'s links to the original saint and his links to God were dramatized every year in a ceremony known as the *Urs* which marked the anniversary of the saint's death when he became 'married' to God.

Multitudes flocked to the shrines, particularly at the time of the *Urs* celebrations. They came in the hope of receiving spiritual and more frequently material blessings. A great trade in amulets was carried on and many shrines were associated with particular miraculous powers. A shrine in Shahpur, for example, was famous for curing toothache,[24] another in Hissar was especially renowned for its power of exorcism, while yet another was resorted to by sufferers from dog bites. Most famous of all was the 'gate of paradise' at Baba Farid's shrine. This was only opened once a year, on the final and most important day of the *Urs* ceremonies. It was believed that anyone who could squeeze through its narrow entrance was assured of a place in Paradise.[25]

The *sajjada nashin's* role as a mediator was formalized by the *piri-muridi* tie between him and the shrine's worshipper. The latter took an oath of obedience (*bayat*) to the Pir and thereafter became his *murid* (disciple). In return for the *murid's* regular offerings, the Pir provided him with access to *baraka*. The *murid* was expected to be absolutely obedient to his Pir and the relationship between them was likened to that between the Prophet and his companions.[26] The leading Pirs had thousands of *murids*. Pir Fazl Shah of Jalalpur in the Jhelum district alone claimed over 200,000 disciples. The size of such followings gave the Pirs great political influence.

In recognition of this fact, governments from the time of the Delhi Sultanate down to the British donated large amounts of land to the shrines in order to secure their *sajjadas*' loyalty. The requirement for becoming a *sajjada nashin* shrine gradually shifted from spiritual merit to political loyalty to the central government.[27] Control of the shrines enabled the State to

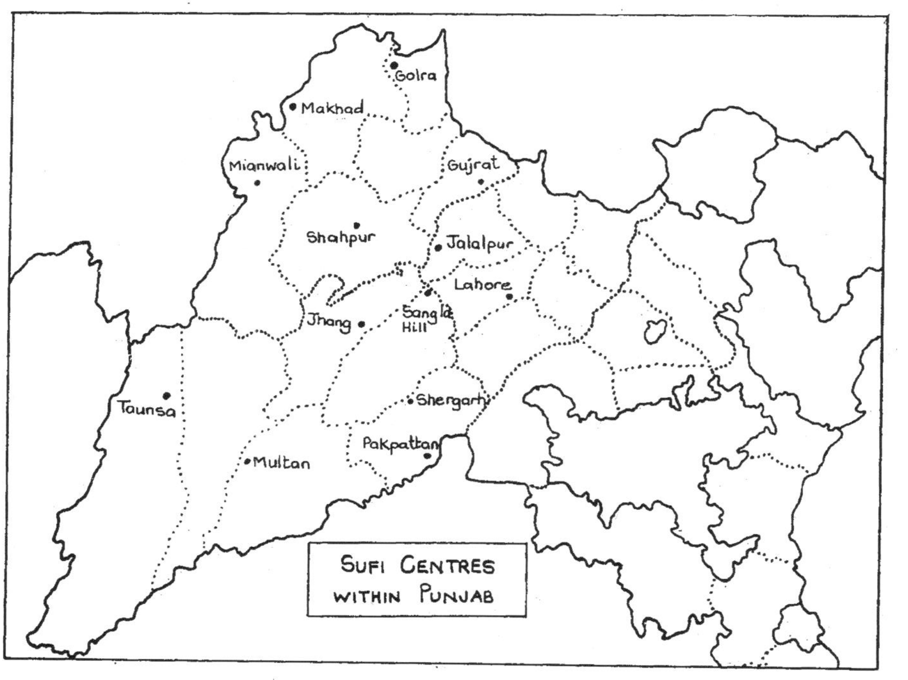
Golra
Makhad
Mianwali
Gujrat
Shahpur
Jalalpur
Lahore
Jhang
Sangla Hill
Taunsa
Shergarh
Pakpattan
Multan
SUFI CENTRES
WITHIN PUNJAB

strengthen the roots of its authority in the countryside. For their part, the Pirs had their own considerable local authority enhanced by collaboration with the government.

Over the years, the leading shrines acquired large amounts of land, as their *inam* grants from the State were in addition to considerable *waqf* endowments which they received from individuals. The descendants of Baba Farid possessed, by the twentieth century, a tenth of all the land in the Pakpattan *tehsil* in which the shrine was situated, some 43,000 acres in all.[28] Part of this land had in fact come to them as State gifts during Sikh rule.[29] The Shia Shah Jiwana Pir family in Jhang owned nearly 10,000 acres of land,[30] whilst the Pirs of Jahanian Shah owned 7,000 acres.[31] Five thousand acres were attached to the leading Suhrawardi shrine of Sheikh Baba-ud-Din Zakariya in Multan.[32]

As the shrines' wealth increased, they became major centres of economic importance for their localities, both as employers and as consumers of local produce. Many of the larger shrines provided dispensaries for the sick and soup kitchens (*langar-khanas*). Food was always distributed at shrines during the *Urs* celebrations. Local fairs were often held at this time on the land near the *dargah*.

The Pirs' social and religious influence did not, however, go unquestioned. The traditional forms of religious practice at the shrines were in fact strongly challenged by the emergence of a reformist Islamic tradition following the collapse of Mughal political power.[33] Within the Punjab, the reformist *ulama*—the *Ahl-i-Hadith*[34]—led the attack on the Pirs' religious practices. But their influence remained confined to the towns and cities right down to the period of British rule, and they were not able to successfully challenge the Pirs' religious influence in the countryside. In urban areas, however, their teachings provided an Islamic justification for the efforts of the emerging Muslim middle class to wrest political leadership from the rural clan leaders and their close Sufi allies.

Among the reasons for the failure of the reformist *ulama* to extend their influence into the countryside was the emergence of a reformist tradition within rural Sufism. This was led by the eighteenth century Chishti reformers such as Khwaja Nur Muhammad of Mihar, Khwaja Muhammad Aqil of Kot Mithan, Hafiz Muhammad Jamal of Multan and Khwaja Muhammad Suleman of Taunsa. They sought to transform the *dargahs* from being the foci of popular devotionalism into centres of Islamic piety and learning.

The Chishti revivalist Pirs made adherence to the *sharia* (the divinely revealed law of Islam) a vital part of their *tariqa* (teaching, way). They also attempted to bring the Sufis and *ulama* closer together.[35] The most famous of these reformers, Khwaja Muhammad Suleman established a *Dar-ul-ulum* (centre for higher religious learning) at his *khanqah* (Sufi hospice) at Taunsa and also established numerous *madrasas* (secondary schools). His *khanqah* soon developed into a large complex with its own cobblers, blacksmiths, barbers and washermen. It became as important a centre of Islamic piety as Baba Farid's had once been.[36]

The prodigious efforts of Khwaja Suleman and his followers led to a network of Chishti revivalist shrines springing up throughout the western areas of the Punjab. Major centres came into existence at Makhad, Golra, Taunsa and Jalalpur. These shrines, because they lacked the historical traditions of involvement with the government of the older established shrines and because they derived their authority more from religious influence than economic power, were much less responsive to State patronage. Even when, for economic reasons, they became involved with the local political system as the Taunsa shrine had done, by the beginning of the twentieth century, their preoccupations and outlook remained considerably different from those of the older shrines.

The Chishti revivalist Pirs were able to form a link between rural Sufism and urban orthodoxy. They used this to help bring about the momentary merging of the region's urban and rural, religious and political traditions during the crucial final days of the Pakistan movement.

2. THE HINDUS OF THE PUNJAB

The most striking feature of Hinduism in the Punjab was the weakness of the Brahmin caste. Its low economic and social status in the region was seen most clearly amongst the Gaur Brahmins of the Rohtak district. They not only took to the plough but exerted strenuous efforts to be classified as an agriculturalist tribe under the terms of the 1901 Alienation of Land Act. They finally achieved this aim in 1909. The Gaur Brahmin Zamindari Association next turned its attention to securing martial caste status for its community so that its low agricultural income could be supplemented by large-scale entry into the Indian Army. The British finally granted this in 1916.

The Brahmin's low status mainly arose from the fact that he not only had to compete with the Muslim Pirs and Sikh gurus for religious leadership, but because he also lacked the economic power which the large Hindu temple complexes gave his brethren elsewhere in India. In the absence of a powerful Brahmin caste, Hindu social leadership had first rested with the Rajput princes but after their power had been smashed by the Mughals it had devolved on the commercial castes of Khatris, Aroras and Banias. During the period of British rule however, their leadership was in turn challenged by the emergence of a rich Jat peasantry.

The distribution of the Hindu population bore witness to the history of Muslim rule in the region. The largest number of Hindus lived in the north-eastern hills where the continuing resistance of the Rajput Rajas had created a barrier to conversion. Over 90 per cent of the population of Kangra was Hindu. The Muslims' tenuous influence during much of their rule in eastern Punjab was also reflected in the size of the Hindu population in this region. East of the Ravi, with the exception of the Sikh-dominated areas of Jullundur, Ludhiana and Ferozepur, Hindus everywhere represented at least 40 per cent of the population. In the extreme south-eastern district of Rohtak, their proportion was as high as 80 per cent. The Rohtak Hindus spoke, for the most part, the Bangura and Ahiravati dialects of western Hindi rather than Punjabi. They were also linked by blood more with

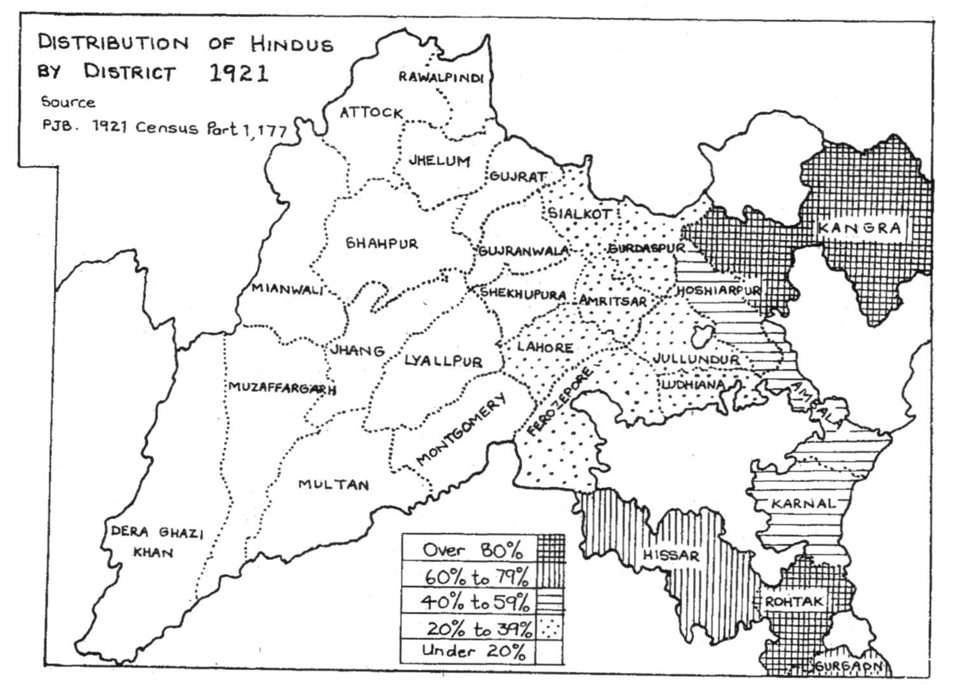
DISTRIBUTION OF HINDUS
BY DISTRICT 1921
Source
PJB. 1921 Census Part 1, 177
RAWALPINDI
ATTOCK
JHELUM
GUJRAT
SIALKOT
KANGRA
SHAHPUR
GUJRANWALA
GURDASPUR
MIANWALI
SHEKHUPURA
AMRITSAR
HOSHIARPUR
JHANG
LAHORE
LYALLPUR
JULLUNDUR
MUZAFFARGARH
LUDHIANA
FEROZEPORE
AMBALA
MONTGOMERY
MULTAN
KARNAL
DERA GHAZI
KHAN
HISSAR
ROHTAK
GURGAON
Over 80%
60% to 79%
40% to 59%
20% to 39%
Under 20%

the population of the Gangetic Plain than with the Punjab.

The further west one journeyed in Punjab the smaller the proportion of the Hindu population became. In Dera Ghazi Khan it was less than 12 per cent and in Attock it was only 5 per cent. Consequently, despite the large numbers of Hindus who lived in the south-east and north-eastern districts, their community formed only just over a quarter of the Punjabi's total population.

The rural Hindus quite frequently borrowed Muslim customs and beliefs. Hindu women in Hoshiarpur district observed purdah.[37] Large numbers of Hindus in the district of Rohtak and Jullundur were followers of a Muslim saint called Sultan Sakhi Sarwar.[38]

In West Punjab, the Hindu population was overwhelmingly urban, made up of traders and shopkeepers, though in the east the majority of Hindus were Jat peasants. The Jat heartland was the Rohtak district, where they owned 60 per cent of all the land.[39] Even before the British encouraged the different rural communities to cooperate, the Hindu Jats from Rohtak had far more in common with the Muslim cultivators than with the Hindu Banias and Khatris. They hated these urban money-lender castes who squeezed the last rupee out of them. For their part these higher castes looked down on the Jats because they practiced widow remarriage.[40]

Even before the advent of colonial rule, the Hindu commercial castes had dominated the economic life of western Punjab's few towns. Thus, when the British introduced new industry and trade into the province, they were well-placed to assume control. They owned, for example, 60 per cent of all the factories registered in Lahore and paid eight times as much sales tax as the Muslim traders. In fact, throughout the British Punjab, the majority of banks, factories, shops and commercial institutions were in Hindu hands.

Lala Harkishan Lal who also played an important part in the growth of the Brahmo Samaj and the Congress in the region was the major representative of the emerging class of Hindu industrialists. He opened the People's Banking and Commercial

Association in 1903 and founded a variety of industrial enterprises including flour mills, cotton mills and soap factories.[41] As elsewhere in India, the Hindu population also led the way in western education. Most jobs in Government service went to the Hindus.

Despite their economic strength, the Punjabi Hindus always felt insecure. They had to be inconspicuous in order to survive in some of the frontier districts of the Punjab, and often suffered high-handed treatment from the tribesmen.[42] Even in the eastern and central districts, the Hindu community had undergone the traumatic experience of losing many of its lower-caste members to Sikhism. The advent of Christian missionaries soon after the British annexed the region increased the Hindus' abiding fear of absorption.

3. THE SIKHS

The Punjab was the homeland of the Sikhs. It contained the major Sikh religious centre of the Golden Temple in Amritsar and all the leading Sikh shrines. Outside of its boundaries and those of its neighbouring Princely States,[43] the Sikhs were an infinitesimal minority. The Sikh faith itself had been founded in the Punjab by Baba Nanak about the year AD 1500.

Nanak had been born into an orthodox Hindu Khatri family in Lahore district. He had not intended to found a religion separate from Hinduism but only to reform it. He thus accepted such important Hindu doctrines as the transmigration of souls and the law of *karma* whilst rejecting idol worship and preaching that there is only one true God. He also sought to do away with caste distinctions. By the time of his death in 1539, he had gathered together a large following of disciples known as Sikhs who regarded him as their guru or spiritual leader.

Nanak's nine successors who were also known by the title Guru, each contributed to the development of the new faith. The second, Guru Angad, gave the Sikhs the distinctive script of Gurumukhi in which they recorded their religious literature and later their everyday affairs. Guru Ramdas, the fourth

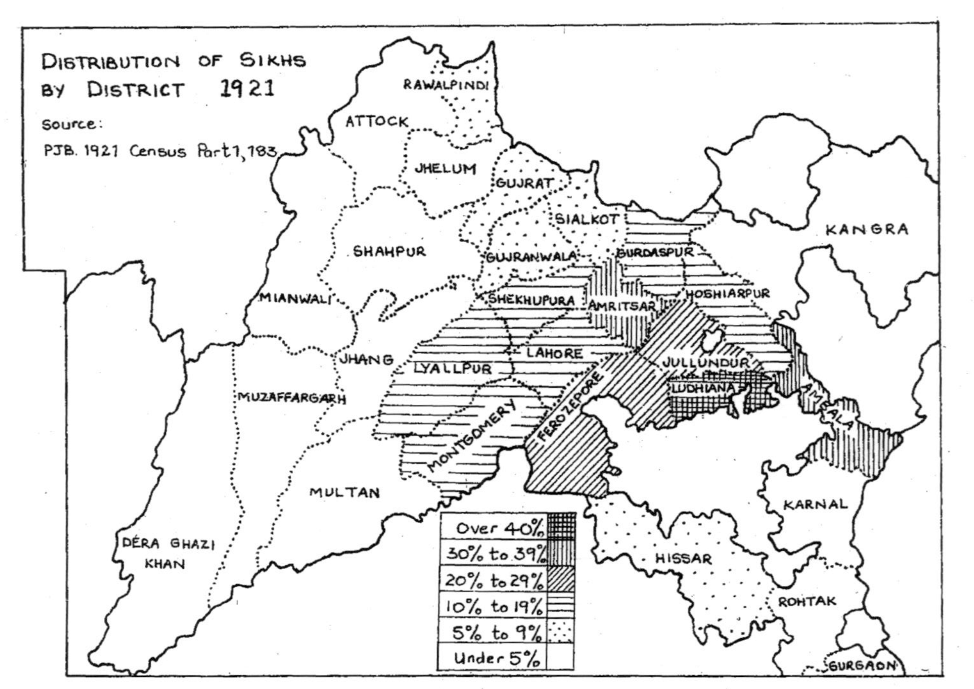
DISTRIBUTION OF SIKHS
BY DISTRICT 1921
Source:
PJB. 1921 Census Part 1, 183
RAWALPINDI
ATTOCK
JHELUM
GUJRAT
SIALKOT
KANGRA
SHAHPUR
GUJRANWALA
GURDASPUR
MIANWALI
SHEKHUPURA
AMRITSAR
HOSHIARPUR
JHANG
LAHORE
LYALLPUR
JULLUNDUR
LUDHIANA
MUZAFFARGARH
FEROZEPORE
MONTGOMERY
AMBALA
MULTAN
KARNAL
Over 40%
30% to 39%
20% to 29%
10% to 19%
5% to 9%
Under 5%
DERA GHAZI KHAN
HISSAR
ROHTAK
GURGAON

Guru, founded the city of Amritsar. His successor, Arjandas added to its importance by completing the building of the Golden Temple which became the focus of the Sikh faith. Other temples known as *gurudwaras* or abodes of the Gurus were also built at that time. Arjandas also finished the compilation of Nanak's teachings which along with other writings formed the Sikh scriptures or Granth Sahib.

From the time of Guru Arjandas, the Sikhs encountered mounting Muslim persecution. This arose partly because they had become too heavily involved in the power struggles of the Mughal court but also stemmed from the Mughal's increasing religious intolerance. Aurangzeb in fact executed the eighth guru Tegh Bahadur in 1675 because he refused to accept Islam. It was in this atmosphere of violence and religious fanaticism that the last Guru, Gobind Singh, completed the transformation of the Sikhs from a passive sect into a militant brotherhood. Gobind Singh called this the 'Khalsa' or 'pure' and ordered its members to wear five things beginning with the letter 'K'. ('Kes': long hair; 'kangha': wooden comb; 'kara': steel bangle; 'kirpan': double-edged sword; and 'kachh': knee-length breeches). He also introduced the ceremony of baptism, 'pahul'. This consisted of a mass baptism and the drinking of a mixture of sugar and water boiled together and stirred by a double-edged sword. Only after he had undergone the 'pahul' initiation could a Sikh carry the title 'Singh'. Those Sikhs who followed the rules laid down by Gobind Singh and had been baptized were known as 'Keshdharis'. The remainder were called 'Sehajdharis'.

The Keshdhari, Sehajdhari division was not the only one in the Sikh community. This in fact overlaid more important caste differences which still existed. The first and most important was that between the high and low-caste Sikhs. Within the upper castes, a further division existed between the Khatris and Aroras and the Jats.

The Mughals exacted a fierce retribution on Gobind Singh and his followers. The Guru was forced to witness his family's execution at Sirhind on Aurangzeb's order and submitted to his successor Bahadur Shah shortly before his death. During the ensuing period of Sikh dispersal, many shrines fell under the protection of Hindu Mahant priests. As Mughal authority began to collapse, the Sikhs re-emerged into the plains of Punjab, and their armed confederacies took advantage of the power vacuum to carve out petty states. The formidable one-eyed lion of Punjab, Ranjit Singh (1781–1839), welded these together to form an extensive Sikh kingdom which, at its height in the early years of the nineteenth century, stretched as far as Bannu and Peshawar.

Ranjit Singh's control of Punjab's western districts was always tenuous and depended on the cooperation of the leading Muslim chiefs. The real base of his power remained in the region's central tracts. Lahore was the political head and Amritsar the religious heart of the Sikh kingdom, which, however, did not survive its architect's death long since the fierce scramble for power which followed weakened it severely at a time when British power was pressing hard against its borders.

The British annexation of the Punjab was a shattering blow for the Sikh community. Sikh soldiers found themselves unemployed as the British recruited Muslims into the military police force and army units, and they often turned to crime to ward off starvation. There was an explosion of armed robbery and cattle theft in the central Sikh districts of the *manjha*. British rule also created an identity crisis for the Sikh community. Loss of political power led to large-scale reconversion to Hinduism and many Sehajdharis slipped back into its fold. Their action aroused acute anxiety because of the Sikh community's relative smallness.

The Sikhs formed just 14 per cent of British Punjab's population. Even in their heartland districts of Lahore, Amritsar and Ludhiana, they were still in a minority, as they were in the neighbouring Sikh-ruled Princely State of Patiala as well.

The Sikhs, however, gradually regained their strength and self-confidence. Indeed, by the beginning of the twentieth century, they had attained a political influence disproportionate to their numbers. This stemmed from their growing importance to the

Punjab's agricultural prosperity and to their massive influx into the Indian Army. Sikh Jats played a major part in clearing the scrub and breaking the soil of the Lyallpur and Montgomery Canal Colonies in which they acquired large amounts of land. They were of course already the principal landowners in central Punjab. The Sikh's loyalty during the revolt of 1857 together with the need for mopping up Sikh unemployment opened up service in the India Army. On the eve of the First World War, Sikhs accounted for a sixth of its total strength.

The British Enter the Punjab

The British did not follow the traditional route down through the passes of Afghanistan and across the Punjab's plains on the way to Delhi. Instead they 'invaded' by sea, slowly extending their power northwards from the coasts of Madras, Bengal and Bombay. The Punjab was thus the last rather than the first region to fall under their control. It was not absorbed into the East India Company's possessions until the Anglo-Sikh Wars of 1841 and 1849. After the first campaign, the Trans-Sutlej territories of Jullundur and Hoshiarpur were annexed by the British. A Regency Council which was under the virtual control and guidance of a permanent British Resident in Lahore was established to govern the remainder of the Sikh Kingdom.

The collapse of this arrangement led to the Second Sikh War. The decisive British victory at the battle of Gujrat on 21 February 1849 brought the whole of the Punjab under the East India Company's control. The boundaries of its new possession stretched from the Afghan frontier to Delhi. The five frontier districts were subsequently separated in 1901 to form the North-West Frontier Province. Delhi district was separated a decade later when the Government of British India transferred its capital from Calcutta to New Delhi. Despite these territorial losses, the Punjab still remained larger than Great Britain and formed just under 10 per cent of British India's total population and area.

The early British rulers faced severe difficulties in controlling the scattered and turbulent population of the Punjab region. They attempted to surmount these by developing a semi-military, despotic system of government. The region was placed under the control of a three-man board of administration, which was dominated by the titan figures of John and Henry Lawrence. The most experienced civilian and military officers were despatched to assist them. All officials were invested with both administrative and judicial powers. Ten Punjabi regiments were raised to assist the 8,000 strong Military Police Force in the maintenance of law and order.

The British sought to govern from a position of moral as well as physical strength. The district officials were thus expected to win the allegiance of the rural population by their example of hard work and fair-mindedness. 'The ideal of a district official was a hard, active man in boots (and) breeches, who almost lived in the saddle, worked all day and night, ate and drank when and where he could and had no family to hamper him', John Beames wrote, looking back on the early days of British rule, 'Such a man must be ready to go anywhere at a moment's notice ... must decide cases sitting on horseback in the village gathering, or under a tree outside the village walls, write his decision on his knee while munching a native chapatty or a fowl cooked in a hole in the ground and then mount his horse and be off to repeat the process in the next village.'[44]

This ideal was frequently realized. The dynamism and sense of duty of the Punjab school of administration as it became known, drew the brightest and best officials to the new province.[45] The Board of Administration initiated a large number of economic reforms. It abolished internal customs duties and improved the roads, thus removing barriers to the development of trade. Work was started on renovating and extending the canal system. The greatest benefit of all, however, was the return of political stability to a region which had known only war and chaos since the death of Ranjit Singh.

The province's loyalty in 1857 enhanced the ideals of the Punjab School of Administration. The paternalistic ethos of British rule thus remained unaltered when the personal rule of the Lawrence era was replaced by the more formalized bureaucracy which grew up after the Punjab Code of Civil Procedure and the Punjab Laws Act of 1862 and 1872.

The province was divided into five administrative divisions, each under the charge of a commissioner. The divisions were further subdivided into twenty-nine districts, each of which contained around a 1,000 villages. The districts were administered by Deputy Commissioners who were aided by up to five Extra Assistant Commissioners drawn from the Indianized provincial civil service. Beneath the districts were the *tehsils*, each of which contained approximately 150 villages. They were under the control of *tehsildars* and *naib-tehsildars* who held revenue and judicial powers. At the bottom of the administrative pyramid there were the *zails* made up of between 10 and 30 villages. Control here rested with the *zaildar* who supervised the village headmen (*lambardars*) and acted as an honorary police officer in charge of the village police. The *zaildar's* position as a mediator between government and society in the localities was a powerful one and highly prized. The British ensured that it was held by local landowners who had demonstrated unquestioning loyalty. The institution of the *zaildar* was in fact unique to the Punjab's local administration. It reflected the importance which the British attached to securing the support of the rural notables. Their collaboration became vital with Punjab's growing value for imperial interests.

Notes

1. Sir Richard Temple, *Men and Events of My Time in India* (London, 1882), p. 51.
2. This was known as the *jajmani* relationship.
3. Tenants for example farmed 75 per cent of the total cultivated area in the western Multan district, but only 43 per cent in eastern Ambala.
4. H. Joseph, *Final Report of the 3rd Regular Settlement of the Rohtak District 1905–10* (Lahore, 1911), p. 11.
5. Ch. Sardar Khan, *Final Report of the 4th Revenue Settlement of the Attock District 1923–7* (Lahore, 1928), p. 17.
6. *Report on the Administration of Estates under the Charge of the Court of Wards for the Year ending 30 September 1911* (Lahore, 1912), L 5 VI (3) IOR.
7. H.S. Williamson, *Final Report of the 4th Regular Settlement of the Gujrat District 1912–16* (Lahore, 1916), p. 4.

8. *Report on the Administration of Estates under the Charge of the Court of Wards for the Year ending 30 September 1928* (Lahore, 1929), L 5 VI (3), IOR.
9. *Imperial Gazetteer of India*, Vol. XV (Oxford, 1908), p. 409 & ff.
10. *Imperial Gazetteer of India*, Vol. XVII (Oxford, 1908), p. 22.
11. *Gazetteer of the Province of Oudh*, Vol. 1 (Lucknow, 1877), p. 199.
12. *Gazetteer of the Province of Oudh*, Vol. 3 (Allahabad, 1878), p. 208.
13. *Ibid.*, (11) above, pp. 220–1.
14. P.J. Musgrave, 'Landlords and Lords of the Land: Estate Management and Social Control in Uttar Pradesh 1860–1920', *Modern Asian Studies*, 6, 3 (1972), p. 274.
15. *Ferozepore District Gazetteer* (Lahore, 1916), p. 222.
16. *Attock District Gazetteer* (Lahore, 1909), p. 229.
17. P. Hardy, *The Muslims of British India* (Cambridge, 1972), p. 4.
18. *1921 Punjab Census*, Part 1 (Lahore, 1923), Subsidiary Table 2, p. 121.
19. H.S. Williamson, *Final Report of the Fourth Regular Settlement of the Gujrat District 1912–16* (Lahore, 1916), p. 2. W.S. Talbot, *Final Report of the Fourth Settlement of the Jhelum District 1895–1901* (Lahore, 1902), p. 7 & ff. Ch. Sardar Khan, *Final Report of the 4th Revenue Settlement of the Attock District 1923–7* (Lahore, 1928), p. 6.
20. Hindus owned well over 60 per cent of the cultivated area in the Rohtak district, Sikhs owned nearly half of the total cultivated area in the Ferozepore district and three-quarters of the total area in the Amritsar district. E. Joseph, *Final Report of the 3rd Regular Settlement of the Rohtak District 1905–10* (Lahore, 1911), p. 10. M.M.L. Cuppie, *Final Report of the Revised Settlement 1910–14 of the Ferozepore District* (Lahore, 1915), p. 8. H.D. Craik, *Final Report of the 4th Regular Settlement of the Amritsar District 1910–14* (Lahore, 1914), p. 3.
21. A. Husain, *Final Settlement Report of the Gurgaon District 1938–43* (Lahore, 1944), p. 9.
22. H.D. Craik, *Final Report of the 4th Regular Settlement of the Amritsar District 1910–14* (Lahore, 1914), p. 3.
23. D.P. Gilmartin, 'Tribe, Land and Religion in the Punjab, Muslim Politics and the Making of Pakistan', Unpublished Ph.D. thesis (Berkeley 1979), p. 4 & ff.
24. *Shahpur District Gazetteer* (Lahore, 1918), p. 127.
25. *Montgomery District Gazetteer* (Lahore, 1933), p. 66.
26. M. Milson (trans.) *Kitab Adab al-Muridin of Abu al-Najib al-Suhrawardi: A Sufi Rule for Novices* (Cambridge, Massachusetts, 1978), p. 46.
27. R.M. Eaton, *Sufis of Bijapur 1300–1700: social roles of Sufis in medieval India* (Princeton, 1978), pp. 217 & 241.
28. M.M.H. Nun, 'Assessment Report of the Pakpattan Tehsil of the Montgomery District' (Lahore, 1921), p. 18. Punjab Proceedings P 11372 (April 1922), Part A IOR.

29. T. G. Singh, *Baba Sheikh Farid* (Delhi, 1974), p. 43.
30. *Report of the Administration of Estates Under the Charge of the Court of Wards for the Year ending 30 September 1921* (Lahore, 1922), Statement No. 1, Punjab Departmental Annual Reports L 5 VI (3), IOR.
31. G. L. Chopra, *Chiefs and Families of Note in the Punjab*, Vol. 2 (Lahore, 1940), p. 242.
32. *Ibid.*, (30) above.
33. This was begun by Shah Waliullah, the Delhi Scholar.
34. They emphasized study of the Quran and the *hadith* rather than the subsequent interpretations of the medieval schools of law, as Shah Waliullah himself had done.
35. M. Z. Siddiqi, 'The Resurgence of the Chishti Silsilah in 18th Century Punjab', *The Punjab Past and Present*, V, 11 (1971), p. 258.
36. *Ibid.*, (35) above, p. 259.
37. Darling/Biervilie Papers 'The Ride', p. 176 of ms., Centre of South Asian Studies, Cambridge.
38. *Jullundur District Gazetteer* (Lahore, 1904), p. 121 & ff.
39. E. Joseph, *Final Report of the 3rd Regular Settlement of the Rohtak District 1905–10* (Lahore, 1911), p. 10.
40. *Rohtak District Gazetteer 1883–4* (Calcutta, 1884), p. 64.
41. M. B. Sen, (ed.) *Punjab's Eminent Hindus* (Lahore, 1944), p. 157.
42. See for example, *Muzaffargarh District Gazetteer* (Lahore, 1884), p. 71. *Dera Ghazi Khan District Gazetteer* (Lahore, 1898), p. 75.
43. The Sikhs formed a large proportion of the population in the Princely States of Patiala, Faridkot, Kapurthala, Nabha, Jind and Malerkotla.
44. J. Beames, *Memoirs of Bengal Citizen* (London, 1961), p. 102 & ff.
45. Also attractive was the region's reputedly healthy climate.

Chapter 2

Punjab and the Raj

> The importance of the Punjab in the history and economy of the (Indian Subcontinent) is not of all proportion to its population, its productive capacity, or even its size.... It has been the arena of conflict between political systems far greater than itself, affording as it does the only practicable highway between the nomad breeding ground of central Asia and the fertile valley of the Ganges.[1]

Punjab comprised around one-tenth of British India's area and population, but its agricultural wealth and military importance gave it a political significance disproportionate to its size. Here the British constructed the world's largest irrigation system, leading to twenty-six million acres being watered by canals and thus transforming the region from one of the poorest agricultural areas in the subcontinent into its granary. By the 1920s, a third of India's wheat was produced in the province. Punjab also emerged as the 'sword arm' of India. Towards the end of the nineteenth century, the region replaced the older areas of Bombay, Madras and Bengal as the major centre of recruitment for the Indian Army. At the outbreak of the First World War, Punjab supplied a half of its troops.

This chapter examines Punjab's increasing importance to the Raj, for it was to have a profound effect on the region's political development during colonial rule.

Punjab's Agricultural Importance

By the 1920s Punjab produced a tenth of British India's total cotton crop and a third of its wheat. Each year, over 500,000 tones of wheat were exported from the province. This was shipped from Karachi, having been sent by rail from the new wheat markets of south-west Punjab, the chief of which, Sargodha, was one of the largest in the world. Whilst other regions such as Bengal, Bihar and Orissa were experiencing a growing agricultural crisis, the Punjab had emerged as the pace-setter of Indian agricultural development. Per capita output of all its crops increased by nearly 45 per cent between 1891 and 1921.[2]

The Punjab owed its agricultural wealth to the massive system of canals which the British constructed. Though other arid areas of India such as parts of the Deccan and the United Provinces had been transformed by irrigation, its impact on the Punjab's agriculture was unparalleled. By 1939, 47 per cent of the region's total cultivated area was watered by canals.[3] Six million acres of land in south-west Punjab had been transformed from arid wasteland populated only by nomadic herders into the richest farming area in the whole of the subcontinent.

Irrigation was nothing new to the Punjab. The Mughals had explored the possibility of harnessing the waters of the region's river system. Though they dug a number of canals in the Punjab's central districts, large-scale irrigation was not technically possible; it only became a reality with the advent of British rule. Their later canal works were stupendous engineering feats, the Triple Project Canal System completed in 1917 being particularly spectacular. This involved the construction of a quarter mile-wide 'level crossing' barrage linking water drawn off from the Chenab river with that from the Ravi in order to irrigate the Montgomery district.

Work began on restoring and extending the Punjab's canal system almost immediately after the region's annexation by the British. The first major canal—the Lower Bari Doab Canal which irrigated the densely populated Amritsar and Lahore districts—was opened in 1861. The Lower Jhelum and Chenab canal systems followed in the 1880s. These transformed the endless waste and scrub of the Jhang, Lyallpur and Shahpur districts into flourishing Canal Colony regions. The Lyallpur district which had only been sparsely populated by nomadic herdsmen before irrigation began possessed a million inhabitants within thirty years. Three and a half million rupees worth of crops were produced annually from its Lower Chenab Canal Colony. The whole area was neatly laid out into plots of land known as squares, with market places, towns and villages spaced at regular intervals along the roads and railways which criss-crossed the colony. By 'creating villages of a type superior in civilization to anything which the region had previously experienced'[4] the British hoped to establish a model for the Punjab's development.

Another aim of the colonies was to relieve the pressure on land in the crowded districts of central Punjab. Large numbers of Sikh Jats emigrated from there to the Lower Chenab Canal Colony where they possessed a third of the land. In all, a million Punjabi peasants emigrated to the nine Canal Colonies. Their regular remittances home boosted the agricultural income of the regions from which they originated, and was further increased by the opportunities for seasonal employment provided by the colonies. Moreover, the agricultural produce of the older regions of the province found a ready market amongst the colonists who specialized in cultivating a narrow range of cash crops.

The creation of the Canal Colonies was closely linked with the other major development of the late nineteenth century, the Punjab's emergence as the leading recruitment centre of the Indian Army. One of the important incentives for enlistment, especially amongst the Sikh Jats, was the British policy of rewarding ex-servicemen with lucrative grants of land in the colonies. Considerable areas of the Lower Bari Doab Canal Colony were distributed in this way.[5] The increased prosperity which irrigation had brought to the Punjab meant that far fewer volunteers for army service were turned away on medical grounds than from poorer regions such as Bihar and Bengal. The vast increase in land available for agriculture enabled the

British to set large areas apart solely for the purpose of breeding horses and cattle for the Army. Over 200,000 acres in the Shahpur district were leased for this purpose. During the First World War, the Lyallpur Canal Colony district provided large amounts of wheat and flour for the troops and gifts of horses and mules were made to the army.[6] Remounts were obtained from the Shahpur district. The Canal Colonies were not of course alone in making this contribution to the war effort; the Hissar district also supplied 2,000 bullocks and 5,000 camels.[7]

PUNJAB AND THE INDIAN ARMY

The Indian Army was of immense importance to British imperial interests. It not only stood in reserve to maintain law and order throughout the subcontinent, but strengthened British influence in the Middle East and ensured that the Indian Ocean remained a British lake. In its heyday, immediately before the outbreak of the First World War, it was the largest volunteer army the world has known. It consisted largely of officers and men drawn from one province—the Punjab.

During the period 1875–1914, the composition of the Indian Army altered dramatically. At the beginning of this period Punjabi troops accounted for just a third of its total strength and the army's main recruiting areas still lay in Bengal, Madras and Bombay. By the end, however, three-fifths of the troops came from the Punjab and the Army had made its home there. The Indian Army entered the First World War with a quarter of a million Punjabis in its ranks. What lay behind this region's overwhelming military importance? Why had the British since the 1870s become so heavily dependent on Punjab's population to defend their colonial empire?

The answer lies partly in the region's turbulent history. This led its people to develop military prowess and martial values long before the British entered it. Generations of Punjabis had been forced to fight to survive as wave after wave of invaders had poured down from the passes of the Frontier. The near anarchy in the Punjab which followed the collapse of Mughal authority greatly strengthened this martial tradition. During the early part of the eighteenth century there was almost continuous fighting as Afghan, Mahratta and Sikh armies marauded across the region. The possession of land became almost entirely dependent on military strength. Military and political leadership went hand in hand.

There thus existed in the Punjab a strong military tradition on which the British could build. Nevertheless, it is unlikely that the region would have assumed importance as a centre of colonial military recruitment if it had not been near the Indian Army's main theatre of war in Afghanistan.

The terrain and climate of the Salt Range hills of the Jhelum and Shahpur districts and of the foothills of the Himalayas in the remote north-eastern region of Kangra was similar to that of the Frontier. Recruits drawn from these areas were ideally suited for the harsh campaigning conditions of the Frontier itself. They were able to survive comfortably in temperatures which froze soldiers from Bengal and Madras to death. They could move as swiftly as any Afghan or Pathan tribesmen across the narrow ridges and steep hillsides of the Frontier passes. Moreover, they were not only better equipped for fighting in this region than troops from South India but they could be paid less. Soldiers serving on the Frontier from more distant parts of India had to be paid extra 'foreign service' allowances, unlike the Punjabis who only qualified for the local service basic rate of pay.[8]

Despite this, the British were able to secure large numbers of recruits from the Muslim tribesmen of the Salt Range and the Hindu Dogras from Kangra. The Muslim warrior tribes of Tiwanas and Khattars had for generations turned to military service in order to supplement their agricultural income derived from rents and haphazard cultivation. They eagerly accepted the opportunity which the British provided for them to perpetuate their military way of life. For the Dogras too, military service was a heaven-sent opportunity to keep intact their martial values and to boost the income of their impoverished Kangra region

Both on the grounds of economy and military efficiency, it was sensible for the British to greatly expand the Punjabi contingent within an Indian Army whose major role at the end of the nineteenth century was seen to be that of policing the Frontier. The British had already fought two wars with Afghanistan and expected a third in which there might also possibly be Russian involvement. Any criticism that the Indian Army's military effectiveness in other theatres of war was being put at risk by its Punjabization was answered by pointing at the large numbers of Sikh Jats included in the contingents. The Sikhs were acknowledged by experts to be the perfect foil for the skirmishing forces of Muslims and Dogras as they were excellent fighters in less hilly terrain.

The domination of the Indian Army by recruits drawn from the Punjab was thus based on sound pragmatic grounds, though this policy became enshrined in the mythology of the martial castes theory which maintained that the ethnic origins and racial characteristics of the main groups of Punjabi recruits particularly fitted them for military service. They were designated as martial castes whose racial superiority made them natural warriors. The martial castes theory gained considerable official support during the period of Lord Roberts' command of the Indian Army (1885–1893). He believed that the 'civilising' effects of British rule had undermined the martial instincts of the populations of the Indian Army's oldest recruiting areas of Madras and Bengal. Truly martial castes only existed in the recently conquered territory of the Punjab. This theory of the superiority of the Punjab's martial castes, the Muslims of the Salt Range, the Sikh Jats and the Hindu Dogras gained general acceptance in Indian Army circles. It also came in for considerable embellishment.[9]

Nationalist opponents of the Raj completely rejected this theory. They maintained that the British had shifted their main area of army recruitment to the Punjab because its uneducated and backward population readily collaborated with them. This had not in fact been an important factor in the decision to transfer recruiting operations to north-west India. Nevertheless, once the Indian Army had made its home in the Punjab, the political loyalty of the region's population became vitally important.

It was especially necessary for the British to secure the loyalty of the clan leaders of the Muslim tribes of the Salt Range. The Muslim martial castes of this region not only greatly outnumbered their Hindu and Sikh counterparts, but their leaders played a far more active role in actually procuring recruits. Many clan leaders not only served as officers themselves in the Indian Army but enlisted their rural followers as *sepoys* and *sowars*. This practice not only simplified the recruiting procedure for the British but greatly assisted army discipline. Such recruits naturally obeyed officers who had acted as their patrons in their home villages. The most famous clan of military contractors for the Army was the Tiwanas. They officered, equipped and enlisted their own men.

The value of relying on clan loyalties to ensure a constant supply of recruits was clearly seen during the First World War. Such leaders of Muslim martial castes as Sardar Muhammad Nawaz Khan and Sikander Hayat Khan played an active role in raising recruits. They were assisted by the Pirs of their followers. Pir Ghulam Abbas of Makhad personally enrolled 4,000 recruits.[10] Pir Fazl Shah of Jalalpur,[11] Pir Badshah of Bhera,[12] Pir Chan,[13] and Pir Sultan Ali Shah of Jehanian Shah[14] all encouraged their disciples amongst the Muslim martial castes of the Shahpur and Jhelum districts to enlist. The brother of the *Sajjada Nashin* of Alipur, Abbas Ali Shah, joined the army himself.

The Tiwanas provided no less than eighteen commissioned officers during the war, as well as large numbers of ordinary soldiers. The presence of the Tiwana clan leader, Umar Hayat Khan, was particularly important in alleviating the disquiet amongst the Punjabi Muslim troops during the campaign against the Ottoman armies in Mesopotamia. The Tiwana chief saw active service in France also and met all his own expenses and that of his large retinue while doing so.[15]

Sikh rural society was far more egalitarian than the Muslim. The British were consequently unable to rely on a few leading families to supply army recruits for them. Economic incentives always played a larger part in securing Sikh enlistment. During the First World War, when there was a huge increase in the demand for Sikh Jat soldiers, the British were forced to rely heavily on these landowners and religious leaders who possessed local influence. The *mahants* of Sikh gurudwaras were, for example, called on to assist the war effort. The most active were, Mahant Parannath of Bohar in the Rohtak district, Mahant Raghbir Singh of Ramdas in Amritsar and Mahant Basheshar Nath of Gurdaspur.[16] The influential Bedi family of Gurus of the Rawalpindi district and the family of Bhai Arjan Singh of Bagarian in the Ludhiana district were also relied on by the British. Arjan Singh used his great spiritual influence in the Malwa to good effect. He made extensive tours throughout the Ludhiana and Ferozepore districts encouraging Sikhs to join the army. He also subscribed over forty thousand rupees to various war loans and funds. The Punjab Government considered his support to have been so important that both the Governor and the Viceroy visited him at Bagarian in 1919 to thank him.[17]

The First World War highlighted Punjab's domination of the Indian Army. During the course of this conflict, over three-quarters of a million Punjabis served in its ranks. This was by far the largest contingent from any province and accounted for nearly two-thirds of the Army's total strength. It was a remarkable achievement for a province which contained less than a tenth of India's population. Punjabis saw action in the mud of Flanders, in the deserts of Arabia and in the bush of East Africa. During these campaigns they won over 2,000 decorations, including 19 Military Crosses and 3 Victoria Crosses. The recruits were drawn from all the rural communities of Punjab. Over half were Muslims, the remainder were almost equally divided between the Hindus and Sikhs.

The Indian Army continued to be dominated by the Punjabi martial castes throughout the inter-war years. At no time did the Punjabi element within it drop below three-fifths of its total strength. During the Second World War, when the Army reached its greatest ever strength, a million Punjabis served in its ranks. The region's domination of the military profession survived independence itself, particularly in Pakistan but also to a lesser extent in India.

The impact of army recruitment on Punjab's social and political life was considerable. It increased still further the rural population's prosperity as soldiers dutifully despatched a stream of remittances home to their villages. Income derived from military service enabled the tribal *maliks* of West Punjab to transform themselves into a wealthy landowning class. The declining Dogra martial caste was given at least a temporary reprieve from total impoverishment. When a degree of democracy was introduced into the province, servicemen and their retired comrades exerted a powerful political influence. Through investing their savings wisely or being granted land or government office as a reward for their loyalty, they came to dominate the restricted electorate. Significantly, such important representatives of the Muslim martial castes as Sikander Hayat and Khizr Hayat Khan Tiwana played a leading role in the Unionist Party, the rural inter-communal group which dominated provincial politics during the final decades of the British rule.

Notes

1. H. K. Trevaskis, *The Land of the Five Rivers* (Oxford, 1928), p. iv.
2. N. Charlesworth, *British Rule and the Indian Economy 1800–1914* (London, 1982), p. 26.
3. B. N. Singh, 'Punjab Canals' in G. C. Chatterji (ed.), *The Punjab Past and Present* (Lahore, 1939), p. 129.
4. M. L. Darling, *The Punjab Peasant in Prosperity and Debt* (New Delhi, 1977), p. 116.
5. F. C. Bourne, *Final Settlement Report of the Lower Bari Doab Canal Colony 1927–1935* (Lahore, 1935), p. 3.
6. G. F. D. Montmorency, *History of the War in the Lyallpur District* (Lahore), p. 36.
7. 'Hissar's War Work. The Efforts of the Punjab District 1914–1919 , IOR Pos 5545, p. 9.
8. For the development of this point see C. Dewey's excellent unpublished paper, 'The Rise of the "Martial Castes". Changes in the Composition of the Indian Army 1878–1914'.
9. See S. P. Cohen, *The Indian Army* (Berkeley, 1971), p. 47 & ff.

10. M. S. D. Butler, *Record of War Services in the Attock District 1914–1919* (Lahore, 1921), Statement C, IOR Pos 5545.
11. *War Services of the Shahpur District*, IOR Pos 5545, p. 86.
12. *Ibid.*, (11) above, p. 89.
13. *Ibid.*, (11) above, p. 85.
14. *Ibid.*, (11) above, p. 39.
15. *Ibid.*, (11) above, p. 73.
16. *Ibid.*, (9) above, p. 121.
17. G. L. Chopra, *Chiefs and Families of Note in the Punjab*, Vol. 1 (Lahore, 1940), p. 207.

CHAPTER 3

The British and Their Allies

> Apply any practical test—the prevention of religious riots, the composing of sectional differences, the raising of recruits for the ... army ... when any of these questions is to the fore, the politician usually retires to the background. His influence for good is usually nil but he can and sometimes does add to the trouble by injudicious or malicious interference. In the Punjab though sectarian feeling often runs very high it rarely leads to riot or bloodshed because the local authorities know on whom to depend to compose matters. These are not politicians but quiet men of local influence.[1]

By the beginning of the twentieth century, Punjab had assumed immense importance to British imperial interests. The loyalty of its rural population from which the Indian Army drew the bulk of its recruits was vitally important. It was particularly necessary to win the support of the Muslim clan leaders and large landowners of West Punjab who acted in effect as the Raj's military contractors.

THE SEARCH FOR ALLIES

The Punjab Government decided in the aftermath of the Indian Mutiny to use the region's native aristocracy as, 'a great bulwark for the state'.[2] It had expected the worst in the newly-annexed region and had been genuinely surprised by the extent of the Muslim and Sikh landowners' loyalty. The previous policy of 'bringing all to a dead level' which had been strongly advocated by the Chief Commissioner, John Lawrence, was finally repudiated and the large landowners responded eagerly to this change of heart. They were prepared to cooperate closely with the colonial regime in return for its patronage and access to its decision-making process. In this way they hoped to increase their standing amongst their rural followers. The Government's policy of coopting the rural elites took an added significance following the Indian Army's decision to switch its main area of recruitment to the Punjab.

From the 1860s onwards, the British were constantly searching for allies amongst the region's rural population. They made great efforts to identify every important family in each locality and compiled and recorded their history in the District Gazetteers and Caste Handbooks of the Indian Army. In the Muslim West Punjab, the task of identifying the local social elites did not present any problems, but in the more egalitarian Sikh and Hindu societies of the Central and East Punjab it was not always easy to discover 'men of influence'. The Rohtak District Gazetteer lamented the lack of old established aristocratic families. After the attempt to engineer the creation of a landowning elite had failed,[3] the British contented themselves with patronising the Jat community as a whole in its efforts to raise its status. They regarded the Jats' collaboration as extremely important, as it provided the necessary Hindu ingredient for a provincial inter-communal rural alliance.

The possession of power and influence did not by itself earn a local elite the patronage of the colonial regime. It had to be accompanied by a demonstration of political loyalty. The British attached great importance to the 'steadfastness' or 'treachery' which the landowners displayed during the crises of the Sikh Wars and the Mutiny. Significantly, most of the elite groups which developed the closest ties with the British had sided with them at these times of difficulty.

The four most important Sikh landowning families, the

Ramgarhias, Sindhanwalias, Ahulwalias and Majithas, who collaborated closely with the British, are a good illustration of this point. Sardar Mangal Singh of Ramgarhia was the head of one of the most powerful Sikh confederacies at the time of the British annexation of Punjab. During the Second Anglo-Sikh War he had sided with the British who amply rewarded him with a *jagir* worth Rs. 37,000. His eldest son served as a Police Inspector from 1859–1887 and held the offices of Honorary Magistrate, Municipal Commissioner, and member of the Provincial Durbar. This tradition of loyalty in return for Government patronage was transmitted through successive generations. In 1916, for example, the family was granted 7 squares of land in the Montgomery district in recognition of its wartime work of raising army recruits.[4]

The Sindhanwalias and Ahluwalias vied for the highest rank in Sikh society during the late eighteenth century. The Ahluwalia lands were situated in the Jullundur Doab, the Sindhanwalia between the Beas and the Indus. Sardar Shamsher Singh Sindhanwalia supported the British during the Second Sikh War and raised a troop of 125 horsemen which formed part of the famous 'flamingoes' force of Hodson's Horse.[5] The Sikh Sardar was made an honorary magistrate by the British in reward for this service, though his family did not prosper under their rule. Shamsher Singh finally had to leave the Punjab and settle in Pondicherry to escape his creditors. The Ahluwalia family which had also fought on the British side during the Sikh Wars adapted more readily to the social and economic changes brought by colonial rule. Its leading member, Pratap Singh Ahluwalia, served as a nominated representative of the Punjab Legislative Council during the 1890s and in 1907 formed the first loyalist inter-communal grouping within it.

The Majithas differed from the other three leading Sikh families in that they initially blotted their copy-book when the head of the family, Sardar Surjit Singh, served with the 'rebel army' during the Second Sikh War. By way of punishment he was exiled to Banaras and had Rs. 22,500 worth of *jagirs* confiscated by the British. He eagerly grasped, however, the opportunity afforded by the revolt of 1857 to restore his family's fortunes. At the cost of a flesh wound in the thigh which he received while fighting for the British, he not only received permission to return to the Punjab but was granted a pension of Rs. 4,800 per annum and a *jagir* in the Gorakhpur district of UP. In 1875 he was made an honorary magistrate and two years later received the title Raja. Both his sons, Umrao Singh and Sunder Singh, were educated at Aitchison College.[6] The latter, after making his fortune as a sugar manufacturer[7] went on to a successful 'loyalist' political career. He was Revenue member in the Punjab Legislative Council from 1920–1926 and Revenue Minister in Sikander Hayat Khan's government in the Legislative Council from 1937 onwards. Sunder Singh Majitha also played a leading role in the development of Khalsa College, Amritsar, and in the Chief Khalsa Diwan.[8]

Most of the leading Muslim families of West Punjab supported the British during the Sikh Wars and the Mutiny and went on to develop close ties with the colonial administration. The two most striking examples of this were the Hayat, Khattar family from Wah in the Attock district and the Tiwanas from the Shahpur region. The head of the Hayat family had been killed while fighting on the British side during the Second Sikh War of 1848–9, and his son, Sardar Hayat Khan, stood loyally by John Nicholson, the Rawalpindi Deputy Commissioner in 1857. He became the first Indian in the Punjab to rise to the rank of Assistant Commissioner in 1871. A generation later, his son Sikandar Hayat Khan after wartime service in the Indian Army and a successful spell as acting-Governor became the first Premier of the Punjab in 1937. The Tiwanas were able to boast an equally lengthy and distinguished record of service to the British. They raised a 400-strong cavalry troop to aid the British during both periods of crisis. Umar Hayat Khan Tiwana served the British in a number of capacities from the beginning of the twentieth century until the 1940s. His son, Khizr Hayat Khan Tiwana, became the last Premier of British Punjab in 1944.

The British were less confident, however, in developing alliances with the Sufi Pirs of West Punjab, in spite of their demonstration of loyalty to the colonial regime. Makhdum Shah Muhammad, head of the influential Qureshi Pir family of Multan, not only supplied troops during the Second Sikh War but had severely demoralized the 'local rebels' by joining in the campaign against them. Although the British at first fought shy of developing too close a link with such Pirs in case it endangered their policy of religious impartiality, they found it impossible to isolate the Pirs from its system of local political alliances. The British increasingly treated them in the same way as the large landowners and clan leaders, taking their encumbered estates under the Court of Wards wing, awarding them positions of authority in the local administration and granting them land in the Canal Colonies.

There was naturally some criticism of this policy. It was stretching the imagination to call all the Pirs members of the Punjab's 'landed gentry'. But on grounds of real-politik it was necessary to do so. Sir Michael O'Dwyer, the province's Governor during the First World War, summed up the situation most clearly. 'If a man has political influence and uses it well', he declared, 'the fact that he is connected with a religious institution and even to a certain extent derives his influence from that connection should not in my opinion stand in his way of obtaining a (Government) land grant.[9]

Once the British had decided to enlist the Pirs' support, they also developed links with the Sikh religious leaders. In return for patronage, the *mahants* of leading shrines obliged them by issuing *Hukamnamas*[10] in support of the Punjab Government at times of political crisis. The British also developed alliances with two important families of Gurus, the family of Bhai Arjan Singh of the Ludhiana district and of Baba Khem Singh Bedi from Rawalpindi. The latter family claimed descent from Guru Nanak. Although it originated in the Rawalpindi district by the time the British annexed the Punjab, it had migrated to Jullundur and held *jagirs* there worth over Rs. 12,000. During the Mutiny, Baba Khem Singh raised troops for the British and helped keep open communications. He was later rewarded with a *khilat*[11] worth Rs. 3000. During the next forty years,

Baba Khem Singh became ever more closely allied to the Government. He pioneered the introduction of vaccination amongst his followers in the north-west of Punjab and sponsored female education. He also became involved in the life of the Lower Bari Doab Canal Colony in which he amassed an estate of over 14,000 Acres, serving as an honorary magistrate from 1877 onwards. He was knighted shortly before his death in 1904. His son, Baba Kartar Singh Bedi, well aware of the advantages which it brought, naturally continued the family tradition of service to the British.

The Bagarian family of Bhai Arjan Singh possessed great spiritual influence amongst the Sikhs of the Malwa and the Phulkian States. The British responded to this by investing each successive head of the family with the powers of a magistrate and Civil Judge in their home district. Bhai Arjan Singh gave invaluable support to the British during the First World War.

BRITISH POLICY TOWARDS RURAL ALLIES

Leading rural families maintained their close links with the British through successive generations for two main reasons. They shared in the general prosperity which British rule brought to the countryside and they remained tied to the colonial regime through complex webs of patronage.

From the 1860s onwards there was a massive increase in agricultural prices and land values in the Punjab. This stemmed from the ending of political insecurity in the region and from vastly improved communications and irrigation facilities. New cash crops such as tobacco, sugar-cane and cotton were introduced. Wheat, which had previously rotted whenever a bumper crop had occurred, was exported in vast quantities via the new railway network. Agricultural output, because of the vast increase in irrigation, easily outstripped population growth. All this added up to a bonanza for Punjab's cultivators who soon ranked amongst the richest farmers in Asia.

Unlike any traditional oriental despot, the Punjab Government allowed most of the increased agricultural profit to remain in the cultivators' hands. It pitched its revenue demand as low as possible. At first it was set at half a cultivator's assessed profit, but by the 1930s it had fallen to a 'quarter net assets'. The farmers not only benefited from this low revenue demand but also from the fact that the land settlement was only reassessed every twenty years or so. This meant that the proportion of the produce which a cultivator had to sell to meet the revenue demand fell steadily because of the increase in agricultural prices. By the time British rule ended, the farmer probably had to sell as little as 10 per cent of his crop to pay his land revenue. In consequence, the rural population experienced an unprecedented rise in standards of living. Nowhere else in India did colonial rule bring so tangible a benefit.

The boom in agricultural prices and land in Punjab had one important drawback. It led to a rapid growth in agricultural indebtedness. When the British recognized that this was undermining their system of rule based on the support of the leading landowning groups, they swallowed their *laissez faire* principles and acted to avert this danger. The resultant 1901 Alienation of Land Act provided an important stimulus to future intercommunal political cooperation within the region.

British rule had swept away the barriers which had previously prevented the Hindu moneylenders from acquiring land in the countryside.[12] As land prices soared, it became increasingly tempting for improvident landowners to pledge their land in return for easy credit. Land began to pass into the moneylenders' hands at an alarming rate, particularly in the backward regions of Muzaffargarh and Dera Ghazi Khan. By 1916 Hindu moneylenders owned over 490,000 acres in the Dera Ghazi Khan district.[13] In Muzaffargarh it was estimated that about 1 per cent of the total cultivated area changed hands each year from the time of the Regular Settlement onwards. All this land virtually passed into the hands of absentee Hindu moneylenders who, despite the fact that over 90 per cent of the population was Muslim, owned a quarter of the cultivated area by the 1920s.[14]

The Muslim cultivators of West Punjab were not alone in

suffering at the hands of the Hindu moneylenders. The Hindu Rajputs of the submontane districts of Ambala Division were also victims of powerful moneylenders who, 'exact free services (*begar*) and free fuel, fodder and *ghi* and (take their) dues as much in grain as in cash'.[15] The Hindu Jats of Rohtak suffered from the moneylenders' exploitation as well. Their subservience was vividly illustrated in village meetings where the moneylender sat in the place of honour at the head of the *charpoy* (stringed cot) with his peasant clients at his feet.

The moneylenders' increasing influence posed a serious threat to rural stability. From the 1860s onwards, local officials warned of the possible danger of unrest as a result of the large-scale transfer of land to them. Their warnings took on a sense of urgency when S. S. Thorburn published his book entitled *Mussulmans and Moneylenders in the Punjab*. Thorburn, a Deputy Commissioner in the Dera Ghazi Khan district, highlighted the rural population's loss of land to the urban moneylenders in the frontier regions of the province. The Punjab Government was nevertheless loathe to interfere with the freedom of land transactions. But its fears remained, as the following Revenue departments' 'Note on Land Transfer' which was written in October 1895 clearly reveals.

> It is essential on the one hand that the management of the villages should be in the hands of men who possess the confidence of the villagers, and it is equally essential on the other that if the executive is to be obeyed and its objects rightly understood, there should be a class of men intermediate between the Government and the mass of the people who, while trusted by government, should have influence over their neighbours. In this respect the moneylender can never take the place of the large ancestral landlord or the substantial yeoman whom he disposes.

At first the British attempted to solve this problem with piece-meal measures. They took a large number of encumbered estates under the wing of the Court of Wards Administration. By the beginning of the twentieth century, however, it had become apparent that wider action needed to be taken in order to bolster the position of the rural leaders who acted as their allies.

During the fifty years of its existence, the Court of Wards Administration played an important part in reinforcing the landowners' loyalty to the British. It supervised most of the Punjab's leading estates either as a result of their indebtedness or of their inheritance by minors. In 1895, it was managing as many as 65 estates with a total area of over 344,000 acres.[17] It revitalized them by introducing sound management techniques and improving irrigation, stock breeding and cultivation. During the sixteen and a half years that the Tiwana family's Kalra estate was under its control, its annual revenue was raised by Rs. 25,000. It spectacularly cleared the Nawab of Mamdot's estate's debt of over Rs. 357,000. All but the smallest and most impoverished estates had their debts liquidated under the Court of Wards' judicious management. It annually ploughed back as much as 20 per cent of an estate's rental income in agricultural improvements. Many estate managers negotiated loans so that Canal Colony land could be purchased on behalf of the wards. The Kalra estate in this way acquired substantial holdings in the Chenab Colony. In 1908 alone, just under 2,000 acres within the Colony were purchased on behalf of estates under the Court of Wards' management. Although its policies were primarily motivated by economic considerations, the British were well aware of the favourable repercussions of its activities.

In 1901, the British introduced major legislation to curb the moneylenders' growing influence. The Punjab Alienation of Land Act divided the population into what it called agriculturalist and non-agriculturalist tribes. Included in the former category were not only the Jats, Rajputs, Arains and Gujars but the Muslim religious elites—the Syeds, Sheikhs and Qureshis. The non-agriculturalist tribes which included the moneylending castes were forbidden to permanently acquire land in the countryside. This measure not only halted the increasing exproporiation of impoverished landowners but encouraged inter-communal political cooperation by giving concrete expression to the Muslim, Hindu and Sikh cultivators' common economic interests.[18]

The British went a stage further in encouraging the creation of an inter-communal rural interest group when they granted agriculturalists a preferential right of recruitment to Government service. They had set up in 1918 a commission under the chairmanship of H. J. Maynard to consider the agriculturalist tribes' representation in the public services. Its recommendation that this should be greatly increased was readily accepted by Michael O'Dwyer. The proportion of agriculturalist Extra Assistant Commissioners was to be raised from 40 to 50 per cent, of *tahsildars* and *naib-tahsildars* from 42 to 66 per cent and of *munsifs* from 29 to 66 per cent. The largest percentage increase of all was to take place in the Irrigation Branch of the Public Works Department where agriculturalist representation was to be increased from 29 to 66 per cent of the officials.[19] Such favouritism by the British reinforced the importance of tribal rather than religious identification amongst the rural population. It drew the Muslim, Hindu and Sikh Jats closer together while at the same time driving a wedge between the Hindu Jats and the banias and khatris.

British educational policy was another factor in securing loyal allies amongst the Punjab landowners. Aitchison College was founded in Lahore in 1886 to provide education for the sons of leading landlords. It restricted admission to all but a few of the province's rural elite. Its ethos and syllabus was similar to that of the English public schools, and it provided its pupils with a sense of pride and emotional attachment to the British Empire. They received an early training as future officials and legislators through regularly taking part in the College's Council of State which 'enabled a considerable number of boys to speak without notes or preparation and to reply in debating points'.[20] Many Aitchison College old boys went on to have important political careers. Most notable of all was Malik Khizr Hayat Khan Tiwana who had been an outstanding pupil at the College.

In addition to these policies aimed at the general advancement and protection of rural interests, the British dispensed large amounts of patronage to individual landholders and rural social groups in order to secure their alliance. This patronage took the form of honorary ranks and titles, positions in local government and most importantly, grants of land in the Canal Colonies. Their creation gave the Punjab Government an almost inexhaustible supply of patronage. It was thus in a much stronger position than was usual for colonial administrations which seldom had sufficient patronage to satisfy all their local allies.

THE BRITISH AND THE MUSLIM LANDOWNERS AND MARTIAL CASTES

The British attached importance to the well-being and views of the martial castes. Their leading representative Umar Hayat Khan Tiwana rose to a position of all-India political importance as spokesman of the Punjab's important military lobby. The land revenue demand was deliberately kept low in tracts which contained martial castes and generous grants of land were made to servicemen in the fertile canal colonies.[21] At the end of the First World War, over 420,000 acres of Colony land were distributed to just over 6,000 Commissioned and Non-Commissioned Army officers.[22] Ex-servicemen received generous pensions in addition to such grants of land. By 1928, over Rs. 140 lakhs* was being paid out each year in pensions for retired Punjabi servicemen. There were 16,000 military pensioners in the Rawalpindi district alone.

Apart from such individual rewards, the British continued their policy after the First World War of rewarding the martial castes as a whole in their Land Settlement policies. The settlement period of the Salt Range and Jhelum riverain circles of the Shahpur district was extended from 20–30 years in recognition of their population's war service. In the adjoining Thal circle, on the other hand, 'where recruiting was very poor' the term was fixed at 15 years.[23]

The large Muslim landowners of West Punjab eagerly sought land in the Canal Colonies as by the 1920s its value had increased to over £80 an acre in Lyallpur and about £40 an acre in Shahpur

*1 lakh represents Rs. 100,000.

and Montgomery.[24] Although the bulk of the land in the Canal Colony areas was sold to peasant proprietors, the Punjab Government reserved areas for the large landowners, some of which was sold to them; the remainder was given in reward for Government service. Seven and a half per cent of the Lower Bari Doab Canal Colony was in this way earmarked for the landed aristocracy.[25]

Cash and land grants were not the only kind of rewards which the British dispensed to the Muslim elite of West Punjab. They also liberally distributed honorary titles and ranks. Umar Hayat Khan Tiwana was knighted in appreciation of his wartime services. The receipt of such titles was considered a fitting reward for loyalty in a society which attached so much importance to individual and family *izzat* (honour).

Patronizing the Pirs

After initial hesitation, the Punjab Government set about drawing the Pirs into its administrative structure through bonds of patronage in the same way as the other landowners. In true Mughal tradition, the Pirs were rewarded by having membership of the provincial and divisional Durbars conferred upon them. The Diwan of Pakpattan and the *Sajjada Nashin* of the shrine of Baha-ud-Din Zakariya were both leading members of the provincial Durbar. Throughout West Punjab, the Pirs were encouraged by the British to play a leading role in local life as *zaildars*, honorary magistrates and later as district board members.

The Pirs were also given 'landed gentry' grants in the Canal Colonies where some of them played an important part both as *zaildars* and improving landlords. The *Sajjada Nashin* of the shrine of Hazrat Daud Karmani at Shergarh in Montgomery District was, for example, the focus of a scheme to improve the famous breed of Montgomery Cattle in the Lower Bari Doab Canal Colony, and his brother managed a very successful dairy farm there.[26] Not all Pirs were so forward-looking, a fact which drew unfavourable comment from some British administrators.

'The tribal characteristics (of the Syeds and Qureshis) are reproduced in their Colony holdings', wrote B. H. Dobson, the Chenab Colony Settlement Officer in 1915, 'subsisting largely on doles from their religious adherents and affecting an odour of sanctity, they are of no great usefulness in the capacity of Colony landlords'.[27] Yet they remained powerful local political figures and had thus to be treated with care by the British.

The Punjab Government's recognition of the Pirs as part of the 'landed gentry' had important political repercussions in establishing a unity of political interests between the landlords and the Pirs. Close religious and social ties already, of course, existed between them. The basis for cooperation between the two dominant social groups in West Punjab had thus been well established by the British before the first efforts were made to create a provincial rural political party in the early 1920s.

The British and Their Sikh Allies

The British drew the Sikh 'men of local influence' to their support in the same way. Cash, land grants and honorary titles were all freely offered in exchange for pledges of loyalty. In addition they lent their patronage to the efforts of the Sikh aristocracy to raise their community's educational and social status through the activities of the Singh Sabha movement.

The Singh Sabha's twin aims were to spread education amongst the Sikh community and to restore Sikhism to its pristine purity. The first Sabha was formed in Amritsar in 1873. Six years later a rival branch was founded in Lahore. The Sabhas sought Government patronage for a project to establish a Sikh College at Amritsar in addition to gaining support from the rulers of the neighbouring Sikh states. The British responded positively to the scheme and gave it their active support. This was symbolized on 5 March 1892 when the Punjab Lieutenant-Governor James Lyall laid the foundation stone of the future Khalsa College at Amritsar.

At the beginning of the twentieth century the Singh Sabhas were merged into the Chief Khalsa Diwan which was formed to represent the Sikhs' political demands to the Government. Its influence soon spread into Sind and the North-West Frontier Province. By 1910, its membership within the Punjab had risen to 10,000. This was grouped in four important regional branches, the Manjha Diwan at Taran Taran, the Malwa Khalsa Diwan at Choohar Chak in the Ferozepur district, the Doaba Khalsa Diwan at Jullundur, and finally, the Khalsa Diwan centred in the neighbouring princely State of Patiala.[28]

The Chief Khalsa Diwan was impeccably loyal to the British. Its memorials to the Punjab Government always began with a recitation of the 'glorious actions of friendship of the Government and favours done to the Sikh community' and ended with 'humble prayers for more concessions'.[29] In spite of such expressions of loyalty, the Punjab Government's sponsorship of the Singh Sabhas ultimately had dangerous consequences. Their activities strengthened growing Sikh religious self-awareness,[30] exploding into violence in the movement for gurdwara reform in the early 1920s which was not only directed against a loyal group of rural collaborators—the *mahants*—but wrested Sikh political leadership from the landed gentry. Most importantly, the movement's religious appeal ran directly counter to the British attempt to organize rural society along non-sectarian lines.

Jat Uplift

It was impossible for the British to control eastern Punjab through a class of landlord intermediaries. Unlike the western regions of the province this was the heartland of the peasant proprietor. British political control reached right down to the villages in East Punjab through an army of revenue and irrigation officials. It was nevertheless still important for the Punjab Government to maintain good relations with the dominant caste of Hindu Jat peasants.

Despite their vigour and agricultural skill, the Jats suffered under the twin burdens of indebtedness and famine. They, in fact, inhabited some of the poorest agricultural tracts in the province including the notorious famine area of Hissar. Their position gradually improved as a result of the increase in irrigation introduced by the British and the starting of the Cooperative movement in the Jat heartland of Rohtak.

During the early years of the twentieth century a new generation of educated Jat leaders emerged who were determined to secure Government support for the uplift of their people. The most notable of these leaders was Chaudhri Chhotu Ram, a young Jat leader from the Rohtak district about whom much was soon to be heard. It was largely as a result of his efforts that an Anglo-Sanskrit Jat High School was built in Rohtak in 1913. Chhotu Ram also encouraged Jat enlistment in the Indian Army during the First World War as he was well aware of the benefits this would bring his community. An immediate spin-off was Michael O'Dwyer's decision in 1915 to recommend the heads of all Government departments to increase the number of Jats in their employment.[31]

The movement for Jat uplift soon spread outwards from Rohtak district. It was also taken into politics where Jatism was to become an important political slogan and source of identity in the hands of Chhotu Ram. When the Unionist Party came into existence in the 1920s based on a pro-rural agriculturalist ideology and led by the Muslim landed gentry of West Punjab, it also contained a powerful Hindu Jat grouping within it.

The Beginnings of a New Era

By the beginning of the twentieth century, the British had established informal political alliances with the major land-owning groups in the Punjab who could be relied on to support the colonial regime. Their rural allies, however, lacked the organization and political expertise of the new generation of urban politicians. It was therefore with considerable reluctance that the Punjab officials responded to the Government of India's promptings concerning the spread of representative institutions within the region.

Successive Governors of Punjab procrastinated over the

establishment of a provincial legislative council despite the introduction of such councils in other parts of India. Almost half a century of British rule had elapsed before a Punjab Legislative Council was created. Even then, the officials saw to it that its powers were severely limited.

The first Punjab Legislative Council which met at Government House, Lahore, on 1 November 1897 did not possess the powers of interpellation which the 1892 Indian Councils Act had given to other legislative councils, nor the privilege of discussing the annual budget. All of its five Indian members were nominated. They were flanked by four Government officials besides the Governor himself who acted as the Council's President. He alone had the power to convene a meeting and also possessed complete control over the discussion of business.

Between 1897 and 1909, when the Council was extended in the wake of the Morley-Minto Reforms, it met just twenty-six times.[32] Virtually all its business was transacted by the British members. Indeed, some of its rural members scarcely opened their mouths. The 1909 Indian Councils Act increased the powers and membership of the Council, introducing an element of indirect election into this. But most of its Indian representatives were still drawn from the landowning classes. They continued to leave the bulk of the committee work and debating to the officials. Only half a dozen questions concerning the Financial Statements of 1910–12 were asked by the Indian members and no resolutions were passed.[33]

The Punjab Government guided a number of items through the Council which were directly to the advantage of its rural allies. The 1902 Descent of Jagirs Act enabled *jagirdars* to regulate their succession by legally adhering to the practice of primogeniture. A year later, the Punjab Court of Wards Act increased the efficiency of the Court of Wards Administration by replacing the 29 district organizations with a single province-wide body. The Act also improved the wards' legal position by removing their liability to be sued in person. Finally, it laid down that an estates' debts would be automatically wiped out if they were not legally contested within three years of its passing under the jurisdiction of the Court of Wards Administration.

Despite this successful use of the legislative council to bolster the position of the landowners, the British recognised that legislative politics could not be completely isolated from the political influences emanating from the cities. If the alliance between the Punjab Government and the rural elites was to survive the approaching era of mass politics it would have to become more formalized. Considerable official support was thus lent to the efforts of the Sikh Council member Sardar Partap Singh Ahluwalia to create a loyalist political association in 1907. This was called the Association of the Landed Aristocracy of the Punjab, later renamed the Punjab Chiefs Association. As its name implied, it was politically conservative organization which served the British and the landowners' interests alike by limiting the Congress' influence. Its development was particularly reassuring for the Government, as it came at a time when communal tension and violence was becoming an everyday feature of urban social and political life.

Notes

1. Sir Michael O'Dwyer, 5 March, 1914.
2. T. R. Metcalf, *The Aftermath of Revolt 1857–1870* (Princeton, 1965), p. 163.
3. *Rohtak District Gazetteer 1883–4* (Calcutta, 1884), p. 69.
4. G. L. Chopra, *Chiefs and Families of Note in the Punjab*, Vol. 2 (Lahore, 1940), p. 427 & ff.
5. They gained this nickname because of their red turbans and cummerbunds and khaki uniforms.
6. This Chiefs College had great importance in inculcating loyalty to the British.
7. He pioneered the development of India's biggest sugar factory in the U.P.
8. W. L. Contan & D. Craik, *Chiefs and Families of Note in Punjab*, Vol. 1 (Lahore, 1909), p. 417 & ff.
9. Quoted in D. Gilmartin, 'Religious Leadership and the Pakistan Movement in the Punjab', *Modern Asian Studies*, 13, 3 (1979), p. 495.
10. Directive from a Guru or a seat of Sikh religious authority.
11. A dress of honour bestowed by a ruler. It could include arms or a horse.
12. British rule made land a valuable commodity, created a private property

right in it and established a legal system in which individual ownership of land could be contested.

13. 'Forecast Report of the Dera Ghazi Khan District' (Lahore, 1916), Punjab Proceedings P 9926, June 1916, Part A, No. 48, IOR.
14. J. D. Anderson, 'Final Settlement Report of the Muzaffargarh District 1920–25' (Lahore, 1929), p. 7, Punjab Proceedings P 12048, Part A, IOR.
15. M. Darling, *Rusticus Loqitor* (Lahore, 1929), p. 74 & ff.
16. N. G. Barrier, *The Punjab Alienation of Land Bill of 1900* (Duke University, 1966), p. 37.
17. 'Report on the Administration of estates under the charge of the Court of Wards for the year ending 30 September 1895' (Lahore, 1896), p. 3. Punjab Departmental Annual Reports L 5 VI (3), IOR.
18. The Unionist Party later rallied support around the issue of maintaining the Act's safeguards for the rural population.
19. Punjab Legislative Council Debates, 12 March 1925, p. 408 & ff, V/9/3424, IOR.
20. 'Annual Report of Aitchison College 1937–38' (Lahore, 1938), p. 6, V/24/944, IOR.
21. F. C. Bourne, 'Assessment Report of the Okara Tehsil of the Montgomery District', Punjab Proceedings P 12048, May 1934, Part A, p. 18, IOR.
22. B. Josh, *Communist Movement in the Punjab 1921–1947* (Delhi, 1979), p. 25.
23. War Services of the Shahpur District, IOR, Pos. 5545, p. 51.
24. M. Darling, *The Punjab Peasant in Prosperity and Debt* (New Delhi, 1977), p. 129.
25. F. C. Bourne, *Final Settlement Report of the Lower Bari Doab Canal Colony 1927–35* (Lahore, 1935), p. 3.
26. *Ibid.*, (21) above.
27. B. H. Dobson, *Final Settlement Report of the Chenab Canal Colony Settlement* (Lahore, 1915), p. 44.
28. D. Petrie, 'Secret C.I.D. Memorandum on recent developments in Sikh Politics' (Lahore, 1911), in, *The Punjab Past and Present*, Vol. IV, Pt. 2 (April 1970), p. 358.
29. M. Singh, *The Akali Movement* (Delhi, 1978), p. 156.
30. The Indian Army had also encouraged this by only accepting baptized Sikhs as recruits and expecting them to observe the five external symbols of Sikhism.
31. War History of the Rohtak District, IOR Pos 5547, p. 8.
32. *Punjab Legislative Council Debates 1897–1936*, V/9/3419–V/9/3455, IOR.
33. W. W. Reinhardt, *The Legislative Council of the Punjab 1897–1912* (Duke University, 1972), p. 169.

CHAPTER 4

The Communalist Threat to British Rule

> What little power and influence the Reforms have conferred on India have been conferred not on Indians as such but on Muslims and Non-Muslims. By this subtle means they have instead of uniting the people only divided them and produced mutual jealousy, hatred and bitterness.[1]

> The existing strained relations between Muslim and Hindu are largely due to the writings of a couple of Hindu and eight or ten Muhammadan newspapers which are doing their best to fan the flame of bigotry in the country by their virulent writings. These papers are ruining the country by their mischievous writings merely for personal gain, simply because such writings sell.[2]

Communalism presented a major threat to the British system of political control in the Punjab. This was based on alliances with the landowners who were drawn from all the religious communities. The British had knitted together these powerful but fragmented groups of local collaborators by encouraging the development of an overarching agriculturalist ideology. It was manifested most clearly in the 1901 Alienation of Land Act which not only stressed the landowners' common economic interests but reinforced the importance of kinship and tribal loyalties over and above religious solidarity.

Any increase in religious self-awareness amongst the Punjab's villagers would thus strike at the heart of the system of colonial, social and political control. There was a real danger that this might happen as from the end of the nineteenth century there was increasing communal competition and rivalry in the cities. This chapter examines the dynamics behind this and explains why the countryside remained largely unaffected by it.

The Causes of Communalism in Punjab's Cities

Communal rivalry became so intense in Punjab's cities towards the end of the nineteenth century that the province gained the nickname, the 'Ulster' of India. It did not spill over into the countryside partly because of its backwardness and isolation. In the main, however, it was the result of the differential impact of colonial rule. In the countryside, the British had created a framework in which inter-communal cooperation thrived; in the cities they had inadvertently stimulated intense communal competition.

Communal, Economic and Political Rivalry

Educated Indian opinion in the Punjab, expressed especially through the columns of the *Tribune*, claimed that the British deliberately encouraged communal tension in order to divide and rule. There is in fact no evidence that the Punjab Government ever followed such a policy. Nevertheless, the British decision to open up opportunities for Muslims in Government service and their introduction of separate electorates in the Municipal Committees undoubtedly encouraged and increased communal rivalry and awareness amongst the urban elites.

The British at first adopted an attitude of strict impartiality concerning all religious and communal issues. This was summed up in Henry Lawrence's orders that, 'my men are expected to extend equal rights to all native religions and to align with none'.[3] Favouritism in Government recruitment policy was directed not towards any particular religious community but towards the landowners who were the 'natural leaders of the country'. This policy was, however, reversed during James Lyall's governorship (1887–1892). He recommended that the Hindus' monopoly of Government posts should be broken by favouring suitable Muslim applicants until the Hindu-Muslim ratio in Government service bore 'some relation' to their numerical proportions 'among the upper and middle classes of the population'.[4] Lyall's recommendation was at first kept secret. It was certainly not part of a devious plot to divide and rule, but rather a serious attempt to ease the communal tension created by the Hindus' domination of the Punjab civil service.

During the first decades of colonial rule there were few Indian officials and the British Deputy Commissioners kept a close personal control over local administration. As government became steadily bureaucratized there was not only a large influx of Indian officials, but the Deputy Commissioners' tours in the *mofussil* became less frequent. Nepotism and communal favouritism became rife in some regions. The emerging Muslim professional class latched on to this to agitate[5] for an opening up of employment opportunities. Lyall hoped that his intervention would quieten this. But his action had a disastrous impact on communal relations. Soon, every Government appointment from the lowliest village *patwari* to the most exalted High Court Judge was keenly scrutinized for its effect on the communal balance of power within the services.

Lyall's innovation revealed that agitation could influence government decisions. It encouraged petitioning and the discussion of communal issues which frequently served only to inflame the situation. Much heat, for instance, was generated at the time of the 1881 Hunter Education Commission. Muslims hoped it would recommend special privileges for them. The Hindus countered by demanding that Hindi should replace Urdu as the official vernacular language as it had done recently in Bihar. The educated Muslim classes in the cities sprang to Urdu's defence. They formed an *Anjuman-i-Himayat-i-Urdu* and organized petitions against its replacement.

Agitations occurred five years later at the time of the Aitchison Public Service Commission and again in 1883 when the Ripon Local Government Reforms were introduced. They revealed the extent to which urban politics had developed along communal lines. The Ripon Reforms initiated the element of election in local government, and increased the powers of municipal committees and district boards over such matters as education, public works and health. A new arena for communal competition emerged in which the Muslims, Hindus and Sikhs struggled for patronage and power. The municipal committees formed the most glittering prizes as they possessed more power and popular representation. Their election contests turned rapidly into bitter communal clashes and intimidation and bribery were commonplace. The Muslims were usually the losers as the Hindus dominated the restricted electorate. Not all Hindu leaders used their newly acquired power wisely. At Hoshiarpur, for example, they attempted to ban the sale of beef within the city. Although the Deputy Commissioner stepped in to prevent this, he could not forestall the outbreak of a serious communal riot.[6]

The Muslims responded to their exclusion from power by demanding separate electorates. The British were not at first prepared to acquiesce. Instead, they threw the most notoriously corrupt Hindus off the committees and in especially troublesome places invoked the right of having a British official as president. It was only after these expedients had failed to allay Muslim fears that they reluctantly agreed to the introduction of separate electorates. Even then they were only introduced piecemeal. It was not until the control of local self-government became a transferred power in 1919 that a concerted effort was made to increase them by the Muslim minister Mian Fazl-i-Husain.[7] He simultaneously instituted the principle of communal representation into the admission's policy of Government College, Lahore, and the Lahore Medical College. These actions aroused vehement protests from the urban Hindu population which culminated in a censure motion being moved against Fazl-i-Husain in the 1923 Legislative Council session. The Governor,

Sir Malcolm Hailey, saw no justification for the portrayal of the Muslim minister as an arch-communalist.[8] Nevertheless, his actions unintentionally increased communal tension as they threatened still further the Hindus' political and economic pre-eminence in the cities. Some Hindus feared this undermining of their position so much that they opposed any further constitutional reforms which they feared could accelerate this process and they yearned for a return to the bureaucratic rule of the 1870s.[9]

The British not only provided new arenas of conflict for Punjab's urban communities, but also encouraged a greater communal awareness. This again was unintentional. It resulted from the unexpected indigenous response to the widespread Christian missionary activity which followed Punjab's annexation.

Religious Revivalism

Although the Punjab Government adopted a policy of strict religious neutrality from the outset, many officials openly supported missionary activity. The Lawrences likened their punitive expeditions against the Sikhs to those of the Israelites against the surrounding heathen populations as they entered the Promised Land. For them and many of their colleagues, 'the conversion of the natives to Christianity was the greatest blessing our rule could confer ... and as far as human reason could see, one of the greatest objects for which our rule was permitted'.[10]

During the early years of British rule, no Punjabi official moved his camp on a Sunday, no regiments marched and no work was undertaken on public works projects. This was the result of the 'quiet and unostentatious example and orders of God-fearing men in authority'.[11] In 1868, the Government moved into open support for missionary activity when it granted 2,000 acres of irrigated land in Chunian to the Church Missionary Society so that it could establish a Christian Colony there.[12] By the 1880s, a network of mission stations covered the province. The largest number of these belonged to the

Church Missionary Society which also ran 113 schools.[13] During the next twenty years, the number of copies of Christian newspapers and tracts rose to over 300,000 annually.[14] The American Missions Board, Urdu weekly, *Nur-i-Afshan*, regularly sold over 500 copies in the Ludhiana district alone.[15]

Although the Christian community remained small, numbering only 163,994 persons at the time of the 1911 Census, it was growing rapidly. It had increased fortyfold since 1881. This success which was highly publicized increased the fears of the native communities. The strongest reaction came from the Hindus who felt particularly endangered by the missionaries' activities. Their response also stirred the urban Muslims into a defence of Islam against both Christianity and revitalized Hinduism.

Hindu religious revivalism in the Punjab was spearheaded by the Arya Samaj. It had been founded in Bombay in 1875 by Swami Dayanand Saraswati, but had made little impact as orthodox Hindus rejected its attacks on caste restrictions, idol worship and elaborate brahminical ritual. It found a far more congenial environment in the Punjab where the brahmins wielded little influence.[16] Dayanand's forthright defence of Hinduism from Christian proselytizing soon attracted attention, especially as it was cloaked in the full scriptural authority of the Vedas. He borrowed such Christian evangelical techniques as street-corner preaching, the establishment of orphanages and the publication of religious tracts.

During the late 1880s, the Arya Samaj spread rapidly. Its network of local branches covered the whole of the Punjab with the exception of the Montgomery district.[17] Importantly, however, for the future of communal relations, despite considerable efforts it had made little progress amongst the Hindu agriculturalists of the Rohtak and Hissar districts. The Samaj's greatest support remained amongst the urban Hindu populations of Lahore, Amritsar, Rawalpindi and Multan. They looked to it to help defend their economic and political power which was now coming under attack from the Muslims and they were also attracted by its increasing educational activities. On June 1886 a

Dayanand Anglo-Vedic High School was established in Lahore. It was soon to become a constituent college of the Punjab University. Arya high schools grew up in many of the cities as also did *gurukuls* (seminaries) to train Arya *updeshaks* (missionaries). The schools established a reputation for providing low-cost, high-quality education. More importantly, schooling along Anglo-Vedic lines provided the opportunity to learn within a secure Hindu environment the modern skills required to obtain employment in the Government's service. Previously, when middle class parents had sent their sons to government and mission schools in order to gain western education, they had always feared that this would lead to a conversion to Christianity. These anxieties were now banished.

The Arya Samaj grew increasingly militant towards other religious groups, partly because of growing ideological and personal rivalries within it. The devotional faction of Pandit Guru Datta, Lala Durga Prasad and Lala Munshi Ram hoped that their belligerence would cut the ground from under the feet of the secular group led by Lala Hans Raj and Lala Lajpat Rai. Tension with the orthodox Hindus was heightened by the sponsorship of widow remarriage, female education and the introduction of de-brahmanized marriage and funeral rituals.[18] Confrontation was also stepped up with Christian missionaries and Muslim and Sikh religious leaders. The *Satyarth Prakash* (Light of Truth) which Dayanand had first published in 1875 had devoted great attention to its attacks on other religions. Arya missionaries eagerly embellished this. The ranting of rival street-corner preachers in the Anarkali bazaar, Lahore became so violent that it was widely denounced as a 'public nuisance which was likely to result in a serious breach of the peace'.[19]

Relations grew particularly bad between the Aryas and the Muslims. Serious violence broke out in 1897 when a leading Arya Samajist called Pandit Lekh Ram was assassinated. Lekh Ram's greatest influence was in the north-west of Punjab. He had in fact joined the Peshawar Arya Samaj in 1880 and rose to prominence first as a missionary and then as the editor of the Arya Gazette. At first he had limited his attacks to the Ahmadi movement of Mirza Ghulam Ahmad, but he increasingly attacked orthodox Muslims as well. His pamphlet, *Risala-i-Jihad ya'ri Din-i-Muhammadi ki Bunyad* (A Treatise on waging holy war, or the foundation of the Muhammadan Religion) caused a considerable outcry, when it was published in 1892. Until his murder by a Muslim five years later, Lekh Ram continued to stir up animosity by his vituperative writings.

Lekh Ram's death came at the end of a period of increasing Muslim-Hindu tension in the cities. Arya agitation over the slaughter of cattle had precipitated fifteen serious riots in the years 1883–1891 alone. The Samaj had also put new life into the controversy concerning the Hindus' right to play musical instruments at all times outside mosques. When Muslims complained that the Samajists had deliberately encouraged this practice, a leading member of the militant faction, Bhai Parmanand, declared that if this right was removed at the first sign of complaint it could only mean that '(we) are permitted to live in India (only) through the kindness of (our) Muslim countrymen'.[20] Even the activities of the moderate, secular Arya Samajists did little to improve relations between the urban communities. The most famous of these, Lala Lajpat Rai (1865–1923) for example, founded the communalist Hindu Mahasabha in order to uphold Hindu interests more vigorously than the Congress. At the same time he never broke entirely with the Congress, hoping to win it over to his view. This qualified support did little to improve the Congress' standing with the Muslims as well as leading to an importation of Arya-Brahmo rivalry into its ranks.

The first two decades of the twentieth century saw an intensification of the Arya Samaj's activities. Muslims complained bitterly that it was 'ripping open old sores'.[21] Most controversial of all was the new emphasis which it placed on converting low-caste Muslims and Sikhs to Hinduism. It transformed the traditional concept of ritual purification (*shuddhi*) through which individuals who had lost caste could be restored into Hindu society into a new weapon of mass conversion. In August 1909 the Arya Samaj held a series of meetings in Jullundur district in an attempt to convert low-caste Sikh Rahtias and

Mazhbis.[22] This brought it into conflict with the Singh Sabha movement, some of whose members had previously enjoyed cordial relations with it. These ties were now sundered and the Sikh community further distanced itself from the Hindus. But the greatest conflict over *shuddhi* occurred, as a result of the Aryas' efforts to reconvert the Muslim Rajput community of south eastern Punjab during the early 1920s. Serious disturbances broke out in 1923 in Amritsar and Rawalpindi following the Muslims' retaliatory social and economic boycott of the Arya community. They also created new institutions to defend Islam in addition to the long established *Anjuman-i-Islamia* and *Anjuman-i-Himayat-i-Islam*. These counterparts of the *shuddhi* movement were known as the *tabligh* and *tansim* movements.

The *Anjuman-i-Islamia* and the *Anjuman-i-Himayat-i-Islam* were both founded in the wake of the Arya Samaj, although the former's original purpose was not to counteract it, but rather to organize efforts to restore Lahore's Badshahi Mosque which had been converted into an arsenal by Ranjit Singh. Like the Arya Samaj, both organizations founded schools and colleges and published religious tracts and journals. The Amritsar branch of the *Anjuman-i-Islamia* founded an Anglo-Oriental College on the line of Syed Ahmad Khan's famous Muhammadan Anglo-Oriental College at Aligarh. The *Anjuman-i-Himayat-i-Islam* ran the influential Islamia College in Lahore. Shortly after its foundation in 1884, the *Anjuman-i-Himayat-i-Islam* eclipsed its rival and gradually spread its influence outwards from Lahore and Amritsar to the Jhang, Ferozepur and Montgomery districts. Unlike the Chishti revivalist movement of the eighteenth century, it did not, however, win support in the countryside. It remained, throughout, the organization of the Muslim professional class and as such did not challenge the intercommunal agriculturalist ideology of the cultivators.

The *shuddhi* movement led the Muslims to organize themselves still further in defence of their community. The Punjabi Congressman, Dr. Saifudin Kitchlew formed the *Jamiat-i-Tansim* movement in 1923 partly with the aim of achieving *swaraj* but mainly to counteract the Arya Samaj's activities. It organized Muslim volunteer corps and engaged in social work and educational activities. *Tabligh* movements were also created in various parts of the Punjab to work amongst low-caste Muslims. The Ahmadis founded a *Jamiat-i-Tabligh* in Ambala to counteract *shuddhi*. In the Sialkot district where the Arya Samaj was also active amongst the Chamars and Batwals, a *Jamiat-i-Divaat-O-Tabligh* was formed. By the time the *shuddhi* and *tabligh* movements petered out at the end of the 1920s, they had gravely damaged communal relations. The activities of the native press hampered any improvement.

The Press and Communalism

The rapidly growing[23] Punjabi press exacerbated communal tension. Many newspapers and periodicals were the aggressive mouthpieces of revivalist movements. The Arya Samaj alone published 30 papers. Sikh views were expressed in a further 10 newspapers. The *Anjuman-i-Himayat-i-Islam* ran its own monthly magazine, *Risala Anjuman-i-Himayat-i-Islam*, which publicized its activities and refuted Christian missionary teaching. The *Hidayat-ul-Akhbar*, the short-lived voice of the 'Muhammadan Faizi Fauj' devoted itself to a similar attack, especially on the work of the Salvation Army. Apart from such specialist papers, most of the ordinary papers devoted considerable coverage to the discussion of religious and communal affairs. The British tried to control the tone of such articles but laboured under the difficulty that 'A Muhammadan paper finds it to its interest to attack the Hindus and a Hindu paper sells well if it falls foul of the Muhammadans ... to write quarrels requires no learning so a man of ordinary learning can successfully run a popular newspaper.'[24] Popular Punjabi journalism plumbed the depths during the 1920s and papers vied with each other to foment antagonism. Each community published numerous books and pamphlets calculated to give offence. The publication of such inflammatory material as the *Rangila Rasul*[25] in May 1924 not only reflected communal animosity, but contributed to it considerably.

The rural areas of Punjab, on the other hand, remained largely unaffected by the war of words. Though the 'effective' readership of newspapers through their being read aloud to illiterate villagers was much larger than their meagre circulation figures,[26] their impact was small outside the cities. Even in 1945, well over half the Punjab's papers and periodicals were published in Amritsar and Lahore. The rural regions of Jhelum, Mianwali, Muzaffargarh and Dera Ghazi Khan together produced just two newspapers.[27] Significantly, it was in the major centres of publication, Rawalpindi, Lahore and Amritsar that serious communal riots broke out in the 1920s.

Communal Riots

In the background of the riots in the Punjab was mounting Hindu-Muslim tension throughout India after the collapse of the brief period of political cooperation during the Khilafat movement. They were the symptom of the underlying hostility between the rival urban communities and perpetuated ill-will by further polarizing attitudes. Indicative of the widespread distrust was the fact that a serious riot broke out in Amritsar in April 1923 over a petty quarrel between a Muslim boy and a Hindu girl.[28] Three years later a serious clash occurred in Rawalpindi over the siting of a cinema. It reveals much, not only about the psychology of communal riots, but the ways in which urban factional rivalries were often intimately connected with them.

On 11 February 1926, Malik Mohan Singh, President of the Rawalpindi Municipal Committee, leased a plot of land immediately behind the chief mosque to a Sikh from Peshawar who planned to build a cinema there. He was given planning permission by the General Committee of the Council just over a month later, despite the complaints of a Hindu whose house adjoined the site. There the matter would have ended if it had not coincided with a quarrel amongst the Muslims of the Juma Masjid Committee and of the Municipal Committee in the wake of the recent elections. Malik Mohan Singh's ally, Chaudhri

Shah Din, had lost control to a faction led by Qazi Nazir Ahmed and Malik Ghulam Haider. They saw in the 'cinema incident' an opportunity to consolidate their position and settle old scores.[29] They claimed that the erection of a cinema close to the mosque was a deliberate insult to Islam. The dispute soon snowballed as an ailing local newspaper, *Tarjan-i-Sarhad*, whipped up Muslim frenzy in order to boost its sales. In the tense atmosphere, an annual Sikh procession which had always previously passed off peacefully led to rioting which resulted in over a 100 casualties and 200 buildings gutted by fire.[30]

Moderate opinion deplored such manipulation of communal feeling in order to serve self-interest. *The Nation* (Lahore) declared for example, 'The middle class leaders find that they must consolidate their power. They are ... not adverse to utilising communal prejudices in order to gain their ends.'[31] The politics of the towns and the countryside contrasted sharply in this as in other respects.

Punjab's Divergent Political Traditions

Distinct rural and urban political traditions had developed in the Punjab by the beginning of the twentieth century. Whilst communal issues and identities dominated urban politics, in the countryside common economic interests and tribal loyalties held sway. The mainsprings of communal tension, elite economic tension, heightened religious solidarity and political manipulation of differences were by and large absent. The newspapers which also helped to stir up animosity had little influence in the villages.

The countryside's isolation from communal political influences emanating from the cities was deliberately maintained by the 1919 Montagu-Chelmsford Reforms. They introduced separate electorates for the urban and rural areas. Only members of the 'agriculturalist' tribes were allowed to stand as candidates for the rural constituencies. Moreover, the small electorate which included just 3 per cent of the Punjab's population was dominated by the loyalist landowning groups. In the cities, the franchise was restricted to those individuals who annually paid at least Rs. 2,000 income tax or Rs. 50 municipal tax. In the villages, the right to vote was as much the result of political loyalty as of meeting property qualifications. All commissioned and non-commissioned officers of the Indian Army, *jagirdars*, *zaildars*, *lambardars* and *safedposhes* were enfranchised in addition to those landlords and tenants who annually paid Rs. 25 in Land Revenue. As a result, over 420,000 of the province's 500,000 voters came from the countryside.[32] Within the Sikh community, there were twenty times as many rural as urban voters. The figures for the Muslim and Hindu populations were in a proportion of 7:1 and 3:1 respectively. The British had safeguarded their rural allies and firmly institutionalized the division between Punjab's cities and villages.

Notes

1. *Tribune*, 16 April, 1926.
2. *The Army News*, 12 August 1911.
3. N.G. Barrier, 'The Punjab Government and Communal Politics', *Journal of Asian Studies*, Vol. XXVIII, No. 3 (May 1968), p. 525.
4. *Ibid.*, (3) above, p. 534.
5. This was coordinated by the Muhammadan Association and the *Anjuman-i-Islamia.*
6. *Ibid.*, (3) above, p. 536.
7. Minister for Education and Local Self-Government, 1921–1926.
8. Hailey to the Viceroy 22 January 1925, Hailey Papers, Mss. Eur. E220/7A, IOR.
9. Hailey to Sir William Vincent 8 July 1927, Hailey Papers, Mss. Eur. E220/11A, IOR.
10. P. Woodruff, *The men who ruled India*, Vol. 2, *The Guardians* (London, 1971), p. 37.
11. R. Clark, *The Missions of the C.M.S. and C.M.S. Zenana Missionary Society in the Punjab and Sindh* (London, 1904), p. 235.
12. K. W. Jones, *Arya Dharm. Hindu Consciousness in 19th Century Punjab* (Berkeley, 1976), p. 10.
13. *Ibid.*, (11) above, p. 13.
14. *Ibid.*, (11) above, p. 19.
15. H.G. Barrier & P. Wallace, *The Punjab Press 1880–1905* (Michigan, 1970), p. 23.

16. Shraddha Ram led an unsuccessful Sanatanist opposition to the Arya Samaj in the Punjab until his death in 1882.
17. *Ibid.*, (12) above, p. 155.
18. The Jullundur branch of the Arya Samaj led the way in encouraging female education, for example.
19. *Ibid.*, (12) above, p. 129, see also, *Tribune* (Ambala), 12 May 1894.
20. Reports on 'Native Newspapers in the Punjab', week ending 1 May 1926, NAI.
21. *Ibid.*, (20) above.
22. Weekly Report of the 'Political Situation in the Punjab', 7 August 1909, IOR, Pos. 3094.
23. Between 1891 and 1931 the number of newspapers and periodicals published in the Punjab rose from 74 to 579.
24. Reports on 'Native Newspapers in the Punjab', week Ending 11 November 1911, NAI.
25. This was a skit on Muhammad's life which portrayed him as the merry debauchee.
26. The paper with the largest circulation in 1900, the *Paisa Akhbar* only sold 13,000 copies a week. Report on 'Native Newspapers in the Punjab', week ending 11 November 1900, NAI.
27. Statement of Newspapers & Periodicals published in the Punjab 1945–6 (Lahore, 1946), p. 11.
28. L/P&J/2130, IOR.
29. Mohan Singh had refused to employ Ghulam Haider's son as a secretary.
30. L/P&J/6/2603.
31. Report on 'Native Newspapers in the Punjab', for the week ending 8 May 1926, NAI.
32. *Punjab Electoral Statistics 1920* (Lahore, 1921), IOR Pos 5546. Statement of the grand total of electors to the Punjab's general constituencies.

Chapter 5

The Unionist Party and Punjab Politics 1919–1937

> Purely landowners' interests should be represented in the Legislature ... they have the greatest stake in the country.[1]

The Punjab's rural political tradition of loyalty to the colonial regime and inter-communal cooperation culminated in the emergence of the Unionist Party. It was built on the foundations of the agriculturalist ideology created by the Punjab Government and its leadership was drawn from the main groups of rural collaborators. The British continued to exert, through the Unionist Party, the same kind of local political control they had secured by informal alliances with the leading landowners.

Creation of the Unionist Party

Amongst the rural members of the new legislative council created by the Montagu-Chelmsford Reforms were such well-known Muslim and Sikh landowners as Firoz Khan Noon, Ahmad Yar Khan Daulatana, Makhdum Reza Shah Gilani, Sunder Singh Majithia, Jogendra Singh and Baba Kartar Singh Bedi. Representatives of the emerging class of rich Jat peasant farmers such as Chaudhri Lal Chand and later Chaudhri Chhotu Ram took their seats alongside them. During the first Council of 1920–23, the agriculturalist members operated informally as a rural bloc. The difficult task of welding them together more closely into a political party was not achieved until just before the 1923 Council elections. This was the work of two men—Mian Fazl-i-Husain and Chhotu Ram.

Fazl-i-Husain was a Lahore-based politician who had risen to prominence by way of a successful legal practice and involvement in the *Anjuman-i-Himayat-i-Islam*. He had first enterd the Legislative Council as a member for the Punjab University constituency—not the background from which one would imagine the successful leader of a rural political party would emerge. But his political acumen and influence[2] were so great, that the Muslim landowners turned to him for guidance. Chhotu Ram's roots were buried far more deeply in the Punjab countryside. His father was a fairly prosperous, but nevertheless illiterate Hindu Jat peasant proprietor. Chhotu Ram's great good fortune was to be in the position, through this background and his education and legal training,[3] to assume the leadership of his community at the time when it was rapidly increasing its economic and political importance.

Fazl-i-Husain and Chhotu Ram both had good reasons for seeking cooperation among the rural council members. The former realized that without this he would not possess a sufficient majority to use to the full the new powers which had been devolved by the British. Moreover, he was well aware that the overwhelmingly rural Muslim population would take the lion's share of any benefits deriving from a programme of agrarian reform. For this reason he hoped to even win over such urban Council members and potential rivals as Abdul Qadir and Muhammad Iqbal. The latter recognized that the changes brought about by the Montagu-Chelmsford Reforms provided an ideal opportunity for extending his work of improving his community's position. An alliance between the Hindu Jats and the Muslim and Sikh landowners would secure a safe majority for policies favouring the agriculturalist tribes. It would also prevent any attacks on the 1901 Alienation of Land Act by the urban Hindus. The Jats were in the position to lead the Hindu agriculturalists into such an alliance, as the other politically important group—the Rajputs—were so divided that they were incapable of such action.[4]

Fazl-i-Husain and Chhotu Ram worked together to form the Punjab Unionist Party in 1923. They issued an election manifesto which defined its aim as being to assist and encourage the backward classes and communities of the province, irrespective of their caste or creed.[5] The party had a clear majority after the 1923 Council elections. It would be a mistake, however, to imagine that its members were elected on a party platform, or that the elections were fought along party lines. The Unionists had been elected because of their individual influence within their constituencies, either as landowners, Pirs or prominent *biradari* leaders. All thirty-two Muslim members came from leading landlord or Pir families. Amongst them were representatives of the Tiwana, Noon, Daultana and Gurmani landlord families and the Shah Jiwana, Makhad, Rajoa and Gilani Pirs.

The colonial administration had, at first, somewhat hesitantly encouraged Fazl-i-Husain and Chhotu Ram in their task of uniting the rural representatives. Indeed, initially, the Jats had been passed over completely and an urban Hindu politician, Lala Harkishan Lal appointed as Minister for Agriculture in 1921. But the difficulties which his lack of support caused in the Council convinced the British that the Reforms could only be effectively operated by a combination of the rural members.[6] They therefore replaced him with the Jat politician Chaudhri Lal Chand. Never before had a Hindu Jat held such high office. The Hindu professional and commercial classes were deeply offended and struck back immediately by bringing a successful election petition against Chaudhri Lal Chand which forced his resignation. It was a Pyrrhic victory. The Governor, Sir Malcolm Hailey, responded by appointing Chhotu Ram as Agriculture Minister, thus boosting the career of the urban classes' most implacable opponent. The Governor noted with some satisfaction that Chhotu Ram's appointment (would), 'at all events keep together the agricultural elements who have felt very deeply the fate of Chaudhri Lal Chand and ... besides afford a fair certainty of combination between the (Hindu and Muslim) ministers'.[7] Three years later, Hailey greeted the appointment of another agriculturalist, the Muslim, Firoz Khan Noon, as Minister for Local Government with similar enthusiasm and hoped that it would encouraged the landowners to take an even greater role in politics in the future.

The colonial administration showed itself responsive to the emerging rural political group in other ways than by patronizing its leading representatives. A striking example of the rewards which could be obtained by united action was given to the agriculturalists in 1924, when the Punjab Government considerably reduced its enhancement of the canal water rates after Unionist protests, even though this meant that it had to rearrange the budget and increase urban taxation.[8]

Fazl-i-Husain and Chhotu Ram were also aided in their task of uniting the rural members by their measures to protect the landowners from expropriation by the moneylenders. Cultivators had experienced uprecedented prosperity during the boom years of the First World War. When agricultural prices slumped thereafter, an increasing number were forced to borrow in order to maintain the higher standard of living to which they had grown accustomed. In the years 1921–29, the province's agricultural debt consequently rose from around Rs. 90 crores* to Rs. 135 crores.[9] Despite the growth of agricultural banks and Cooperative Credit Societies, the bulk of this money was owed to moneylenders. Moneylending became such a profitable business during these years, that it was reckoned that nearly 60,000 people derived their livelihood from it[10] and in 1928–29, over a third of the total income tax paid by industry and business came from it.[11]

This situation revived old fears and hatreds amongst the landowners and led to demands for the maintenance of the safeguards of the 1901 Alienation of Land Act and for the removal of the loopholes in it which the moneylenders were exploiting. When Fazl-i-Husain and Chhotu Ram embarked on a programme which emphasized these twin demands, they

*Rs 1 crore is equal to Rs 10 million.

were easily able to command the support of all the rural Legislative Council members. In quick succession they brought forward such measures as the Moneylenders Registration Bill, The Punjab Court Fees (Amendment) Bill and the Punjab (Urban Property) Rent Regulation Bill which which were in favour of the agriculturalists' interests. Loopholes, which the Punjab High Court had discovered in the 1901 Legislation, were closed by the 1926 Punjab Alienation of Land Amendment Act. They also attempted to improve the position of the landowners whose land revenue assessments had been calculated at the time of artificially high agricultural prices during the First World War. By the late 1920s, prices had fallen so much that such landowners were unable to pay their land taxes. In order to remedy the situation, the Unionist Party introduced a Bill in 1926 which reduced the land revenue demand from a half to a third of a proprietor's calculated net assets. This proposal was, however, too much for the British and the Governor vetoed the Bill. The Unionists, nevertheless, stepped up their demands for reform of the land revenue system of taxation. Their pressure once more paid off as the colonial administration introduced a Land Revenue Act in 1928 which incorporated many of the earlier measure's proposals. This victory for the Unionist Party was particularly welcome as it came at a time when its influence was slightly waning.

Chhotu Ram was replaced as a Minister in the Legislative Council from 1926 onwards by the urban politician Manohar Lal. Malcolm Hailey, during his final years as Governor, no longer appointed purely Unionist ministries.[12] This change in policy weakened the Unionist Party and made it more difficult for Chhotu Ram to hold it together during the five years from 1930 onwards when Fazl-i-Husain was away serving on the Viceroy's Executive Council.

Azim Husain in his biography of his father has maintained that Hailey's action was a deliberate attempt to prevent the Unionist Party becoming too powerful in provincial politics and thus more independent of the British in outlook.[13] This interpretation is based on the comment Fazl-i-Husain wrote in his diary in July 1935. 'Government policy is responsible for there being no leader in any community', he noted, 'as soon as Government officials find an Indian wielding influence, the tendency is to counteract his influence. This has come to be a Government policy. Ministers cannot really be useful if their position is no better than that of glorified *tehsildars* to do the bidding of the Government.'[14] Hailey, looking back in 1961, denied that any ulterior motives lay behind his replacement of solely Unionist ministries by coalitions which included representatives of the urban classes. His earlier career as a secretary and disciple of S. S. Thorburn (1844–1924), the great defender of the landowners against the moneylenders, could hardly have encouraged him to undertake lightly a policy of building up the power of the Unionists' urban opponents. Moreover, whilst he was Governor of the United Provinces from 1928–34 he supported the growth of strong landlord parties. There is therefore little reason to doubt the sincerity of his explanation. 'The whole object of the introduction of the system of Dyarchy', he recalled in 1961, 'was educative and this purpose would have been frustrated if one party had secured an (unchallenged) position of control.... It would have been very easy for me ... to throw my weight on the side of the Unionists and to overlook all claims of the non-agriculturalists ... but this was not my duty as I saw it.'[15]

The Unionist Party's Eclipse of its Rivals

Despite Hailey's initiative, no other single party approached the Unionists' influence after 1926. When the countryside was hit by the agricultural slump in the early 1930s, their minority position in the Transferred Departments of Government worked in fact to their own and British advantage. They were able to act as a loyal opposition whilst still having access to the Governor's ear. In any case, the Punjab's electoral system ensured that the landowners' setback would only be temporary. The urban groups, despite their superior education and organization, were locked out of power as they possessed neither a landed base or agriculturalist status. Both remained essential prerequisites for political power. It was thus the rural Akali Dal, Kisan Sabha and Ahrar parties rather than the urban Congress and Muslim League which mounted the greatest challenge to the Unionists during this period.

Congress and Muslim League Weakness

Both the Congress and the Muslim League failed to offer a credible challenge to the Unionist Party during the years 1919–1937. They were victims of the same circumstances, an electoral system which conspired against them and an inability to pick up rural support without alienating their urban adherents. In addition, there were specific causes for their weakness. Thus, the Congress, after 1932, suffered from its unpopular attitude to the Communal Award; the Muslim League from Fazl-i-Husain's predominant position in both All-India and provincial Muslim politics during the 1930s. Finally, the more they threatened to destabilize the region's politics, the more the British were convinced that they should develop closer ties with the Unionists.

The Congress had the longest history of any political party within the Punjab. The Punjab Provincial Committee of the Indian National Congress had in fact been founded as early as 1885. However, though its district and primary branches existed throughout the region its influence was minimal. This resulted from its total lack of support amongst the rural Muslim and Hindu communities. The emerging Muslim professional class also shunned it to such an extent that only forty-nine Muslims were included at the 1893 Indian National Congress Session at Lahore in a 481-strong Punjabi delegation. Only very briefly during the Khilafat movement was the Congress able to win over any appreciable Muslim support within the region. The Hindu Jats steered clear of it because of its identification with the moneylenders' interests. The Punjab Congress never in fact fully recovered from its blundering attitude towards the 1901 Alienation of Land Act. At first it opposed this charter of the agriculturalists' economic freedom before hastily changing its mind. The Hindu and Muslim cultivators remained unconvinced that it had their interests at heart whilst the moneylenders and traders felt betrayed. They formed a rival party, the Mahasabha, to orchestrate opposition to the Act. Whenever agricultural legislation came to the fore, the Congress was put on the spot. It found it impossible to square its need for rural support with its urban paymasters' demands for protection. Whilst its sister organisation in the United Provinces exploited the conditions of the agriculturally depressed early 1930s to undermine the landlord parties, the Punjab Congress remained cut off from the countryside. It failed to make any inroads into the rural support for the Unionist Party. The Hindu and Muslim cultivators remained aloof, whilst the Sikhs were preoccupied with communal interests.

The publication of the Communal Award in 1932 made it even more difficult for the Congress to develop close ties with the Sikhs. They had hoped that it would grant them at least 30 per cent communal representation in a future Legislative Assembly. They received, however, a mere 18 per cent of the seats.[16] Despite advice to the contrary,[17] the Punjab Congress leader Dr. Satyapal accepted this decision without demur. He did not want to jeopardize the chance of winning the Muslims' support by opposing the Award which they had greeted so enthusiastically. Moreover, he realised that the Sikhs' position could only be improved at the expense of the Hindus as the British would not reduce the Muslims' already slim majority. It was not, however, the time for such cool logic and Satyapal was attacked bitterly by both his Hindu opponents and the Sikhs. Thereafter, the Congress was in a weaker position than ever to unite the Hindu and Sikh communities. Yet only by doing so could it greatly improve its standing within the Punjab. It was never able to become the major focus of Sikh political aspirations despite the fact that it gained the support of such respected figures as Kharak Singh[18] and even from time to time that of Master Tara Singh himself.

The Punjab Congress did not contest Legislative Council

elections until 1926 on the orders of the All-India Congress Committee. It therefore lost the initiative to those groups of urban Hindus who argued that their community's interests must be defended in the Legislature come what may. Included amongst these were leading Arya Samajists, (Dr Gokul Chand Narang), Brahmos, (Ruchi Ram Sahni) and Sanatanists (Gulshan Rai). They united to fight the 1926 Council elections and inflicted a heavy defeat on the Congress,[19] which received a similar drubbing in 1934, this time mainly because of its unpopular attitude towards the Communal Award. Its difficulties were compounded by intense factionalism. The bitter rivalry between the Arya Samaj and the Brahmo Samaj spilled over into it. The Arya faction led by Lajpat Rai competed with Harkishen Lal's Brahmo group for political control.[20]

The Congress' continued weakness disillusioned the professional and trading classes. Conservatives flocked to the Mahasabha, radicals gravitated to the terriorist Nau Jawan Bharat Sabha. Until Lajpat Rai's death in 1928, the gap between the Mahasabha and the Congress remained narrow. Thereafter, it widened as such Congress leaders as Duni Chand and Satyapal became vocal in their criticism of its 'communalism'. The dispute rumbled on within the Congress itself, as Lajpat Rai's disciple, Gopichand Bhargava[21] fought a running battle with Dr Satyapal for over a decade.

The Gandhian Satyagraha had little impact in the Punjab because of the Congress' weakness. It went almost unnoticed in the eastern Ambala Division and in the predominantly Muslim, north-western regions of the province. The Congress' difficulties were blatantly revealed when its Secretary warned that it would be impossible to step up the agitation by launching a no-tax campaign because of the rival communities' mutual suspicions. Neither Muslims nor Hindus would risk their rivals being able to buy up cattle and land auctioned by the British to realize tax from defaulters.[22]

The Gandhi-Irwin Pact of 5 March 1931 gave the Punjab Congress a ten-month breathing space in which to put its house in order. The old weaknesses still remained, however, and when satyagraha resumed after Gandhi's arrest on 4 January 1932, there was even less enthusiasm than before.[23] The Civil Disobedience campaign was largely overshadowed by the controvesy caused by the Communal Award and events in neighbouring Kashmir which led a large number of Muslims to leave the Congress and form the *Majlis-i-Ahrar-i-Islam-i-Hind*. By the mid-1930s, the Punjab Congress Committee was at an all-time low. What little energy it had left was directed away from politics towards the laudable aim of Harijan uplift enshrined in Gandhi's constructive programme.

The Punjab Muslim League had a similarly chequered history during the years 1919–37. It did not even hold any annual sessions from 1920–24, then fitfully came to life in 1924 when the All-India Muslim League met in Punjab's capital, Lahore. The main reason for its inactivity was that Fazl-i-Husain, the driving force in Muslim politics, saw the Unionist Party as a better vehicle for his community's interests. He had in fact invited the All-India body to Lahore to ensure that the Punjabi Muslims' interests did not suffer as a result of its efforts to win safeguards for the Muslims who lived in Hindu-dominated provinces. Fazl-i-Husain's plan worked in that, although Jinnah presided, the League's session was dominated by Muslim Unionists. The danger remained, however, that the UP and Bombay members of All-India Muslim League would encourage constitutional changes to the detriment of the Muslim majority in the Punjab.

When Jinnah seemed to be prepared to barter away separate electorates in 1929,[24] Fazl-i-Husain moved quickly to safeguard the Punjabi Muslims' interests. Along with his cousin, Mian Muhammad Shafi, a former member of the Viceroy's Executive Council, he founded the All-India Muslim Conference to oppose Jinnah's adoption of these so-called Delhi proposals and his decision not to cooperate with the Simon Commission. The All-India Muslim Conference, despite its title, was dominated by Muslim Unionists from the Punjab. It had a considerable advantage over the All-India Muslim League because of Fazl-i-Husain's ready access to the Viceroy. The All-India Muslim

Conference had considerable influence on the Government of India's decisions concerning separate electorates and the Communal Award. The All-India Muslim League on the other hand withered away and almost died during the early 1930s. In such circumstances, it was impossible for its Punjab branch to challenge the Unionist Party.

Rural Challenges to the Unionist Party

The greatest challenge to the Unionist Party's rural power came from the Akali Dal, Ahrar movement and Kisan Sabha. British officials anxiously monitored their activities, worried that they might disrupt their local control and endanger army recruitment by introducing communalism or communism into the countryside. Especially during the agricultural depression of 1929–33, British fortnightly reports were peppered with references to the 'communist menace' of the Kisan Sabha.

The Sabha identified itself with the rural poor and claimed that the Unionist Party was the tool of the large landowners. It called for extensive reforms in rural taxation and the landholding system. Behind the Unionist Party it saw the colonial state propping up the inequalities in Punjabi society. The Sabha's leaders knew that agitation would be ruthlessly repressed. Parliamentary activity also held out little hope of success, however, because many of the Sabha's natural supporters were disenfranchised. Nevertheless, the disturbed conditions of the early 1930s held out fresh hope for advance.

The Punjab was badly hit by world depression. Wheat fell in value by 64 per cent in 1930–31 and cotton by 56 per cent. Cultivators found it almost impossible to offset low prices by restricting output or by switching to alternative crops. Costs of production remained high. The result was a further rise in agricultural indebtedness. Gold ornaments had to be sold to meet the land revenue demands which continued to be levied at the pre-crisis rate.

The Kisan Sabha gained a political boost from the mounting economic crisis. It gradually extended its support in the Jullundur,

Amritsar, Sheikhupura and Gujrat districts.[25] It was also able in April 1930 to lead a successful campaign in Hissar against the payment of rents in kind to landowners.[26] Soon afterwards, the Unionists made strong representations to the Governor to alleviate the cultivators' distress. Their advice was wisely heeded and the land revenue demand for the 1931 *rabi* crop was reduced by 50 per cent. Similar remissions were made until 1933. These undoubtedly limited the Kisan Sabha's advance. The Unionists further deflected the cultivators' wrath from the large landowners and the British by blaming the moneylenders for the prevailing distress. The Kisan Sabha, as a result, made little headway except in the Sikh villages of central Punjab. Their inhabitants were more receptive to its appeals because they had been radicalized by the events of the 1920s.

The struggle at that time by the Sikh Akalis (immortals) to wrest control of the gurdwaras from the *mahant* priests had launched the largest mass movement in British Punjab's history. The Akali movement's communal outlook had, of course, completely challenged the view of rural society which the British had so assiduously encouraged. From the beginning of the struggle in 1920, until its uneasy conclusion in October 1925, over 30,000 arrests had been made.[27] The Akalis clashed violently both with the *mahants* and the British authorities. They sympathized with the latter partly because they saw the sturggle as an attack on the sanctity of private property, but also because the *mahants* had loyally collaborated with their rule.

Sikh opposition to the *mahants* had been brewing for some time. The reforming zeal brought by the Singh Sabha movement refused to turn a blind eye to the *mahants*' corrupt life-styles, paid for by the rich landholdings attached to most gurdwaras. The belief grew that whatever their legal rights, the *mahants* had forfeited all moral rights to the control of the shrines. When legal efforts to evict them failed, a section of the Sikh community decided to use more direct methods. On 15 November 1920, a 175-member committee known as the Shiromani Gurdwara Prabandhak Committee (Society for Gurdwara Protection) was established to manage all the Sikh shrines. Its spearhead was to be a mass movement called the Akali Dal (army of the immortals). Its aim was to emulate the Gandhian techniques of non-cooperation and non-violence. The *mahants*, however, used force to keep control of the shrines. The first violent clash occurred in February 1921 at Nankana Sahib. Thereafter, the struggle became increasingly bitter. It centred on three main agitations, the so-called 'Keys Affair',[28] the Guruka Bagh agitation in the Amritsar district and the Jaito 'Morcha' in the neighbouring Princely State of Nabha.

The Guruka Bagh agitation began early in 1922 and continued for over fifteen months. It was caused by the Akalis' challenging the *mahant*'s ownership of the land surrounding the Guruka Bagh shrine by cutting wood from it. The increasing use of force by the police to control the daily non-violent demonstrations embarrassed the British. They eventually engineered a simple solution to the dispute, by encouraging a Sikh official to rent the land next to the gurdwara from the *mahant*. He then allowed the Akalis to gather their firewood in peace.

The Akali agitation in Nabha State was less successful, partly because it was more overtly political, but also because the Maharaja and his officials were less sensitive to criticism of their policing techniques. The initial cause of the agitation was the abdication of the State's Maharaja, Ripudman Singh. The Akalis claimed that he had been forced into this by the British because he sympathized with the Akali cause. The dispute took on a wider significance following police disruption of an Akali Akhand Path at the village of Jaito. The issue was now over the Akalis' right to freedom of worship. Sikhs flocked from the neighbouring districts of the Punjab to join the Akali demonstrations at Jaito. These ended only after the passage of the 1925 Gurdwara and Shrines Act and the Nabha authorities' granting permission for the completion of the interrupted Akhand Path at Jaito.

The Akalis were divided in their response to the 1925 Legislation. The majority of the General Committee of the Shiromani Gurdwara Prabandhak Committee eventually came down in favour of acceptance. The Act gave it control over most of the gurdwaras including the Golden Temple in Amritsar. This had important political consequences as it meant that it not only controlled the substantial financial resources of the shrines but also their vast powers of patronage. Henceforth, these became available to the Akali Dal which dominated the Shiromani Gurdwara Prabandhak Committee. It thus had a considerable advantage over other Sikh political parties.

The Akali Dal was made up of a new generation of leaders drawn mainly from the Khatri and Arora castes who rejected the landed aristocracy's domination of Sikh politics.[29] The latter's position had always been insecure because of the predominantly egalitarian character of rural Sikh society. There were simply too few 'good families' to dominate in the way in which their Muslim counterparts did in West Punjab. The most important of the new Sikh leaders was Master Tara Singh.[30] Ever since the time of the Gurdwara movement, he became almost synonymous with the Sikh community, reflecting in his approach to politics both its major strengths and weaknesses.

The Akalis pointed the way forward for urban Muslim politicians who wanted to wrest leadership from the landowners. Control of the Sufi shrines would in the same way give them access to new resources and political influence. The villagers' respect for the Pirs precluded, however, a similar frontal assault on their position. Instead, their cooperation and support would have to be secured. The Ahrars during the early 1930s made the first attempt to wean away the Pirs from the Unionist Party. Another decade was to elapse, however, before the Muslim League more successfully clothed itself in the robes of popular Islam.

The *Majlis-i-Ahrar-i-Islam* was founded in 1931 by Chaudhri Afżal Haq. Its nucleus consisted of urban, middle-class Muslims who were former members of the Congress and the Punjab Khilafat Committee. Its leadership was primarily religious.[31] The Ahrars rose to prominence in the confrontation between the Hindu Maharaja of Kashmir and his Muslim subjects. The Punjab's proximity to the Dogra Kingdom and its large Kashmiri community aroused intense Muslim feelings about the dispute.

The All-India Kashmir Committee which was formed to organize the Muslim protests was totally dominated by Punjabis. The Ahrars who were represented on this Committee resorted to direct action within Kashmir. Their protests were rewarded in January 1932 when the Maharaja dismissed his unpopular Hindu Premier, Hari Kishan Kaul.[32] The Ahrars' popularity soared amongst the large Kashmiri populations of Amritsar, Ludhiana and Sialkot. Most importantly, they began to forge alliances with such leading Pirs as Pir Jamaat Ali Shah and Pir Fazl Shah of Jalalpur. Here was the opportunity to link urban and rural Islam in a common political cause. The Ahrars, however, lacked the patience and discipline to succeed in this delicate operation. Many Pirs were suspicious of them because of their close relationship with the pro-Congress *Jamiat-i-Ulama-i-Hind*. They were further alienated when the Ahrars turned on the loyalist rural Ahmadi community.[33] Although the Ahmadis were regarded by most Punjabi Muslims as heretics, they shared common political interests and outlooks with the Pirs and other landowning groups.

For nearly five years, the Ahrars launched bitter attacks on the Ahmadi religious centre of Qadian. They attempted, for example, to prevent the Ahmadis from burying their dead in Muslim graveyards. At a Conference at Sialkot in November 1935, the Ahrars publicly demanded that the Ahmadis should no longer be recognized as Muslims. They depicted the Ahmadis as religiously threatening to subvert Muslim unity and strength and to politically stand in the way of independence because of their loyalty to the British.

Whilst the Ahrars' attacks on the Ahmadis alienated the Pirs, they did win them considerable support amongst the lower classes in the cities. There too, however, they received a major setback as a result of the Shahidgunj dispute. This flared up in 1935 between the Muslims and Sikhs over the demolition of the Shahidgunj Mosque site in Lahore.[34] The Ahrar leaders were already preparing to fight the forthcoming provincial elections and did not wish to risk imprisonment by joining in an agitation which they rightly believed was doomed to failure. Their caution was very unpopular amongst their new followers. Local leaders resented the central *majlis'* decision to stand idly by.[35] Public opposition was so great that the Ahrars found it virtually impossible to hold a successful meeting in Lahore for the best part of a year.[36]

The attacks on the Ahrars were orchestrated by the *Majlis-i-Ittehad-i-Millat.* This organization was founded in 1935 by Maulana Zafar Ali Khan to lead the Muslims who were taking part in the Shahidgunj agitation. Maulana Zafar Ali Khan edited the popular Urdu newspaper *Zamindar* and was a former leading Khilafatist. He still retained his old influence amongst the Muslim middle-class groups of Lahore and the Punjab's other towns. His condemnation of the Ahrars thus carried considerable weight.

The Shahidgunj dispute effectively ended the Ahrars' threat to the Unionists. The first attempt to unite urban and rural Muslim politics had failed. The Muslim landowners, unlike their Sikh counterparts, still controlled the political leadership of their community. The terms of the 1935 Government of India Act conspired to perpetuate this state of affairs.

The Unionist Party and the 1935 Government of India

Fazl-i-Husain used his influence to protect the interests of the rural Muslims during the period of constitutional revision which culminated in the 1935 Government of India Act. They had been worried since the time of the 1929 Simon Commission about the effects of an extension of the franchise. Mian Mushtaq Ahmad Gurmani, Syed Mubarak Ali Shah and Mian Ahmad Yar Khan Daultana demanded that if the franchise was increased, the number of seats reserved for landholders should be raised from 4 to 10. 'We would like', Syed Mubarak Ali Shah had declared, 'that purely landowners' interests should be represented in the legislature ... they have the greatest stake in the country ... the tenant is apt to be influenced by many persons say the moneylender or some other things. The big landowners, landowners who have big estates having an independent living are not likely to be influenced by such persons.'[37] Here spoke the voice of British officialdom mediated through the Unionist Party.

Under the system of dyarchy, only 745,000 Punjabis (3.1 per cent of the total population) had the right to vote.[38] The Punjab Government, at first, proposed that in any future reform this number should only be doubled. The Government of India, itself under pressure from London, could not accept this blatant attempt to retard political development in the Punjab. Even so, the final total was only raised to two and a quarter million.

This new electorate consisted of 1,398,000 landowners, 407,000 tenants, 251,000 other rural voters and 225,000 municipal voters.[39] The qualifications for the landowners were lowered from annual payment of land revenue of Rs. 25 and upwards to Rs. 5 and upwards, and for tenants from occupation of more than 25 acres of irrigated land or 48 acres of unirrigated land, to holdings of 6 acres 'wet' and 12 acres 'dry'. In the towns, the house rent qualification was reduced from Rs. 8 to Rs. 5. This did not placate urban politicians who attacked the conservative nature of the proposals. Sir Gokul Chand Narang for example, astutely pointed out that only a quarter of the electorate would consist of members of non-agriculturalist tribes.[40] The Lothian Franchise Committee, partly as a result of such criticisms, added another 400,000 voters to the Punjab's electorate. But most of these additional voters were women who had their own separate constituencies.[41] The Government of India Act of 1935 thus could hardly be said to have revolutionized electoral conditions in the Punjab. Only 1 in 10 Punjabis still had the right to vote.[42] Landowners still dominated the restricted electorate. Moreover, non-agriculturalists were still disallowed from contesting rural constituencies.

British officials had quite unashamedly worked for the continued political predominance in the Punjab of the main landholding groups. They saw this as the best means of reproducing in the new era of provincial autonomy the mechanisms of imperial control which had worked so well earlier. Men committed to the imperial connection dominated every government which was elected from 1937 onwards.

Notes

1. Syed Mubarik Ali Shah, *Indian Franchise Committee* (London, 1932), Vol. V, *Selections from Memoranda Submitted by Individuals and Oral Evidence*, p. 142.
2. During the years 1917–20, he was simultaneously General Secretary of the Punjab Muslim League and President of the Punjab Congress. He was also President of the High Court Bar Association and influential within the Punjab University.
3. He set up practice at Rohtak in October 1912. He encouraged education and tribal unity, founding and editing The *Jat Gazette*. He also helped to organize an All-India Jat Conference similar to the Rajput and Brahmin caste associations.
4. See, for example, *Civil and Military Gazette* (Lahore), 11 November 1936.
5. Chhotu Ram considerably expanded this agriculturalist ideology in 1932. See, Mian Fazl-i-Husain Papers, Mss. Eur. E 352/21, IOR.
6. Letter of Sir Malcolm Hailey, 15 September 1924. Hailey Collection, Mss. Eur. E 220/6B, IOR.
7. *Ibid.*, (6).
8. The British did not want a repeat of the serious disturbances which had occurred in 1907 over the raising of canal water rates. *Ibid.*, (6 B).
9. A. Ullah, *The Cooperative Movement in the Punjab* (London, 1937), p. 47 & ff.
10. *Report of the Punjab Provincial Banking Enquiry Committee 1929–30*, Vol. 1 (Lahore, 1930), p. 129.
11. *Ibid.*, (10).
12. From 1926 onwards just 1 of the 3 ministerial positions was filled by a member of the Unionist Party.
13. A. Hussain, *Mian Fazl-i-Husain: A Political Biography* (London, 1944), pp. 160–2.
14. Fazl-i-Husain Papers, *ibid.*, (5) above.
15. Note by Sir Malcolm Hailey, 10 January 1961. Fazl-i-Husain Papers (7).
16. The Sikhs were particularly angry that they did not receive similar representation to that enjoyed by the minority Muslim community in the neighbouring United Provinces.
17. This was expressed through the columns of *Tribune* and by the Muslim Congressman from Amritsar, Saifuddin Kitchlew.
18. Born 1869; Graduate of the Punjab University; President of the Sikh Education Conference from 1916; pioneer of the Gurdwara Reform

Movement; first President of the old Gurdwara Prabandhak Committee; President of the Punjab Congress.

19. G. A. Heeger, 'The Growth of the Congress Movement in the Punjab', in *Journal of Asian Studies* 32, 1 (1972), p. 41.
20. K. W. Jones, *Arya Dharma. Hindu Consciousness in 19th Century Punjab* (Berkeley, 1976), p. 249.
21. Born 1889 Sirsa, Hissar district; educated at D.A.V. College, Lahore and Lahore Medical School; elected Secretary Lahore City Congress Committee 1919; member of All-India Harijan Sewak Sangh.
22. S. L. Malhotra, *Gandhi's Experiment with Communal Politics* (Delhi, 1975), p. 137.
23. S. L. Malhotra, *From Civil Disobedience to Quit India* (Chandigarh, 1979), p. 13.
24. This was to be in return for Sind's separation from the Bombay Presidency, the introduction of reforms in the NWFP and Baluchistan and the reservation of seats for Muslims in the Central Legislature.
25. Bhagwan Josh, *The Communist Movement in the Punjab 1926–1947* (Delhi, 1979), p. 105.
26. *Ibid.*, (25) above, p. 102.
27. Mohinder Singh, *The Akali Movement* (Delhi, 1978), p. 137.
28. This agitation successfully secured the return of the keys of the Golden Temple in Amritsar from the British authorities, *ibid.*, (27 above), p. 41.
29. Sunder Singh Majitha had been attacked as early as 1915 because of his opposition to the Ghadr Movement. Baba Kartar Songh Bedi was publicly denounced as a Tankhahia in 1921 because of his anti-Akali activities.
30. Born 1885 into a Hindu Khatri family from the Rawalpindi district; adopted Sikhism graduated from Khalsa College, Amritsar in 1907 during which time he acquired the title 'Master' which thereafter stuck with him.
31. The leading Ahrars were Maulana Ataullah Shah Bukhari, Maulana Habibur Rahman, Maulana Daud Ghaznavi and Maulana Mazhar Ali Azhar.
32. S. Lavan, *The Ahmadiyah Movement* (Delhi, 1974), p. 149 & ff.
33. Founded by Mirza Ghulam Ahmad who in March 1889 claimed revelations from God. He identified himself as the Messiah and the promised Mahdi who would conquer the world for Islam. Despite bitter opposition his movement spread rapidly.
34. The site had formerly been owned by the *mahants*. The courts gave it to the S.G.P.C. in 1934. Its intention to demolish the site which had once had a mosque and build shops there, sparked off the dispute.
35. Punjab FR for the first half of July 1936. 18/7/1936-Poll., NAI.
36. Punjab FR for the second half of May 1936. 18/5/1936-Poll., NAI.

37. *Indian Franchise Committee* (London, 1932), Vol. V, p. 142.
38. *Ibid.*, (38), Vol. I, p. 64.
39. File No. 9/1/33-R & K.W. Reforms Office, NAI.
40. Note by Gokul Chand Narang, File 102/32-R & K.W., Reforms Office, NAI.
41. File 9/1/33-R & K.W. and 9/7/33-R & K.W., Reforms Office, NAI.
42. In the neighbouring U.P. the figure was 1 in 7. File 102/32-R & K.W., Reforms Office, NAI.

Chapter 6

The Unionist Party in Triumph

> The Ahrars have begun with an awfully vigorous propaganda. At least they presume to have captured the towns. Still we don't fear if they do not begin with the villages. Villagers, you know, follow these 'Pirs' blindly.... Take care of the 'Pirs'. Ask them only to keep silent on the matter of the elections. We don't require their help but they should not oppose us.[1]

The Unionist Party was swept to power in the 1937 elections. The Congress and the Muslim League, having crushed their landlord rivals elsewhere in India, were reduced to just 19 seats in the 175-member Punjab Assembly. Their only hope was that factional rivalry would tear the Unionist Party asunder. The Party's new leader Sikander Hayat Khan was, however, as successful as Fazl-i-Husain had been in welding the rural grouping into a strong parliamentary party. He also emulated his predecessor in exerting a powerful influence in All-India Muslim politics. In return for bolstering Jinnah's shaky position, he was able to assume complete control of the Punjab Muslim League organization. With the League in its pocket and the Congress in disarray, the Unionist Party stood at the zenith of its power on the eve of the Second World War.

This chapter describes the background to the Unionist Party's spectacular success in the 1937 elections, examines the reasons for its success at a time of defeat for landlord parties elsewhere in India, and describes the way in which Sikander Hayat Khan was able to consolidate his power during the period 1937–40.

THE 1937 PUNJAB ELECTIONS

The Unionist Party, unlike the Congress and the Muslim League, enthusiastically greeted the new reforms. The Congress contested the 1937 elections explicitly in order to wreck the new constitution, whilst the Muslim League had very reluctantly decided to work it 'for what it was worth'. The Unionist Party, on the other hand, saw the new constitution as the embodiment of many of the principles for which it had been struggling in national politics from 1929 onwards. Provincial Autonomy[2] afforded it the opportunity to create an agriculturalist raj within the Punjab.

Fazl-i-Husain returned to the region in 1935. It was commonly expected that he would resume the party's leadership in order to fight the elections. Two possible barriers stood in his way: his failing health and his growing rivalry with Sikander Hayat Khan. The latter was a member of the Khattar landlord family of Wah in the Attock district. He had been elected in 1926 for the Muhammadan landholders seat which Fazl-i-Husain had previously occupied and in 1930 he had become Revenue Minister. Thereafter, he twice served for a short period as acting Governor. Early in 1935, he resigned from the Punjab Executive Council in order to take up the post of Deputy-Governor of the Reserve Bank of India. Almost immediately after Fazl-i-Husain's retirement from the Viceroy's Executive Council, rumours began to circulate that Sikander intended to challenge him for the future leadership of the Unionist Party. On several occasions a split between the two men appeared likely. Only Fazl-i-Husain's caution and Sikander's knowledge that his rival was dying prevented a major division in the Unionist Party.

It was not until February 1936 that Fazl-i-Husain issued his plan for leading the Unionist Party in the rapidly approaching elections. His caution was prompted by the support which

Sikander was receiving from the large Khattar landlord faction. The press also rumoured that Sikander was attempting to use his links with the urban Hindu politician Raja Narendra Nath to form a new party. The Hindus remained hostile to Fazl-i-Husain because of the 'communalist' policies which he had pursued whilst Minister for Local Government. There was also Muslim opposition to his re-entry into politics on account of his alleged pro-Ahmadi sympathies. The *Ehsan*, for example, made the demand that 'before Mian Fazl-i-Husain enters the field of Muslim politics again he would have to remove the blot from his fair name which has been caused by his pro-Qadian policy'.[3] Fazl-i-Husain dispelled any lingering doubts about his intentions when he issued the pamphlet 'Punjab Politics' in February 1936. It called for the Unionist Party's reorganization in preparation for the elections. It was to be transformed from a narrow landlord group in the Legislative Council into a mass party which had district branches throughout the province. The first steps were taken in April 1936 when the new party headquarters in Lahore was opened and the Unionist Party's manifesto issued. It pledged the party to stand by the 1901 Alienation of Land Act as a measure for the protection of the agriculturalists and advocated a policy of 'limited liability socialism' akin to the National Congress policy[4] which would achieve agrarian reform while at the same time not unduly encroaching on the landlords' interests. Political workers were to be trained to carry the party's message to the villages. Fazl-i-Husain aimed to create in this way the first mass political party in the province's history. It was never achieved. His failing health prevented him from taking an active role to force this plan through to a successful conclusion. Factional rivalries amongst the landlords of Multan, Jhang, Muzaffargarh and Dera Ghazi Khan districts frustrated his efforts to create Unionist district branches there. Little progress had been made in this direction by the time of his death. Sikander, who succeeded him as party leader in October 1936, was content to rely on the landlord and Pirs' traditional influence in these areas to win votes.

The Muslim League suffered a series of major setbacks in the period immediately preceding the elections. Jinnah returned to India in October 1935 to reorganize the Muslim League to fight the forthcoming elections. The party's constitution was revised at its 1936 session at Bombay and a parliamentary board set up to coordinate its electioneering. The Unionist Party remained the biggest stumbling block to Jinnah's success. It not only threatened to exclude the League from power in the key Punjab province but its control of the All-India Muslim Conference was a major threat at the centre. It even exerted influence within the Muslim League itself as the fifty Punjab members of the Muslim League Council were mainly Unionists. Jinnah attempted to reduce their influence in the 1936 Punjab delegation[5] but this only created a background of suspicion and ill-will because of his endeavours to persuade Fazl-i-Husain to support the Muslim League Parliamentary Board. He had begun negotiations with him in May 1936 but these made little progress. 'Why has Jinnah not done what any ordinary practical man would have done—revive the Provincial League and give it a good start and stress the need of opening its branches in all districts'. Fazl-i-Husain noted almost contemptuously at the time, 'he has done seemingly nothing except talk and talk and talk. He apparently believed that he was so clever that he (would) get people to agree to become his nominees and serve on the Central (Parliamentary) Board and they (would) be responsible for running the election in the province.'[6] Fazl-i-Husain had in fact already turned down a suggestion by Firoz Khan Noon to create a Punjab Muslim Zamindara League to fight the elections. He realised that if he contested them solely on a Muslim platform it would be difficult to establish an inter-communal ministry. Yet, only the latter type of government could effectively wield power and consolidate the gains which the Unionist Party had already made for the agriculturalists, most of whom were Muslims. Fazl-i-Husain had little choice but to reconcile to an inter-communal government, even if it meant weakening the Muslim League's influence in all-India politics.[7]

Jinnah continued his preparations despite his rebuff by the Unionists and announced in May 1936 the formation of a Muslim League Central Parliamentary Board. Most of the Punjab's eleven representatives were members of the rival Ahrar and *Ittehad-i-Millat* parties to which he had turned following the collapse of his talks with Fazl-i-Husain.[8] Cracks soon began to appear in this ramshackle coalition. Maulana Zafar Ali, the leader of the *Ittehad-i-Millat* Party, resigned from the Board in June along with three of his prominent supporters.[9] The Ahrars quickly followed suit, angered by the measures which the more moderate members had taken to curb their influence.[10] Mian Abdul Aziz's resignation later that month was an even greater blow. He was the leading landlord member of the Parliamentary Board and had considerable influence within the Arain *biradari*. He could thus have delivered the Arain vote to the League in a number of key constituencies in the east Punjab as well as in the Lyallpur Canal Colony. The Unionists naturally made strenuous efforts to win back his support. Firoz Khan Noon and Ahmad Yar Khan Daultana directly approached him, whilst Nur Ilahi tried to persuade Begum Shah Nawaz to intercede with her brother-in-law. Their success signalled the Election Board's virtual collapse, Jinnah was back where he had started with his support limited to Iqbal's small group of followers.

The Ahrars had only flirted with membership of the Muslim League Board in an attempt to recover the ground which they had lost since the Shahidgunj dispute. Shortly after their resignation, they held an All-India Political and *Tabligh* Conference in Lahore, which was presided over by Syed Muhammad Ahmad Kazni of Saharanpur. It evoked little enthusiasm, although they tried to put a brave face on the proceedings by organizing their Red Shirt parades and processions. Their inactivity during the Shahidgunj dispute had still not been forgiven. The Ahrars complained bitterly that the Ahmadis and the Unionists had engineered the dispute in order to discredit them. Their belief in this implausible conspiracy thesis was confirmed by the publication, on the eve of the election, of a series of letters allegedly written by their leaders in which the Shahidgunj Agitation was strongly condemned.[11]

The Congress approached the elections in almost as troubled a state as the Ahrars and the Muslim League. The factional rivalries between Dr. Satyapal and Gopichand Bhargava still weakened it and it had yet to establish itself in the countryside. Like the Muslim League, it tried to cash in on the Ahrars' remaining popular support. Its attempt, at the end of 1935, to ally itself with an urban Islamic party revealed how weak its support had become. In complete contrast was its position in the United Provinces, where it had just launched a vigorous campaign amongst the kisans and tenants which threatened the traditional dominance of the landlord parties. Even in Punjab's towns the Congress faced serious opposition from the Hindu Election Board which was supported by the Manohar Lal 'loyalist' Hindu group in the Legislature and by the Sanatanists and the Arya Samaj.

As the elections approached, the parties stepped up their preparations. Jinnah inaugurated the Punjab Muslim League's election campaign on 12 October. Four subcommittees were created by the Muslim League's Working Committee to run it and steps were taken to organize district committees throughout the province. The Congress also established a Punjab Parliamentary Board and planned a concerted propaganda drive. Its desperate search for allies was finally rewarded when the Sikh Akalis and the Hindu Nationalist Party agreed to work with it.[12] Even the *Majlis-i-Ittehad-i-Millat* Party tried to widen its appeal by publishing a detailed 12-point manifesto and decided to contest seats in the countryside as well as the towns.

By the eve of polling, the province had reached a fever pitch of excitement. Both the Muslim League and the Congress climaxed their campaigns by bringing in political heavy-weights from outside the province. Maulana Shaukat Ali, who had played a leading role in the Khilafat agitation, toured the Punjab on the Muslim League's behalf and addressed meetings at Lahore, Amritsar and Jullundur. Vallabhbhai Patel, Bulabhai Desai,

Sarat Chandra Bose, Pandit Pant and Sarojini Naidu held meetings for the Congress.[13] In the last few days before polling, the Congress president, Jawaharlal Nehru, flew the length and breadth of the province to hold meetings.[14]

The Unionist Party, in complete contrast to its rivals, held no mass meetings or rallies. Sikander made no effort to match the publicity which Nehru's flying visit to the province had made. Jinnah smelt a rat. 'Why', he asked at a rally in Lahore, 'do the Unionists leaders not come out to the people to seek their suffrage? Why do they not address public meetings?' The answer, he declared, was that, 'the Unionists believe that the officials of the Government (are) working for them in the districts and the villages'.[15] Although this charge was unfounded, the Unionist leaders certainly believe that they need not engage in electioneering in the same way as their rivals. The natural leadership of the landlords and Pirs in the countryside would ensure the party's success. They would act as brokers in the localities, mobilising their kinsmen, *murids* and clients to vote for the Unionist Party in return for its promise of access to Government patronage.[16]

The National Agriculturalist Parties of Agra and Oudh adopted a similar policy.[17] They lacked, however, the influence to carry it out successfully. Changes in the composition of the landowning class, withdrawal of patronage and absentee landlordism had all combined to reduce the 'legitimacy' of the *taluqdars*' influence in the eyes of the peasants. The old face-to-face, reciprocal exchange of services and duties had been replaced by an impersonal business contract which increasingly needed to be bolstered by the Government. The UP tenants, as a result, had no legal rights of occupancy or of compensation for eviction, unlike their Punjabi counterparts. There was no longer a community of interests between the landlord and his tenants, as there was in the Punjab, where many tenants were themselves also small landowners. The agricultural depression of 1929–33 starkly revealed the different state of affairs in the two areas. In the Punjab, landlords responded to the crisis by granting their tenants remission of rent,[18] in the United Provinces the *taluqdars* compensated for the fall in agricultural prices by stepping up their exactions.[19] Loss of 'legitimacy' reduced the *taluqdars*' ability to mobilize political support. Some were even driven to use force during the 1937 elections in order to obtain the votes of their tenants.[20] These circumstances made it much easier for the Congress to gain a foothold in UP than in the Punjab countryside, particularly as the *taluqdars* were chronically divided amongst themselves.[21]

Factional rivalries split the two UP landlord parties and encouraged the defection of so many of the Muslim *taluqdars* to the Muslim League that the Oudh Party was only able to field fifteen *taluqdars* amongst its forty-five Legislative Assembly candidates.[22] Regarding the rural Hindu seats, the Congress triumphed, not only by attacking the landlords' repression but also by taking advantage of the disunity within the *taluqdars*' ranks. In the Sultanpur East General Rural Constituency, for example, a weak Congress candidate was able to win because of the rivalry between his three landlord opponents.[23] This was repeated in the neighbouring Fyzabad East seat where the clash between the *taluqdars* of Khajrahat and Kapradih presented the Congress with victory.[24] Wherever possible, it used caste and religious loyalties to mobilize support[25] as well as by promising the tenants a 'new heaven and a new earth'.[26] P. D. Reeves is thus wrong when he attributes the UP landlord parties' defeat mainly to the collapse of the old-style brokerage system of politics.[27] The comments of the Assistant Secretary of the Agra Province Zamindar's Association immediately after the election appear much nearer the truth. 'There was enmity and rivalry in their own rank', Nurul Hasan Siddiqi declared in his post mortem, 'as at the time of the election, the landholders were trying to defeat their own men by siding with the Congress simply that their rivals might be in a position to secure supremacy over them'.[28]

The Unionist Party was well aware of the dangers of similar disunity amongst the Punjabi landlords. In particular, it did not want to risk disappointed would-be candidates flocking to the ranks of the Congress and the Muslim League. It, therefore, never published a list of official candidates before polling began and in most constituencies adopted the policy of allowing the local landlord factions to fight it out amongst themselves, the winning faction leader being declared the official Unionist candidate.[29] In the Batala constituency, for example, immediately after polling, the victorious independent candidate, Mian Badr Mohyuddin, was claimed as a Unionist despite the fact that he had defeated two 'official Unionist' candidates.[30] Mahomed Hassan who was elected at Ludhiana was variously described in the electoral returns as an Independent, a Congressman and a Unionist![31]

The faction leaders who fought so loosely under the Unionist Party's banner in 1937 relied on their 'traditional' religious, social and economic influence to gather votes. Amongst the voters of East Punjab and the Canal Colonies where strong groups of peasant proprietors existed, *biradari* played a vital role in mobilizing political support. The faction leaders who succeeded in these areas were those with the strongest *biradari* backing. Mian Nurullah, for example, the President of the provincial Arain Anjuman (Council) romped home in the Lyallpur Canal Colony constituency in which most voters were Arains. The Secretary of the Punjab Anjuman-i-Rajputan, Chaudhri Faqir Hussain Khan, likewise won the Tarn Taran constituency in which the Rajput *biradari* was dominant. In the eastern Rohtak district of the province, 'Unionist' candidates swept the board in both the rural Muslim and Hindu seats because they had the backing of the leading Jat *biradari*. In the western areas of the province where peasant proprietors were far fewer in number, ties of economic dependency between the tenant and his landlord were more important in deciding voting than the *biradari*. The leading landlords marshalled their tenants and clients to support them in their internecine struggles, often taking their tenants by lorry to the polls. Where the boundaries of estate and constituency neatly coincided, there was of course no need to have a troublesome electoral contest at all. The increased number of seats within the legislature rather than opening the way for smaller landlords and tenants to win access to power consolidated the influence of the leading landlords. They were now able to accommodate nephews and younger sons in the 'spare' seats which came under their influence.[32]

The Pirs' political influence was also extended. The increased electorate made their province-wide social networks and multifaceted influence more important than ever before in vote gathering. The importance which the Unionists attached to their cooperation in the 1937 elections comes out clearly in the words of Mohammad Bashir, the Unionist Party organizer for the Gurdaspur district.

> Villagers, you know, follow these 'Pirs' blindly. . . . Take care of the 'Pirs'. Ask them only to keep silent on the matter of the elections. We don't require their help but (that) they should not oppose us.[33]

Shortly before his death, Mian Fazl-i-Husain approved plans for winning the assistance of the leading Pirs of Punjab and its surrounding areas. In June 1936, the Unionists approached eleven of the most influential Pirs in the region to issue a statement on their behalf.[34] They were: Pir Taunsa, Pir Golra, Pir Makhad, Pir Fazal Shah of Jalalpur, Pir Jamiat Ali Shah of Alipur, the Diwan of Pakpattan, the Gilani and Qureshi Pirs of Multan, the Sajjada Nashin of the Chishti Revivalist Shrine of Mahar Sharif in Bahawalpur State and the Sajjada Nashins of the two leading Chishti shrines in India—the *dargah* of Hazrat Khwaja Moinuddin Chishti at Ajmer and the *dargah* of Nizamuddin Aulia in Delhi. They all rendered at least tacit support to the Unionists with the exception of Pir Fazal Shah. Pir Makhad and the Gilani and Qureshi Pirs of Multan all entered the Unionist Party's ranks once they had been elected, as did the Pirs of Shergarh and Shah Jiwana who controlled many votes in the Canal Colony districts.

The Pirs supported the 'loyalist' Unionist Party rather than the Muslim League or the Islamic, Ahrar and *Ittehad-i-Millat* Parties in part because they were less politically influenced by religious considerations than the orthodox *ulema* of Deoband and Firangi Mahal,[35] but in the main because they were large landowners who wanted to see the status quo maintained within the countryside. Many of them had benefited from Government patronage and had close political, and in some cases, family links with the leading Unionist landlords. They were naturally influenced, and in some cases no doubt manipulated, by their landed followers to support the Unionist Party.

The Muslim League and the Congress faced almost insurmountable difficulties in attempting to win support in the rural areas. Lack of elite support meant that they had to somehow circumvent the brokerage system and appeal directly to the peasants. Neither succeeded in this attempt. To rub salt in the wound, they both achieved their most notable success on the sole occasion when they commanded the 'traditional' channels for mobilizing political support. Pir Fazal Shah mobilized his *murids* to ensure his uncle's election (Raja Ghazanfar Ali Khan) for the Muslim League in the Pind Dadan Khan constituency and the young and inexperienced Mian Iftikhar-ud-din[36] manipulated the Arain kinship network in the Kasur seat to defeat the veteran Unionist Khan Bahadur Sardar Habib Ullah Khan.[37] Elsewhere, the Muslim League and the Congress struggled in vain to compensate for their lack of rural influence by holding mass meetings and rallies.

Pir Fazal Shah was the only leading Pir who supported the Muslim League. It tried to counteract the Unionists' Sufi support by issuing an appeal to the Muslim peasants exhorting them in the name of Islam to vote for the candidates of the Muslim League Board.[38] But this had very little influence particularly because it was published in Urdu, the language of the educated townspeople rather than Punjabi. The composition of Muslim League's touring propaganda committee highlighted the difficulties which it faced in mobilizing support in the rural areas. There was only one landlord amongst its fifteen members. Seven of whom were lawyers or urban politicians from Lahore.[39] They had not always shown themselves as enthusiastic for agrarian reform as had the Unionists. Their attack on the Unionist Party during the elections for setting the countryside against the towns raised doubts once more in the minds of many *zamindars* whether the Muslim League would favour their interests in the way which the Unionist Party had done. The Muslim League found it very difficult to find candidates who were willing to oppose the Unionists. Whilst virtually all the Muslim newspapers, and Anglo-Indian press and influential sections of the Hindu press supported the Unionists, the Muslim League only had the backing of the Urdu daily *Ehsan* and the English weekly, *The New Times*, specifically founded as a pro-League paper by Malik Barkat Ali.[40] the situation might still have been retrieved if the League had made overtures to the large number of independent candidates but nothing was done in this respect. A derisory number of candidates, eight in all, finally fought under its banner.

The Congress was also severely handicapped because it had little support amongst the rural population. To make matters worse its internal division spilled over into the election campaign. The Amritsar and Lyallpur Congress Committees actively opposed the candidates approved for their constituencies by the Provincial Parliamentary Board.[41] Dr. Satyapal journeyed to Karachi to address Congress election meetings to avoid having to do any electioneering in Lahore on behalf of Gopichand Bhargava.[42] A further setback was caused by the breakdown of the alliance with the Sikhs Akalis. A number of their leaders went back on their promise to withdraw candidates from the seats which the Congress was contesting.[43]

Neither of the Islamic parties made any impact in the rural seats which they contested. The *Ittehad-i-Millat's* position in the Attock South Constituency was indicative of their weakness. This seat was almost the personal possession of Pir Makhad—his shrine dominated the area's social and religious life, his nominees filled the local district board.[44] The only candidate the *Ittehad-i-Millat* Party could find to oppose him was Mir Ahmad Shah, a *vakil* from Campbellpur.[45]

Polling began on 18 January and continued for the next ten days in some constituencies. During this period, the roads were more crowded than ever as lorries, bullock carts and tongas rushed supporters to the polls. Propagandists plastered walls and lamp-posts with slogans and groups of young boys vied with each other in their vocal support for the candidates. In the Eastern Towns Urban Constituency, 'hundreds of voters rushed to the polling booths ... shouting religious slogans'.[46] The few election clashes which took place all occurred in the towns and usually involved fighting between the supporters of the Ahrar and the *Majlis-i-Ittehad-i-Millat* parties. The worst disturbance in Lahore took place at the women's polling booths, where police had to be called finally to separate the *burqa*-clad female voters.[47] Although much excitement was generated, the turnout was very disappointing. Only just over a third of those entitled to vote did so. This apathy partly reflected the fact that it had been an election of personalities rather than issues. Voters continued to be influenced by personal and 'tribal' considerations as in earlier legislative council elections. All that had changed was that election expenses had risen sharply. In such circumstances, those parties without a firm social base in the countryside were doomed to defeat. Only a split in the ranks of the rural elite could have saved the Muslim League and the Congress from humiliating defeat. The Unionist Party's approach to electioneering made sure that this did not occur.

As soon as the first results were announced on 1 February, it was clear that the Unionist Party hade secured a great victory. This was confirmed when the large number of independent candidates announced their allegiance to the party. At the final count, the Unionists had captured 99 of the 175 seats in the Assembly. The Muslim League and the Congress between them managed only nineteen. The Unionist Party showed the best results in the rural Muslim constituencies in which it won seventy-three of the seventy-five seats. In the towns however, where social and economic influence played a much smaller part in electioneering, it was unable to beat off the combined challenge of the Muslim League, Congress, Ahrar and *Ittehad-i-Millat* parties and, disappointingly, won only one of the nine Muslim seats. Its support among the Hindu Jats was amply testified to by the fact that it captured all but one of the rural

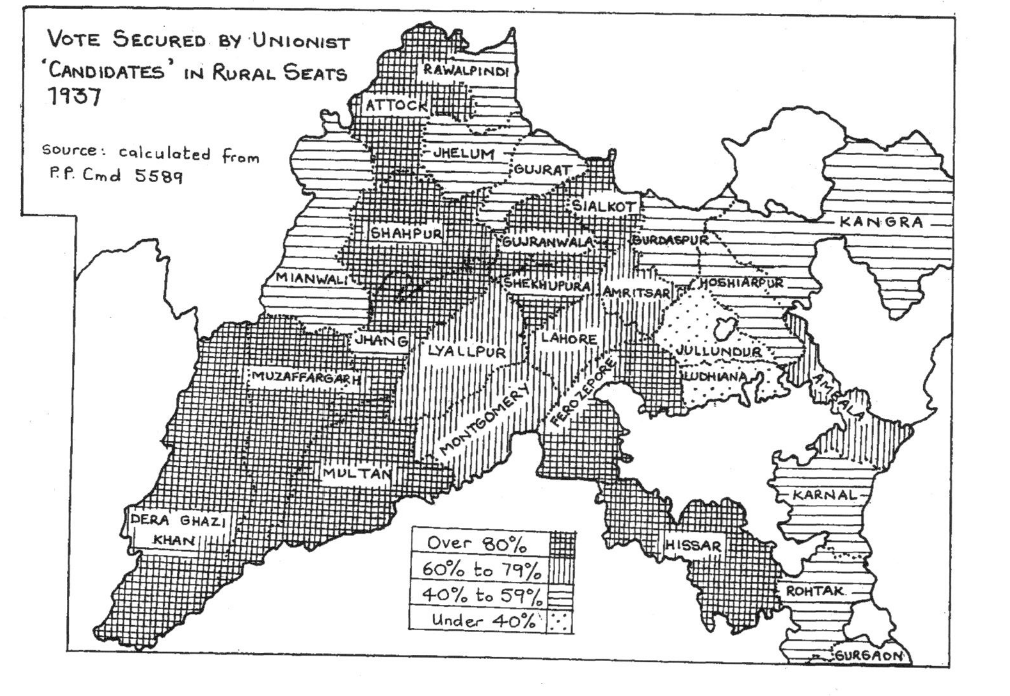
VOTE SECURED BY UNIONIST
'CANDIDATES' IN RURAL SEATS
1937
Source: calculated from
P.P. Cmd 5589
RAWALPINDI
ATTOCK
JHELUM
GUJRAT
SIALKOT
KANGRA
SHAHPUR
GUJRANWALA
GURDASPUR
MIANWALI
SHEKHUPURA
AMRITSAR
HOSHIARPUR
JHANG
LYALLPUR
LAHORE
JULLUNDUR
LUDHIANA
MUZAFFARGARH
AMBALA
MONTGOMERY
FEROZEPORE
MULTAN
KARNAL
DERA GHAZI KHAN
HISSAR
ROHTAK
GURGAON
Over 80%
60% to 79%
40% to 59%
Under 40%

Hindu seats in the Jat heartland of the Ambala Division. The Unionists fared worst in the central tracts of the Jullundur division where they lost the Ludhiana seat to the Congress and received a smaller proportion of the vote than in any other region. The party's greatest success was achieved in the Canal Colony constituencies in which its candidates had been members of the leading *biradaris* of peasant proprietors or had the support of the influential Pirs of Shergarh and Shah Jiwana. In two out of three Jhang constituencies it was unopposed and it faced only token opposition at Montgomery. In Lyallpur, it won 77 per cent of the total vote.

The list of successful Unionists contained most of Punjab's lending landlords and Pirs. The Tiwanas captured the Khushab and Bhulwal seats; the Chathas, Gujranwala North; the Gurmanis, Muzaffargarh; the Sials, Jhang East; the Pirs of Shah Jiwana and Taunsa, Jhang Central and Dera Ghazi Khan. The Nawab of Mamdot and Muhammad Shah Nawaz Khan were returned unopposed for the Ferozepore and Attock constituencies in which their estates were situated and Captain Ashiq Hussain, the nephew of the *Sajjada Nashin* of the Sheikh Bahadudin Zakaria shrine, faced only token opposition at Multan. Pir Makhad swept the *Ittehad-i-Millat* Party's feeble opposition aside at Attock to become one of the large number of successful independent candidates.

The 1937 elections were a resounding victory for Punjab's rural elite. In the new era of provincial autonomy, the levers of power remained firmly in the hands of the landlords and Pirs. The Muslim League had suffered a major setback in this key province. All it could hope was that Sikander would be unable to weld the amorphous body of rural members into a disciplined party within the legislative assembly.

The Unionist Government, 1937–40

The Unionist Party's victory in 1937 was greeted with satisfaction by British officials. The new ministers would be men whom they trusted and knew from past experience to be cooperative.

The Premier, Sikander Hayat Khan and his Minister of Public Works both in fact came from families with long established loyalty to the British. Sikander's grandfather had been killed whilst fighting for the British during the Second Sikh War, his father, Sardar Hayat Khan had been loyal in 1857 and had later become the first Indian in the Punjab to rise to the rank of Assistant Commissioner. The father of Khizr Hayat Khan Tiwana, the young Minister of Public Works, had served the British in various offices for close on thirty years. The control of the Punjab thus seemed to be in the safest possible Indian hands. A further cause for British satisfaction was the new Cabinet's delicate communal balance. The powerful rural communities of Hindu and Sikh Jats were represented by Chhotu Ram and Sunder Singh Majitha[48] respectively, whilst the Finance Minister, Manohar Lal,[49] came from the urban Hindu community. The only slight British anxiety was that Sikander would be unable to unite the rural Muslim Assembly members as well as Fazl-i-Husain had done.

Sikander in fact soon proved himself adept at manipulating *biradari* loyalties in order to maintain the rural Muslims' unity. Because the Hayat family did not always adhere to the customary cross-cousin marriage pattern, it had numerous *biradari* ties with other leading Muslim families. Sikander's relatives within the Assembly included, Nawab Muzaffar Khan, Mir Maqbool Mahmood, Sheikh Muhammad Sadiq, Sheikh Sadiq Hassan, Ahmad Bakhsh Khan, Pir Ashiq Hussain, Mian Bashir Ahmad, Mian Iftikhar-ud-Din, Nawab Shah Nawaz Khan and Begum Shah Nawaz.[50] They formed an impressive and influential bloc, which was rivalled only by the Noon-Tiwana group from the Shahpur district. Its loyalty was assured once Khizr Hayat Khan Tiwana was included in the Government.

Within a year of taking office, Sikander had built up such a personal following within the Assembly that the British Governor Emerson believed that he had become indispensable to the Unionist Party's continued success. 'The Ministers have come through the year very well', he wrote to the Viceroy in April 1938, 'success has depended very largely on the personality and popularity of the Premier. It would be very difficult to replace him, if for any reason he were not able to carry on.'[51] The Unionists' reliance on Sikander's leadership would have been reduced if steps had been taken to introduce a formal decision-making and disciplinary machinery. No progress was in fact made. It was not even decided to hold an annual party conference until 1944.[52] Nor was there an effective grassroots Unionist organization until that date, although a Zamindara League had been created on paper as early as October 1937. This institutional weakness ultimately proved harmful, but matterd little in the favourable circumstances of the years 1937–40.

Sikander relied heavily on patronage as well as kinship ties to keep the Muslim Unionists contented. Within two years of taking office, over a third of the Unionists held honorary titles from the rank of Rai Bahadur to Knight.[53] One of the Unionists' first legislative measures removed the 1935 Government of India Act's disqualification from election after 1937 of such persons as *zaildars*, Sub-Registrars and honorary magistrates. By 1945, a fifth of the Muslim Assembly members held such posts. Sikander also provided his supporters with land grants in the Canal Colonies. The Muslim League attacked the Unionists for making such grants solely as a reward for political loyalty. This practice certainly increased as the 1946 elections approached. Khizr Hayat Khan Tiwana, who was then the Premier, rewarded eighteen people in his Khushab constituency alone with Colony squares of land for allegedly nothing more than their personal loyalty to him. Sikander's earlier award to his close ally Nawab Mehr Shah had not gone unchallenged even within the Unionist Party[54] as neither had his insistence in January 1939 that the Nawab of Mamdot be granted a knighthood and that somewhat ironically, Ahmad Yar Khan Daultana's close friend Qurban Ali be appointed as Anti-Corruption officer.[55] Despite the Muslim League's propaganda claims however, the Unionist Ministers did not, on the whole, greatly misuse their powers of patronage.

Provincial Autonomy not only increased the Unionist Party's ability to provide the rural elite with patronage but extended the opportunity for legislating in the landlords' favour. The Unionist Party continued its earlier policy of clamping down on the moneylenders and made large sums of money available for rural uplift. It did not however bring forward any radical measures of land reform as these were unpalatable to its landlord supporters. The small tenants and kisans who would have gained most from them could bring little pressure to bear on this issue as they remained without the vote throughout this period.[56] The Unionist Party's agrarian reforms had two major effects. They consolidated its hold over its rural supporters and so exacerbated existing tensions within the provincial Congress that its mass contact movement in the countryside lost all its effectiveness.

The need for agrarian reform was strongly pressed by Chhotu Ram, whose experience in rural politics and influence amongst the Haryana Jats was greatly valued by Sikander. Chhotu Ram had an almost pathological hatred of moneylenders and traders which some said stemmed from his childhood memories of their[57] oppression. He had dedicated his life to raising the status of the poor peasants and was determined to grasp the opportunity provided by the Unionists' electoral success to put into practice the policies which he had been advocating for the last twenty years through the columns of the *Jat Gazette*.[58] The Rahbar-i-Azan (friend of the helpless) could not have been easily deflected from this course of action even if Sikander had wanted to do so. Sikander, although more circumspect than Chhotu Ram, was also enthusiastic for agrarian reform. He too believed that the province's root problems were economic rather than religious or communal and that the Unionist Party was uniquely equipped to deal with them.

Early in 1937, Sikander launched a Six-Year Programme of Rural Uplift which aimed to establish medical centres, schools, model farms and improved sanitation and drainage systems. By 1939, work was well under way in such backward districts as Muzaffargarh.[59] Even more popular was the legislation which he introduced during the 1938 summer session of the Provincial Assembly. This was almost entirely concerned with the growing problem of rural indebtedness, the blame for which was placed squarely on the shoulders of the moneylender. By 1937 rural indebtedness amounted to around Rs. 200 crores. The Punjab *zamindars* annually paid back in interest on their loans, four to five times the aggregate amount of land revenue and the water rate.[60] In the Kahuta *tehsil* of the Rawalpindi district the burden of debt per head reached the staggering sum of Rs. 74.[61] Moneylending had grown second only to agriculture as the most important industry in the province.

Sikander introduced the Punjab Alienation of Land Second Amendment Act and the Registration of Moneylenders Act in a bid to curb the moneylenders' influence.[62] These legislative enactments attacked the moneylenders' position by closing the loophole in the 1901 Punjab Alienation of Land Act created by the *benami* transaction and by enforcing a licensing system for moneylenders. Urban moneylenders acquired land in the countryside by a process which became known as the *benami* transaction. They appointed agents in the villages who were members of the statutory agricultural tribes and asked their debtors to transfer the land in the name of the agent so that it never legally passed out of agriculturalist hands. The retrospective nature of the Punjab Alienation of Land Second Amendment Act which rendered void all previous *benami* transactions, aroused great controversy as it destroyed the validity of transactions made over a considerable period of time. Equally controversial was another measure which Sikander introduced at this time, the Restitution of Mortgaged Lands Act. This enabled persons to recover all the land which they had mortgaged before 1901. The mortgage would be compensated if he had not received back from the land twice the value of the principal which he had originally advanced. It was estimated that over 700,000 acres of land would be returned to its original owners.[63] The Hindu and Sikh moneylenders claimed that the measure was merely a cover for expropriating their lands, as most land mortgaged before the 1901 Punjab Alienation of Land Act had been mortgaged by Muslim *zamindars* to them. They wanted the Act to be extended to transactions which had taken place after 1901, many of which were between the small peasants and the growing agriculturalist moneylending class. The Unionists however rejected this proposal as a result of which the urban Hindu and Sikh moneylenders had to bear the brunt of the measure. It was estimated that whereas only 84,617 Muslims had to return land under its terms, over 200,000 Hindus and Sikhs gave back the land to their original owners.[64]

The agrarian reforms made the Unionist Party even more popular amongst the rural population.[65] In Amritsar district alone, over 100 meetings were held to celebrate the passage of what became known as the 'Golden Acts'.[66] Early in September 1938 over one and a half lakh peasants attended the Zamindara Conference which Chhotu Ram and Sikander organized at Lyallpur to explain the significance and benefits of their policy.[67] Included in this audience were many Hindu and Sikh Jats who had suffered as much as the Muslim *zamindars* at the hands of the moneylenders. Support for the reforms united the Unionist Party. 'All these measures have the enthusiastic and practically unanimous support of the Unionist Party and have, I think', wrote the Punjab Governor to the Viceroy in July 1938, 'had the effect of pulling the Party together'.[68]

Congress Weakness

The 'Golden Acts' raised again the dilemma which had dogged the Punjab Congress since the turn of the century, namely how to win the support of the rural population without alienating its wealthy Bania and Khatri benefactors. The Satyapal and Bhargava factions adopted a different approach to this problem and the whole issue soon became inextricably linked with the power struggle between them. The dispute came to a head at the worst possible moment, almost immediately after the Congress had launched a mass movement in the countryside aimed at winning the Muslim peasants' support. Before the 1937 elections, the Congress had steered clear of this approach but many of its leaders now saw it as the only way of making any impact in the province. It hoped to mobilize the peasants' support by appealing to their economic interests and by attacking the landlord composition and outlook of the Unionist Party.[69] In April 1937 two and a half lakh rupees were set aside for propaganda work along these lines. The passage of the 'Golden Acts' however questioned the wisdom of this approach. For here was a Government pursuing policies similar to those which it was now advocating and to those which Congress ministries were carrying out in such provinces as Madras but which had incurred as a result the implacable hatred of the Hindu commercial castes.

The Hindu press led by the *Tribune* had launched a bitter campaign against the measures which it claimed were motivated solely by communal considerations. They were also vehemently opposed by the Mahasabhite members of the Legislative Assembly. 'This is a step calculated to destory the confidence of the people in the present government', declared Sir Gokul Chand Narang during the course of the debates on the Restitution of Mortgaged Lands Bill, 'they may please a number of mortgagers to whom the land is to be restored, but there are at least 50 per cent of the people who look upon these gentlemen as usurpers'.[70] In July 1938 he formed the All-Punjab Non-Agriculturalist Association. Its initial aim was to enroll 25,000 members and to collect 25,000 rupees in order to continue the agitation against the legislation.[71] On July 10, it organised *hartals* by Hindu shopkeepers and businessmen in a number of Punjab towns and at the end of the month held a provincial conference at Lyallpur.[72] The prosperous Jat and Sikh proprietors of this area however boycotted it with the result that the Conference was a complete disaster, raising only the paltry sum of Rs. 1,600.[73] The urban Hindus next sought to broaden their support by turning to the kisans. They knew that the kisans had little love for them but nevertheless believed that they could be mobilized on an anti-landlord platform. They organised a Kisan Conference at Lyallpur in September so that it would coincide with the Unionist-backed Zamindara Conference. The kisans however stayed away in large numbers and this second failure at Lyallpur together with the poor response for the 'Black Week' of protests which the

Non-Agriculturalist Association had organized earlier in August revealed the general apathy towards its aims.[74]

The Punjab Congress had not been involved in the Association's creation and adopted a neutral attitude during the debates on the Unionist legislation,[75] despite the fact that most of its members represented those constituents who were hardest hit by the measures. In the 1937 elections, the Congress had won all nine of the Urban Hindu seats but had captured only two of the twenty-four Rural Hindu seats, both of them being in the Jullundur Division. Why then was it so quiet over this issue? The answer lies in the fact that Dr Satyapal had still not given up hope of winning over Muslim and Hindu peasant support. His approach was supported by the All-India Congress Committee which would have been embarrassed if its Punjab organization had opposed policies of rural uplift similar to those advocated by Congress ministries in other province.[76] The Hindu press, the Mahasabha and the Non-Agriculturalist Association bitterly attacked the Congress attitude. Gopi Chand Bhargava saw an opportunity in this to finally topple Dr. Satyapal. He set about repairing relations with the Non-Agriculturalist Association by persuading it to declare that its quarrel was only with the Unionist Party and not with the Congress as well.[77] In a statement to the Press he declared that although Congress Committees should not become involved with the Non-Agriculturalist Association, individual Congress members could join its agitation.[78] Dr. Satyapal immediately responded by issuing a counter-statement. The Working Council of the Punjab Congress became almost totally inactive as a result of the deadlock which ensued.

Gopi Chand Bhargava worked up sufficient support in the Hindu community to seize the leadership of the provincial Congress organization and to temporarily purge the Satyapal faction from the Working Council. In September 1938, he swung the Congress around to a policy of opposition to the agrarian reforms. Its first action was to help organize the ill-fated Lyallpur Kisan Conference.[79] Although the reversal of its policy prevented the provincial Congress from breaking up, it destroyed all possibility of its mass contact movement succeeding in the villages. The damage which its vacillating attitude had done to its prestige was immediately brought home in the Gurgaon District Board elections. Gurgaon was a district in which the Congress usually did well, but in the elections held there in October 1938 it captured only one of the thirty seats.[80] Far more important was the long-term damage to its prospects caused by Bhargava's new leadership. He headed the most communal and reactionary elements within the Punjab Congress and set it on a course of action which not only lost it the valuable support of such Muslim Congress leaders as Dr. Mohammad Alam, the deputy Congress Assembly Party leader, but destroyed any hope of it building a mass base of support amongst the Muslim peasants. 'The attitude of the party on the Agrarian Bills and particularly the Relief of Indebtedness Bill', Dr. Alam wrote at the time of his resignation, 'reveals its communal mentality without a doubt.... It is no better than the Hindu Mahasabha Party'.[81]

The Punjab Congress could ill afford to risk unpopularity when events outside the province were conspiring against it. Congress ministries had been formed in seven of the eleven Indian Provinces following the 1937 elections. Reports of the oppression of Muslims in these Congress-governed areas soon began to reach the Punjab. Most instances of Congress 'oppression' were not deliberately caused but resulted from its failure to understand and respect the Muslims' cultural and religious sensitivities. A prime example of this was its encouragement of the Wardha Scheme of Education. This had been drawn up by a committee headed by the prominent Muslim educationalist, Dr. Zakir Hussain[82] but its emphasis on craft learning, its Hindi textbooks and its secular character (Muslim primary education had always been mainly religious in content) made it seem to the Muslims that this was a deliberate attempt to 'Hinduize' them. In the same way, the flying of the Congress flag from public buildings and the introduction of the singing of the 'Bande Mataram' with its strong Hindu sentiments[83] in the Congress-ruled provinces also increased Muslim fears of

Hindu domination. The Pirpur Committee Report into Muslim grievances in the Congress provinces was published shortly after the December 1938 Patna Muslim League Session. It was succeeded the following March by the even more lurid Shareef Report on the Congress oppression of the Muslim minority in Bihar. Although many of the claims in these reports were exaggerated,[84] most Muslims believed that they were true. In May 1939, a deputation of prominent All-India Muslim League leaders toured the Punjab to describe the sufferings of the Muslims in the Congress-governed provinces.[85] Their meetings attracted large audiences and destroyed much of the remaining influence which the Congress possessed amongst the Muslims of the province.

GOBBLING UP THE MUSLIM LEAGUE

The Punjab Muslim League was in an even weaker position than the Congress to challenge the Unionist Party's predominance. It had gained just one seat in the 1937 elections. Raja Ghazanfar Ali had joined the Unionists immediately on being offered a Parliamentary Secretaryship leaving Malik Barkat Ali to soldier on alone. The Punjab Muslim League thus remained a small clique of Lahore lawyers rather than being a political party. Moreover, its parent body was almost entirely dependent on the Unionist Party's support in all-India politics. From October 1937 onwards, Sikander exacted a high price for this support—the complete subordination of the Punjab Muslim League to his party.

The Punjab Muslim League emerged from its drubbing in the 1937 elections determined to build a mass base of support in the countryside in order to bypass the brokerage system. During the summer months of 1937, it launched a vigorous rural propaganda campaign. Workers were sent into the villages to form primary branches of the League[86] and its membership fee was reduced to only 4 annas (Re. 0.25) to encourage as many villagers to join as possible. The Punjab League hoped to enroll at this time as many as 20,000 new primary members in the

Lahore district alone.[87] A number of provincial League leaders toured the rural areas to whip up enthusiasm for this membership drive. In September, Malik Zeman Mehdi Khan, the deputy President, and Ghulam Rasul, the Honorary Secretary, toured Gujranwala and established a district branch of the League there and encouraged the formation of primary branches in the villages.[88] The League achieved some success in enrolling new primary members during the summer, but by the end of the year this activity had ceased almost completely and was not resumed again in earnest for nearly another seven years. Throughout this period, the Punjab countryside was sealed off from the Muslim League's influence by the Unionist Party's capture of its organization. This had resulted from the Jinnah-Sikander Pact of October 1937.

The Pact was concluded at the 1937 Lucknow Session of the All-India Muslim League. Under its terms, Sikander agreed to advise all the Muslim members of the Unionist Party to join the Muslim League. They would form a Punjab Muslim League Assembly Party which would be subject to the rules and regulations of the Central and Provincial Parliamentary Boards of the All-India Muslim League. In view of the agreement, the Provincial Parliamentary Board would be reconstituted. The agreement was not however to affect the continuation of the existing Coalition Ministry which would retain its Unionist Party name.

The reason why Sikander agreed to the Pact and what it precisely meant still remains controversial. M. A. H. Isphani has depicted Sikander as joining the Muslim League, 'not out of deep conviction but merely as a matter of necessity' in order to strengthen his ministry in the face of the threat from the Congress' mass contact movement.[89] This seems scarcely credible in the light of the Congress' weakness even before the passage of the 'Golden Acts'. Sajjad Zaheer and Ashiq Husain Batalvi have on the other hand criticized Sikander for agreeing to the Pact solely with the intention of gobbling up the provincial League organization.[90] Even its co-drafters, Sikander and Malik Barkat Ali, completely contradicted each other's interpretation of the political effects of the Pact within the Punjab. Sikander's view was that, 'the position of the parties so far as the Punjab is concerned will remain unaltered by the agreement, the change will be however that Muslim members of the Unionist Party will be advised to join the League if they so desire'.[91] This attempt to reassure the Hindus and Sikhs whose opposition to the agreement was mounting[92] was flatly contradicted by Malik Barkat Ali. 'The status and character of the Unionist Party will under the agreement undergo a radical transformation', he declared 'the Unionist Party will consist of (1) the Muslim League Party within the Legislature as constituted under the agreement and subject to the full control of the All-India Muslim League and bound by its rules and regulations and (2) the party of Sir Chhotu Ram or any other party that agree to form a coalition with the League Party.... The allegiance of the Muslim League members will primarily be to the All-India Muslim League and if ever a conflict arises between the fundamental policy and programme of the League and the coalescing group the Muslim League Party will be bound by the mandate and orders of the parent body.'[93]

The Pact's immediate effect was to strengthen the Muslim League's position in All-India politics. 'No one can deny that without this action on the part of Sikander the Muslim League would have been confined to the minority provinces alone and sooner or later they would have gone under', Choudhry Khaliquzzaman has declared. 'Sikander saved Muslim India by coming to the League session in Lucknow and by infusing life into the organisation. His association with the Muslim League at this crucial hour in the fate of Muslim India is an event in history and must live for ever to remind us of his greatness'.[94] But did Sikander lose anything by this move? For whilst the Pact undoubtedly strengthened the Muslim League's position in all-India politics, Sikander used the opportunity it provided to assume complete control of the Punjab Muslim League, thereby not only removing a potentially dangerous rival provincial party but clearing the ground for any future attempt to challenge Jinnah's position in national politics.

Sikander only acquiesced to the Pact on the understanding that the Punjab Muslim League would be reorganized afterwards.[95] Jinnah was forced to agree to this because he needed the Unionists' support in all-India politics. In order to gain this, he was prepared, for the moment, to see the Punjab League come under Unionist control. His previous intervention in Punjabi politics in May 1936[96] had convinced him that the halt which this would bring to the League's growth in popular support would not damage its eventual chances of coming to power. They key to this would always be the capture of the rural elite's support. The League's provincial leaders, smarting at their exclusion from power by the Unionist landlords, quite naturally saw things in a very different light. Iqbal, who despite his ill-health was still the Punjab League President at this time, wrote to Jinnah on 10 November expressing his concern at the way Sikander was manipulating the Pact. He was backed up soon afterwards by Ghulam Rasul and Malik Barkat Ali. All three were unaware that in less than six months Sikander's efforts to control their party would be given official recognition by Jinnah.

In March 1938, the All-India Muslim League Council appointed a committee under Nawab Ismail Khan's presidency to decide on the applications for reaffiliation of its provincial organizations. It refused to reaffiliate the Punjab Muslim League on the grounds that its constitution was irregular.[97] Allama Iqbal responded by drafting a statement for release to the press in which he condemned the working of the Jinnah-Sikander Pact, but Jinnah dissuaded him from publishing it.[98] At the special 'Shahidgunj' Muslim League Session held at Calcutta in April 1938, less than a month before Iqbal's death, an Organizing Committee was formed under Sikander Hayat Khan's chairmanship with the task of creating a new Muslim League organization in the Punjab.[99] The following month, the Punjab Muslim League which consisted on paper of twenty-seven district and 100 primary leagues was officially dissolved.[100] Sikander, despite Malik Barkat Ali's protests, made sure that Unionists were in the majority on the Organizing Committee.

Only ten of its thirty-five members were 'Old' Leaguers.[101] He was thus in a position to delay the League's formation as long as he wanted and to ensure that when it was finally created it would remain firmly under Unionist control.

The 'Old' Muslim League members of the Organizing Committee grew increasingly restive as the months passed and still no steps had been taken to create a new Muslim League. At the December 1938 Patna Working Committee Meeting of the All-India Muslim League, Malik Barkat Ali voiced their frustration by attempting to move a resolution to the effect that:

... the Organising Committee appointed at Calcutta to set up and establish the Punjab Provincial Muslim League and its branches under the new (League) constitution be dissolved and a new organising committee ... be set up for the same purpose.[102]

Jinnah, who did not wish to upset the leading Unionists, stepped in however and forced Malik Barkat Ali to withdraw his resolution. The Punjab's district Muslim League leaders were not however so easily quietened. At a meeting held in Lahore at the end of February 1939, Mohammad Azam, Secretary of the Sialkot District Muslim League and Mir Ahmad Shah, President of the Campbellpore District League,[103] attempted to pass a resolution demanding action from the Organizing Committee.[104] Sikander's immediate response was to remove Ghulam Rasul, one of the leading spokesmen of the 'Old' Leaguers, from the post of Secretary of the Organizing Committee and replace him with a loyal Unionist, Mian Ramzan Ali.[105]

The split between the Unionists and the 'Old' Leaguers became even wider in August 1939 when a sharp difference of opinion arose between them over the nomination of Muslim League candidates for the Amritsar and Multan Division Towns by-elections. According to the terms of the Jinnah-Sikander Pact:

In future elections and by-elections for the Legislature after the adoption of this arrangement, the groups constituting the present Unionist Party will jointly support the candidates put up by their respective groups.[106]

This somewhat ambiguous statement was capable of being interpreted in a number of ways, it was generally agreed however that as a new Muslim League organization had not yet been created, the task of selecting the candidates fell to the Organizing Committee. Sikander moved quickly and, without consulting its 'Old' League members, nominated his relative, Sheikh Sadiq Hasan, for the Amritsar seat and Khan Sahib Sheikh Mohammad Amin, Bar-at-law, for Multan. He thus hoped to gain influence in the towns, the only area in which the Unionists had failed in 1937, by passing off Unionists as Muslim League candidates. The 'Old' Leaguers however refused to accept this *fait accompli* and nominated Malik Zeman Mehdi Khan as their candidate for Multan. He marshalled an impressive array of support within the constituency,[107] but although Ghulam Rasul pleaded his case with Jinnah, after a brief telegraphic exchange with Sikander, he acquiesced to Mohammad Amin's candidature.[108]

Later that same month, at the Delhi League Council Meeting the 'Old' Leaguers tried once more to secure the Organizing Committee's dissolution.[109] Again, the all-India leaders intervened to prevent open conflict with the Unionists. Nawabzada Liaqat Ali Khan arranged a compromise in which the Organizing Committee was given until 15 November 1939 to set up a Punjab Muslim League. After that date, regardless of whether or not its task was completed, it would be dissolved. The Unionist members of the Organizing Committee reluctantly accepted this, whilst attempting to gain revenge by asking for the removal of Ghulam Rasul, Malik Zeman Mehdi Khan and Ashiq Hussain Batalvi from membership of the Organizing Committee and the All-India Muslim League Council.[110]

The Organizing Committee procrastinated as long as possible before announcing its formation of a Punjab Muslim League just a week before the deadline ran out. Three more months passed before its first meeting was held under Sikander's chairmanship at his Lahore residence. At this meeting, Nawab Shah Nawaz of Mamdot was elected League President, Mian Ramzan Ali, Secretary, Mian Amir-ud-Din, Financial Secretary and Syed Mohammad Ali Jaafari Organizing Secretary. They were loyal Unionists to a man.[111] The Muslim League's activists throughout the province were disgusted at this blatant move and protested to Jinnah that the creation of the new Muslim League was a farce. A number of district officials including the Vice-President of the Ferozepore District Muslim League, Khadim Mohy-ud-Din, resigned.[112] The Montgomery District League begged Jinnah not to affiliate the newly-created League.[113] Mian Nurullah, the Arain member for Lyallpur, who had resigned from the Unionist Party in January 1939, issued a press statement directly challenging Jinnah to take action against this 'bogus' Muslim League.

> Thanks to the policy pursued by the High Command of the Muslim League the Unionist Party has become the complete master of the (Punjab) Muslim League.... So far the Muslim League headquarters do not seem to be realising the peril to which their policy of vacillation and drift pursued during the past two years has exposed the organisation in the Punjab.... I would appeal to Mr Jinnah in the interests of the League to see that a living Muslim League organisation is established in the Punjab. The Muslim League under the leadership of the Premier is merely a creature of the Unionist Party packed by honorary Magistrates and Sub-Registrars.... Their allegiance is first and last to the Unionist Party in power and they can any day flout Mr. Jinnah on the Central Body.[114]

The force of such protests caused the All-India Muslim League to set up a Punjab Committee of Enquiry at the end of February 1939. Its members were Nawab Mohammad Ismail Khan, the Raja of Mahmudabad and Choudhry Khaliquzzaman and they were empowered to decide whether the newly-constituted Punjab Muslim League should be granted affiliation. Nearly two years had now elapsed since the creation of the Organizing Committee. Would the process have to be started all over again? The answer was no. After a short stay in the province, the Enquiry Committee recommended that the Punjab Muslim League's affiliation should be accepted. This decision was a tremendous triumph for Sikander. He had succeeded in gaining control of the Punjab League with Jinnah's permission! It marked the zenith of the Unionist Party's power within the province. Its two main rivals, the Congress and the Muslim League, were now both reduced to impotence.

Malik Barkat Ali and the other provincial League leaders found it almost unbelievable that Jinnah should have allowed the Unionist Party to gain complete control of the Punjab Muslim League.[115] Their incredulity stemmed from their failure to recognize the extent to which Jinnah depended on Sikander's support in all-India politics. In the years before the outbreak of the Second World War which raised the Muslim League's status, it was in a very weak position in comparison with the Congress. This was the legacy of its poor showing in the 1937 elections. It had won only 109 of the 482 Muslim seats in the provincial assemblies, whereas the Congress had captured 716 of the 1161 General (Hindu) seats and 26 of the 58 Muslim seats which it had contested. Whereas the Congress was able to form ministries in seven of the eleven Indian provinces including the Muslim North-West Frontier Province, the Muslim League was nowhere in a position to do so. It therefore had to rely heavily on the support of the two Muslim Premiers of Punjab and Bengal, Sikander Hayat and Fazlul Haq, in order to have a voice at all in all-India politics. Fazlul Haq's Krishak Proja Party played similar role in Bengal politics to the Unionist Party in the Punjab, although as it was mainly a party of small tenants and peasants, it was prepared to go considerably further in tampering with the landlords' interests in order to achieve agrarian reform. The Unionist Party's power base was much stronger than that of its Bengal counterpart. In the Bengal Assembly in which there were no less than forty-one independent Muslim members, the Krishak Proja Party had captured only thirty-five seats.[116] Fazlul Haq needed to include Muslim League members in his first coalition government. However, Jinnah could hardly rely whole-heartedly on Fazlul Haq's support. He had therefore to turn to Sikander for the crucial support which he needed at the Centre.

Sikander played a leading role in All-India Muslim League politics through the years 1937–40. He exerted a strong moderating influence which ultimately worked against his own interests.

For without this influence during these years, the League might have adopted a less 'helpful' attitude to the British war effort. Its cooperation however led the British to elevate it to a position of equality with the Congress in all-India politics. Jinnah was thus eventually freed of his dependence on the Unionists' support and could turn his attention to revitalizing the Punjab Muslim League. All this however was in the distant future in August 1938 when largely as a result of Sikander's efforts, the Muslim members of the Central Assembly supported the Government of India's Dissuasion from Enlistment Bill.[117] A month later, in a speech at Simla, Sikander pledged Punjab's complete and unconditional support for the British in the event of war. This was in opposition to the official Muslim League policy at that time. A. H. Lari, a U.P. Legislative Assembly member, moved a resolution condemning this speech at the December League Council meeting held at Delhi. Contrary to contemporary press reports, Jinnah did not administer a 'stern rebuke' to Sikander but rather spoke in his favour and insisted that the resolution be withdrawn.[118] The same month at the Patna League Session, Sikander again exerted a strong moderating influence throughout the proceedings. Without his support Jinnah would have been unable to secure the amendment to the Civil Disobedience Resolution which left the decision to launch such a campaign in the hands of the Working Committee.[119] In return, Jinnah not only made sure that Malik Barkat Ali's resolution calling for the immediate dissolution of the Organizing Committee was thrown out, but sternly rebuked him for opposing Sikander.[120] Jinnah could ill-afford to displease someone whose assistance was as useful in internal League politics as in dealings with the Congress and the British.

Sikander's greatest influence in the Muslim League was reached five months later in May 1939 when he presided over the Sholapur Muslim League Session. It was a clear demonstration to the Unionist Party's predominance in Muslim politics at that time. Its strong provincial power base made its support in all-India politics indispensable to Jinnah. The Party had become not only the most dominant political force in the Punjab but in the whole of Muslim India. Memories of the bitter struggle with the Khizr Unionist Coalition Ministry in February 1947 together with the needs of nation-building have led many Pakistani historians[121] to ignore this importance. But it would be no exaggeration to say that during the period 1937–40, Sikander, not Jinnah, was the most powerful Muslim political leader.

Sikander's ascendancy however was to be short-lived, as the Second World War brought with it a completely new chapter in the history of the Unionist Party and the Muslim League. During the war years many of the Unionist Party's landed supporters deserted it in favour of the Muslim League. Their transfer of allegiance constituted a radical new dimension in Punjabi politics. By 1946, the Muslim League was a major rival to the Unionist Party in its rural heartland of power. The following two chapters will explain the way in which wartime changes at both the national and provincial level of politics undermined the Unionist dominance in the Punjab countryside.

Notes

1. Mohammad Bashir of Gurdaspur to Unionist Party headquarters, 9 May 1936.
2. The 1935 Government of India Act made Indian Ministers responsible for all the day-to-day government of the provinces. The distinction between reserved and transferred powers was abolished, the official bloc was removed from the provincial legislatures and Governors reduced to the role of constitutional longstop.
3. He had earlier been attacked by the '*Zamindar*' and *Mujahid* for his alleged influence in securing Chaudhri Zafrulla Khan's membership of the Viceroy's Executive Council. Husain, *Mian Fazl-i-Husain*, p. 314.
4. Mian Fazl-i-Husain Papers (5), p. 131.
5. Government of India, Home Department Political Section, File No. 88/36-Poll., NAI.
6. A. Hussain, *Fazl-i-Husain, A Political Biography* (London, 1946), p. 309.
7. Fazl-i-Husain was of course influenced in this decision by the institutional framework in which he worked. Until there was another instalment of reform, real political power and influence lay at the provincial rather than the 'national' sphere of politics.

8. Punjab FR for the second half of April 1936, 18/4/36-Poll., NAI.
9. They were Maulvi Mohammad Ishaq of Mansehra, Pir Zain-ul-Abdin of Multan and Rahim Bakhsh Ghaznavi of Peshawar. Punjab FR for the second half of June 1936, 18/6/1936, NAI.
10. Punjab FR for the second half of August 1936, 18/8/36, Poll., NAI.
11. Punjab FR for the second half of January 1937, 18/1/37, Poll., NAI.
12. *Times of India* (Bombay), 15 December 1936.
13. Punjab FR for the second half of December 1936, 18/12/1936, Poll., NAI.
14. Punjab FR for the first half of January 1937, 18/1/37-Poll., NAI.
15. *Civil and Military Gazette* (Lahore), 14 October 1936.
16. This had been the political approach which the Unionist Party had so successfully adopted in earlier Legislative Council elections. The situation remained the same in 1937.

    > It is by no means uncommon for 2 or 3 candidates of the same party to be fighting the same seat. Whichever candidate is successful will adopt the party programme. But, in the present stage of political development in the Punjab, the party programme represents the policy of the candidate after the election and not the policy on which the election is fought. In many constituencies the voting will be along tribal or personal lines and not according to political convictions.

    Punjab FR for the second half of November 1936, 18/11/36, Poll., NAI.
17. The Oudh NAP based its election campaign solely on the *taluqdars'* 'natural leadership' in the countryside. Under a chief organizer who was to be a landlord there were to be hired organizers appointed for each *tehsil*. These *tehsil* organizers would prepare a list of 'persons who exercised influence in the tehsil' and then obtain from these persons a list of 'the tenants within the scope of their influence'. When their lists were completed, the chief organizer would tour the constituencies to meet the 'influential persons' and to make them responsible for the votes of their circle. In this way the landlords would make sure of their control in each constituency.
18. Note by K. B. Mian Abdul Aziz, Commissioner Ambala Division on the present economic situation in Ambala Division 26 May 1933. Punjab Proceedings P 12017, August 1933, No. 23, p. 78, IOR.
19. The Oudh *taluqdars'* made unrestrained use of their power to enhance rents. They also exacted *nazrana* (premiums for entry to a tenant-holding). Opposition to these in 1920–22 had led to tenant riots but the landlords remained 'unconvinced' of the need to do anything to win over their tenants.
20. *The Leader* (Allahabad), 18 February 1937.
21. In the Oudh NAP there was conflict between Raja Sir Rampal Singh, President of the British Indian Association of Oudh, and Maheshwar Dyal Seth, the party's founder. Nawabzada Liaqat Ali Khan refused to be elected one of the two joint secretaries of the Agra NAP because he felt it was too lowly a post and had to be made treasurer instead. Major

Ranjit Singh, who was one of the party's founders, threatened to leave it after only being offered the post of 'honorary assistant secretary' as all the higher positions had been given to men of superior rank but less ability. Regional rivalries prevented the two NAPs uniting to fight the elections.

22. *Pioneer* (Lucknow), 6 January 1937.
23. *Ibid.*, 19 January 1937.
24. *Ibid.*, (22) above.
25. See *The Leader* (Allahabad), 24 January 1937, and 3 February 1937, and also *Pioneer* (Lucknow), 6 February.
26. P. D. Reeves, *Landlords and Party Politics in the U.P. 1934–7.* Reeves' essay contained in, D.A. Low (ed.), *Soundings in Modern South Asian History* (London, 1968), p. 282.
27. Reeves declares (p. 282), 'an era had passed and the landlords could no longer claim that they were 'the chosen and natural leaders' of the people'. The old brokerage system had not however disappeared overnight. The NAPs had been defeated to a large extent because the *taluqdars* had transferred their allegiance to other parties and were deeply divided amongst themselves.
28. *The Leader* (Allahabad), 27 February 1937.
29. *The Times of India* (Bombay), 13 January 1937.
30. *Ibid.*, (above) 29, 8 February 1937.
31. *Civil and Military Gazette* (Lahore), 3 February 1937.
32. Firoz Khan Noon's cousin, Malik Sardar Khan Noon, was in this way accommodated with a seat from 1943 onwards. The cadet Mundial and Hamoka branches of the Tiwana family which had not been so well represented in the Council as the Mitha Tiwanas were able to secure seats after 1937. The Chathas and the Gilanis were other families which noticeably increased their representation in the new Assembly.
33. D. Gilmartin, 'Religious Leadership and the Pakistan Movement in the Punjab', *Modern Asian Studies*, 13, 3 (1979), p. 504.
34. W. Ahmad (ed.), *Letters of Mian Fazl-i-Husain* (Lahore, 1976), p. 592 & ff.
35. Most Deobandi and Firangi Mahal *ulema* refused to have anything to do with the British government and refused to be sucked in to its web of patronage. Indeed, in defence of Islam they became political activists against the Raj during the Khilafat movement.
36. Mian Iftikhar-ud-Din was a member of the Arain Mian family of Baghbanpura Lahore. Despite his feudal background he had strong Communist leanings and even before his entry into provincial politics had been involved in the Indian Progressive Writer's Association.
37. Sardar Habib Ullah Khan was a Jat. Unfortunately for him the majority of the voters in the Kasur constituency were Arains. Punjab FR for the first half of February 1937, 18/2/1937, Poll., NAI.

38. M. Rafique Afzal, *Malik Barkat Ali: His Life and Writings* (Lahore, 1969), p. 36.
39. The Committee's members were: Sheikh Akbar Ali (Advocate), Professor Inayat Ullah, Mian Abdul Aziz (Bar-at-law, Ex-President of the Lahore Municipal Committee), Abdul Mannan, Sheikh Mohammad Jan (Justice), Pir Taj-ud-Din (Bar-at-law), Mohammad Azim Khan (Municipal Commissioner Lahore), Mohammad Jafri, Malik Nur Elahi, Haji Amir-ud-Din Saharai, Syed Tassaduq Hussain of Bhera (Bar-at-law), Mohammad Shafi (Secretary of the Intercollegiate Muslim Brotherhood Lahore). Ex-Officio members were: Abdul Malik, Nawabzada Muzaffar Ali Khan (he defected to the Unionists in December), Khan Bahadur Malik Zeman Mehdi Khan (the only influential landlord on the Committee) and Ghulam Rasul (Bar-at-law). *Civil and Military Gazette* (Lahore), 17 October 1936.
40. *Ibid.*, (38) above.
41. Punjab FR for the second half of November 1936, 18/11/36, Poll., NAI.
42. Punjab FR for the second half of December 1936, 18/12/36, Poll., NAI.
43. *Ibid.*, (29) above.
44. Pir Makhad's main political rival was the Khan of Makhad, the head of the Sagri Pathans. Pir Makhad attached such importance to the 1937 District Board elections that he personally directed the operations of his 'party' Most of the thirty-two seats were contested by his nominees. *Civil and Military Gazette* (Lahore), 19 September 1937.
45. *Tribune* (Ambala), 4 November 1936.
46. *Ibid.*, 30 January 1937.
47. Punjab FR for the second half of January 1937, 18/1/37, Poll., NAI.
48. His Sikh National Board Party had entered into a coalition with the Unionist Government.
49. He had no personal following, but was the nominee of Raja Narendra Nath.
50. For further details see, C. Baxter, 'The People's Party Vs. the Punjab Feudalists', *Journal of Asian and African Studies*, VIII (1974), p. 171 & ff.
51. Punjab FR, 5 April 1938, L/P&J/5/241, IOR.
52. *Hindustan Times* (Delhi), 1 August 1944.
53. *Tribune* (Ambala), 5 January 1939.
54. Mushtaq Ahmad Gurmani, the Unionist member for Muzaffargarh North, was, for example, very critical not only of this instance but of the Unionist Party's general reliance on patronage to win support. He declared that it would not only bring the party into contempt amongst the general public but would accelerate its disintegration as members came to believe that the best way of satisfying their personal ambitions was to threaten secession. Note of E.P. Moon, Punjab FR for the second half of April 1939, L/P&J/5/242, IOR.
55. Ibid., (53) above.

56. Just over one in ten Punjabis had the right to vote in the 1937 and 1946 Provincial Elections.
57. The story was told of how Chhotu Ram accompanied his father when he went to a *bania* in Sampla village (Rohtak district) to seek advice concerning his son's future career. The moneylender flung the *pankha* cord to Chaudhri Sukhi Ram and asked him to pull it, while he was thinking over the issue. Chhotu Ram could not stand this humiliation and questioned the *bania* about the propriety of such conduct. This incident is said to have acted as a catalyst in Chhotu Ram's decision to dedicate his career to improving the peasant's social and economic status and to destroying the moneylenders' influence. H. L. Agnithori and S. N. Malik, *A Profile in Courage: A Biography of Chaudhri Chhotu Ram* (New Delhi, 1978), p. 2 & ff.
58. Chhotu Ram began a series of articles under the heading 'Bazar Thagi Ki Sair' (Ramble through the Thagi Market) which dealt with bribery, corruption and official high-handedness towards the peasants. He followed these up with another series of articles under the heading 'Bechara Zamindar' (The Helpless Peasant) in which he called for agrarian reform. *Ibid.*, (56) above, p. 43.
59. *Tribune* (Ambala), 19 July 1939.
60. D. Verma, 'Provincial Autonomy in the Punjab April 1937–October 1939', *Indian Journal of Political Science*, Vol. 1 (1940), p. 457 & ff.
61. *Civil and Military Gazette* (Lahore), 19 January 1937.
62. The Punjab Registration of Moneylenders Act provided that a moneylender would not be helped by the law courts to recover his loans unless he was registered and held a licence to carry on a moneylender's trade. His licence could be suspended if he was suspected of malpractice during which time he would be unable to successfully sue for the recovery of his loans without the express permission of the Deputy Commissioner. The Act was applicable to non-agriculturalist and agriculturalist moneylenders alike. The Punjab Alienation of Land 2nd Amendment Act closed the loophole in the original measure created by the *benami* transaction.
63. R. Narendranath, 'The Punjab Agrarian Laws and their Economic and Constitutional bearings', *Modern Review*, 65 (1939), p. 30.
64. *Ibid.*, (63) above.
65. Punjab FR 26 October 1938, L/P&J/5/241, IOR.
66. *Tribune* (Ambala), 31 August 1938.
67. Punjab FR 6 September 1938, L/P&J/5/241, IOR.
68. Punjab FR 8 July 1938, L/P&J/5/241, IOR.
69. *Hindustan Times* (Delhi), 27 March 1937.
70. Extract from the Proceedings of the meetings of the Punjab Legislative Assembly held on 23 June and 4, 8, 18 and 21 July 1938 relating to the

debates on the Punjab Restitution of Mortgaged Lands Bill. File no. L/E9/9/584, Economic Department Collection, IOR.

71. Punjab FR for the first half of July 1938, L/P&J/5/241, IOR.
72. *Ibid.*, (71) above.
73. Punjab FR for the first half of August 1938, L/P&J/5/241, IOR.
74. Although the *Tribune* recorded that the Kisan Conference opened amidst scenes of almost frantic zeal, it was poorly attended in comparison with the Zamindara Conference. Its attendance which steadily declined as the Conference progressed was never more than 15,000 and consisted mainly of Hindus drawn from Lyallpur City. The 'Black Week' of protests from 15–21 August against the 'Golden Acts' was, 'practically a complete failure'. Punjab FR for the first half of September 1938, L/P&J/5/241, IOR.
75. *Ibid.*, (71) above.
76. *Ibid.*, (71) above.
77. Punjab FR for the first half of August 1938, L/P&J/5/241, IOR.
78. Punjab FR for the second half of July 1938, L/P&J/5/241, IOR.
79. *Ibid.*, (74) above.
80. Punjab FR 26 October 1938, L/P&J/5/241, IOR.
81. G. A. Heeger, 'The Growth of the Congress Movement in the Punjab 1920–1940', *Journal of Asian Studies*, 32, 1 (1972), p. 50.
82. P. Hardy, *The Muslims of British India* (Cambridge, 1972), p. 227.
83. Muslims found the third, fourth and final stanzas of the 'Bande Mataram' objectionable. The reason becomes immediately apparent from the following rendering of the third and fourth stanzas (English translation by Sri Aurobindo Ghose).

Who hath said thou art weak in thy lands,
When the swords flash but in seventy million hands,
And seventy million voices roar,
Thy dreadful name from shore to shore?
To thee! call, Mother and Lord!
Thou who Sayest, arise and save!
To her! cry who ever her foemen drave (sic)
Back from plain and sea and shook herself free.

Thou art wisdom, thou art law,
Thou art heart, our soul, our breath,
Thou the love divine, the awe
In our hearts that conquerors death.
Thine the strength that nerves the arm,
Thine the beauty, thine the charm,
Every image divine,
In our temples is but thine.
Thou art Durga, Lady and Queen,
With her hands that strike and her swords of sheen.

> Thou art Lakshmi lotus-throned,
> And the Muse, a hundred-toned.
> Pure and perfect without peer,
> Mother, lend thine perfect ear.

84. G. Rizvi, *Linlithgow and India* (London, 1978), pp. 97–105.
85. *Tribune* (Ambala), 12 May 1939.
86. *Civil and Military Gazette* (Lahore), 4 May 1937.
87. *Civil and Military Gazette* (Lahore), 15 July 1937.
88. *Tribune* (Ambala), 7 October 1937.
89. M. A. H. Isphani, *Qaid-e-Azam Jinnah as I Knew Him* (Karachi, 1966), p. 54 & ff.
99. S. Zaheer, *Light on the League-Unionist Conflict* (Bombay, 1944), A. H. Batalvi, *Iqbal Ke Akhiri Do Sal* (Karachi, 1961), p. 251 & ff. Quoted in S. M. Ikram, *Modern Muslim India and the Birth of Pakistan* (Lahore, 1977), p. 252 & ff.
91. *Tribune* (Ambala), 19 October 1937.
92. Pandit Ram Gopal Shashtri, General Secretary of the Arya Samaj Sabha declared, for example, in a press statement of 19 October:

> The news of the alliance between Mr Jinnah and Sir Sikander comes as a surprise. It forebodes a political somersault and is fraught with dangerous consequences for the inter-communal relations in the Punjab ... (It) is tantamount to a reversal of the non-communal policy enunciated by the leader of the Unionist Party.

A Muslm member of the Punjab Congress Committee, Khalifa Fazal Din also criticized the Pact in similar terms.

> He (Sikander) was very popular among all communities because there was a widespread belief that there was no communal trait in his composition. By entering into an entente cordial with the League communalists he has spoilt bis reputation.

Tribune (Ambala), 21 October 1937.

93. *Tribune* (Ambala), 23 October 1937.
94. C. Khaliquzzaman, *Pathway to Pakistan* (Lahore, 1961), p. 290.
95. The landlord members of the Unionists Party were only persuaded with some difficulty to agree to the Pact and then orly because Jinnah had promised to reorganize the League afterwards so that it would be under Unionist control.

> Everyone assured Sir Sikander that they would obey his orders and join the League when so desired. But they all expressed their alarm and anxiety over the present state of affairs in the Provincial League. I assured them that you had promised about the reconstruction of the Provincial League. They were not prepared to trust their funds in the hands of Mr Ghulam Rasul or to acknowledge the present office-bearers of the Provincial League with the exception of Dr Sir Mohammad Iqbal as their leaders or representatives.... I request you in the interests of the Muslims of the Punjab to be very careful of what the Old

Leaguers of the Punjab write to you, it is impossible for us to carry on with the people like Mr Ghulam Rasul and others of the same type.

A. Y. K. Daultana to Jinnah 15 November 1937. QEAP File 255/6 and 255/7, NAP.

96. On his departure from Lahore after failing to win the Unionists' support for the Muslim League Central Parliamentary Board, Jinnah had said: 'I shall never go back to the Punjab again. It is such a hopeless place.' His despair however proved short-lived. A. Husain, *Mian Fazl-i-Husain. A Political Biography* (London, 1946), p. 311.

97. Ashiq Husain Batalvi has attributed the decision to Nawabzada Liaqat Ali Khan's influence. His social background (he was a large UP landlord as well as owning land in the Karnal district of the Punjab) and his earlier membership of the national Agriculturalist Party would certainly have inclined him in favour of landlord rather than urban control of the Punjab Muslim League. But the decision was most likely part of the general League strategy of this time of allowing the Unionists free rein in the Punjab in return for their support at the Centre. The provincial League was officially refused affiliation because of the provisions in its constitution that any Muslim Association in the Punjab might be affiliated to it and that persons could be enrolled directly into the Punjab League without first becoming Primary League members. These were deemed to be 'contrary to the spirit of the new Constitution of the All India Muslim League'. Evidently more lay behind this decision than concern for constitutional niceties because the Committee refused to reconsider its decision when the Punjab League amended its constitution to comply with the All India Muslim League's.
Extract from the Report of the Sub-Committee appointed to consider and decide the applications for affiliation from various provinces, and from a letter of Ghulam Rasul to the Secretary of the All-India Muslim League, 15 April 1938. Punjab Provincial Muslim League 1938–9, Vol. 131, pt. 4, pp. 20 & 23, FMA.

98. M. R. Afzal, *Malik Barkat Ali. His Life and Writings* (Lahore, 1969), p. 47.

99. Press Message from M. A. Jinnah, 19 April 1938. Punjab Provincial Muslim League 1938–9, Vol. 131, pt. 4, p. 32, FMA.

100. *Tribune* (Ambala), 7 June 1938.

101. The 35 members of the Organizing Committee appointed at Calcutta were as follows:

Dr. Sir Mohammad Iqbal President of the 'Old' Punjab Muslim League; Nawab Shah Nawaz Khan, Nawab of Mamdot (Unionist); Maulana Zafar Ali Khan, Editor, '*Zemindar*' (Muslim League); Ghulam Rasul Secretary 'Old' Punjab Muslim League; Dr Khalifa Shujaddin (Muslim League); Pir Tajuddin (Muslim League); K. B. Malik Zeman Mehdi Khan, Deputy President 'Old' Muslim

League; K. S. Nawab Saadat Ali Khan (Muslim League); Sheikh Sadiq Hasan (Unionist); Mian Abdul Aziz (Muslim League); Malik Barkat Ali (Muslim League); Pir Ashiq Hussain (Unionist); Khan Murtaza Ahmed Khan, Editor, *Ehsan* (Muslim League); Sir Sikander Hayat Khan (Unionist); Nawab Khizr Hayat Khan Tiwana (Unionist); Mian Abdul Haye (Unionist); A.Y.K. Daultana (Unionist); Syed Afzal Ali Hasn (Unionist); K. B. Mian Mushtaq Ahmad Gurmani (Unionist); Mir Maqbool Mahmood (Unionist); Syed Amjad Ali (Unionist); Nawabzada Muzaffar Khan (Unionist); Nawab Fazal Ali (Unionist); Raja Fateh Khan (Unionist); Sir Mohammad Hayat Khan Noon (Unionist); Choudhry Mohammad Yasin Khan (Unionist); Sir Sher Mohammad (Unionist); Sheikh Karamat Ali (Unionist); K. S. Choudhry Riasit Ali (Unionist); Sheikh Faiz Mohammad (Unionist); Moulvi Ghulam Mohy-ud-Din (Unionist); Maulana Ghulam Rasul Mehr, Editor, '*Inqilab*' (Unionist).

102. Muslim League Working Committee Meetings 1932, 1933 and 1938, Vol. 122, p. 115 & ff., FMA.
103. He had transferred his allegiance to the Muslim League shortly after his defeat in the 1937 elections. A large number of other *Ittehad-i-Millat* Party leaders transferred their loyalty at this time. Among them was Abu Saeed Enver who went to become the Punjab League's Propaganda Secretary.
104. Punjab Provincial Muslim League 1938–9, Vol. 131, pt. 4, p. 51, FMA.
105. Punjab Provincial Muslim League 1938–9, Vol. 131, pt. 4, p. 54, FMA.
106. I. Ali, *Punjab Politics in the Decade Before Partition* (Lahore, 1975), p. 22.
107. He gained the signatures of support of 157 office bearers of the leading Muslim, political and educational organizations in the district.
108. Telegrams between Jinnah and Sikander August 1939. File No. 49/256-8, QEAP, NAP.
109. Muslim League Council Meetings 1939, Vol. 253, pt. 2, p. 72, FMA.
110. *Ibid.*, (105) above, p. 61 & ff.
111. Mian Amir-ud-Din was a leading Arain landlord of Lahore and a Sub-Registrar, the Nawab of Mamdot was the largest Muslim landlord in the east Punjab. Mian Ramzan Ali was a retired Postmaster General. *Ibid.*, (98) above, p. 53.
112. *Tribune* (Ambala), 12 February 1940.
113. Muslim League Council Meetings 1940, Vol. 284, pt. 1, p. 52, FMA.
114. *Tribune* (Ambala), 24 January 1940.
115. Malik Barkat Ali wrote many letters to Jinnah warning him of the consequences of Sikander's capture of the Punjab Muslim League. 'The only persons who form the so-called Muslim League are Unionists who owe allegiance first and last to Sir Sikander', Barkat Ali warned in December 1940, 'Sir Sikander's only desire was to capture the organisation of the League in order to keep it inert', Malik Barkat Ali to Jinnah 4 December 1940. QEAP, File 215/60, NAP.

116. S. M. Ikram, *Modern Muslim India and the Birth of Pakistan* (Lahore, 1977), p. 313.
117. Brabourne to Craik 27 August 1938. Linlithgow Papers Mss. Eur. F. 125, File 87, IOR.
118. Craik to Linlithgow 8 December 1938. Linlithgow Papers Mass. Eur. F. 125, File 87, IOR.
119. Copy of His Excellency's Note Recorded on 10 January 1939. Linlithgow Papers Mss. Eur. F. 125, File 88, IOR.
120. *Ibid.*, (119) above.
121. A notable exception is Dr S.M. Ikram. See S. M. Ikram, *Modern Muslim India and the Birth of Pakistan* (Lahore, 1977), p. 230 & ff and p. 255 & ff.

Chapter 7

The Unionist Party in Decline

> The procurement of the necessary surplus wheat from the Punjab is more important than any political considerations, any interests of the ministers and in the last resort, the continuance of Provincial Autonomy in the Punjab.[1]

The Unionist Ministers loyally served British interests during the Second World War. They helped raise nearly a million recruits for the Indian Army, and organized savings and 'grow more food' campaigns on a massive scale.[2] But this notable contribution to the war effort undermined their popularity at the very moment when the Muslim League was beginning to mount its challenge.

The Unionists' ability to provide patronage to its supporters declined because of wartime financial stringency. Moreover, they could no longer feather the landowner's nests at the expense of the commercial class, for its goodwill was essential to the success of the war effort. Despite the wartime increase in agricultural prices, the Unionist Party's popularity in the villages was hit by the widespread shortages of consumer goods, increasing economic controls and the heavy burden of army recruitment. The Unionist Ministry's difficulties were worsened by the untimely deaths of Chhotu Ram and Sikander Hayat Khan which severely undermined its unity. The Muslim League eagerly took advantage of the growing divisions within the Unionist Party. It was also able to exploit the wartime discontent. British demands added to this as the Unionists were forced to carry out policies of grain requisition and the rationing of food supplies. The cardinal principle of maintaining rural stability was thus abandoned because of the pressing needs of the war effort.

THE PUNJAB AND THE SECOND WORLD WAR

The war dominated the life of the province in all its aspects. The Punjab even surpassed its herculean efforts of 1914–18 in raising army recruits and food supplies for the embattled British Empire. The Unionist Party, unlike the Congress or the Muslim League, unconditionally supported the British war effort. It dominated the Punjab National War Front which coordinated the region's contribution to this effort. At the local level, the landowners actively encouraged army recruitment. Initially there was great enthusiasm for the British cause. 'The declaration of war by England', stated, for example, the Deputy Commissioner of Sheikhupura, 'has touched the hearts of the Punjabis and the various communities are vying with each other in offering their services and resources to the Government.'[3]

Economic interest as well as the tradition of loyalty to the King-Emperor played its part in creating this outburst of popular enthusiasm. The province's farmers regarded the outbreak of the war as a boon which would dispel the lingering effects of the agricultural depression by increasing employment and raising the prices of their products. Military service offered the opportunity of an improved standard of living to the recruit and his relatives. Consequently, the non-martial classes of Punjab's central congested districts were as eager to enlist during the early stages of the war as the martial classes of Rawalpindi and Jhelum districts. Far more influential than the official propaganda was the sight of soldiers on leave in clean new clothes, their pockets stuffed with rupees. Large sums of money flowed into the Punjab's villages from abroad. A survey of twenty villages in the Ludhiana district revealed, for example, that during the period April 1943–November 1944 over 20,000 rupees were sent each month by army recruits to their relatives.[4] More still could have been sent if many of the soldiers had not been interested in saving sufficient money to start their own businesses at the end of the war and thus make themselves economically independent of the village.[5] Another stimulus to the rural economy was the large increase in the area under cultivation. As a result of the encouragement of the 'grow more food' campaign, the total cropped area of the province rose from about 30 million acres in 1939–40 to nearly 35 million acres in 1942–43 and thereafter remained steady at around 33 million acres.[6] Punjab's farmers were thus not only securing higher prices for their produce than ever before, but were growing and selling more. Much of the increased agricultural wealth was used to redeem mortgaged land. The total cultivated area which was redeemed rose steadily from 203,669 acres in 1940–41 to 482,641 in 1942–43.[7]

The war, however, did not bring only advantages to the rural population. It also brought considerable hardship in the shape of inflation and growing shortages of consumer goods. Cloth, iron, cement, sugar and kerosene, all became virtually unobtainable in the villages. The large increase in the redemption of mortgaged lands reflected as much the shortage of these goods as the new agricultural prosperity. Unable to spend their increased income on consumer goods, the villagers made a virtue out of necessity by accumulating savings and redeeming their mortgaged lands. As the war progressed, inflation wiped out the profits which resulted from the increase in price of such crops as wheat, maize, gram and *bajra*.[8] As economic dislocation worsened, the Unionist Party's total commitment to the war effort made its position increasingly vulnerable.

Particularly ominous for its future prospects was the breakdown in certain areas of the province of the community of interest between the landlords and their clients. This was almost as vital to its political success as inter-communal cooperation and the support of the rural elite. During the agricultural depression, there had been little tension between the landlords and their tenants and labourers unlike, for example, in Bihar and the U.P. But towards the end of the war, reports were received from the Ludhiana district of a growing breakdown in the relationship between the landlords and the village labourers. The latter paraded their new economic independence (the result of the money which they received from their relatives in the army) by refusing to render *begar* and other services to the landlords who retaliated by withdrawing such concessions as the collection of fuel from the fields. 'The old basis of reciprocal cordiality in social relationships was thus knocked out and any assistance given by one class to the other was invariably considered as a special favour.'[9]

Equally worrying for the Unionist Party was its growing inability to function effectively as a vehicle for the *zamindars*' interests. The commercial castes' exploitation of the agriculturalists[10] could no longer be attacked because of the need for their cooperation in fighting the war. Less patronage was available for the landlords and Pirs because of financial stringency, although the Hindu and Sikh businessmen profited enormously from a new source of Government patronage in the form of civil supply contracts. The traditional sources of the Unionist Party's strength in the countryside were being slowly eroded because of the impact of the war and the very efficiency with which the Party mobilized the province to meet its demands.

The first sign of war-weariness was the drastic decline in army recruitment in 1942. In November and December 1942 recruitment was the lowest since the outbreak of hostilities.[11] At the same time there was an alarming increase in the number of deserters.[12] The major recruiting areas were by this time almost completely exhausted[13] and men were being enlisted in large numbers from the non-martial tribes. Scenes occurred similar to those described in the last years of the First World War when the women of the semi-nomadic home-loving tribes of west Punjab threw themselves in front of the trains which conveyed their husbands to the army depots.[14] Coercion began to be used to sustain the supply of recruits. The Sarpanch of Sham Nagar, Amritsar, complained of the Revenue Officials' recruiting methods. He claimed that the *patwaris* were ordered to produce a certain quota of recruits and threatened with suspension if they failed to meet it.[15] Such actions naturally led to opposition towards the war and the Unionist Party.

A major headache for the Unionist Government was the shortage of consumer goods. The diversion of resources to war production and the curtailment of the imports of ordinary consumer goods were the root cause of this intractable problem. Although its first impact was felt in the towns, the rural population increasingly suffered from its effects. In December 1942, for example, shortages of foodgrains were reported from thirteen districts, of fuel from ten, sugar from six and salt from four.[16] These led to a rapid rise in inflation which caused great distress amongst the poor.[17] The existence of such shortages made the Unionist Party's export of wheat from the province very unpopular even though this was only carried out reluctantly in obedience to the Government of India. Between May and October 1943 alone, 265,100 tons of foodstuffs were sent from the Punjab to Bengal. As early as March 1942, the export of wheat was criticized in the Legislative Assembly. It was an ominous sign for the Unionist Party that the major opposition came from some of its own supporters. A Unionist member moved the adjournment motion on the issue and Khan Bahadur Mushtaq Ahmad Gurmani defied Parliamentary convention to criticize his own government.[18] The Ministry could do nothing about this opposition as its hands were tied by the central authorities.

The Unionist Party incurred even more hostility by obeying the Government of India's policy concerning the rationing and requisitioning of foodgrains. A storm of protest greeted its introduction in 1943. The Unionists had fought hard against this issue and its introduction over their heads constituted a major setback. Grain requisitioning which was particularly unpopular was introduced in September. At the command of the central authorities, the Punjab Government ordered its district officials, 'to induce the release of all surplus stocks of foodgrains lying in the villages or in the *mandis*'.[19] The Unionists had been forced to completely reverse their attitude to this policy. Chhotu Ram, during his tour of the villages just three months earlier, had repeatedly urged his audiences to hold back their stocks of wheat until they could get the highest possible rate and so offset the rising prices for consumer articles. When the Viceroy learnt of this he wrote angrily to the Punjab Governor:

> It is impossible to reconcile such ruthless political opportunism with the general food position in India and the overriding calls of the war.... [20] It is intolerable that a Minister of the Crown (and representative of a community that owes everything to us) should venture to make a statement of this character in public. I should like you to send for Chhotu Ram and admonish him very severely.[21]

Sir Bertrand Glancy, who was well aware of the Unionists' need to use every possible means to retain their popularity in the countryside, attempted to defend Chhotu Ram. He pointed out that the Jat minister's attitude resulted from the fact that many *zamindars* had blamed him for the losses which they had suffered when the price of wheat had been decontrolled the previous year.[22] Lord Linlithgow remained unmoved by such arguments, although he knew that requisitioning would be very unpopular. 'I have very little doubt that if a policy of active requisition backed where necessary by force were to follow', he wrote to the Secretary of State in September, 'there would be something very like an agrarian revolution in the province. Apart from that there has of course to be considered the reaction of the very large numbers of the Punjab soldiers of every religion and community who are serving overseas of (sic) the receipt of letters from the Province representing that their houses were being invaded and their families insulted, under the pretext of requisitioning, and that their legitimate claims out of food profits were being taken from them.'[23] He had to agree to requisitioning despite his anxieties about its political consequences because he was under great pressure from the

Cabinet to ensure that grain was adequately supplied to the famine-stricken areas of Bengal.[24] 'To put it quite clearly', he wrote to Glancy in September 1943, 'the procurement of the necessary surplus wheat from the Punjab is more important than any political considerations, any interests of the Ministers, and even, in the last resort, the continuance of Provincial Autonomy in the Punjab.'[25] This attitude signalled the end of the traditional policy of putting the Punjabi *zamindars*' loyalty above all other political considerations. The British were unwittingly destroying the political system which they had so carefully created.

The introduction of requisitioning and rationing of grain angered the Unionist Party's rural supporters. It seemed to them that they were being discriminated against, as the Hindu and Sikh businessmen were free to make large wartime profits. They also resented the increase in Government interference which accompanied requisitioning. During the latter years of the war, the Punjab's rural population became subject to a wide range of Government regulations. The District Officer became a hated figure in the village. This was an important change, as in the early years of British rule, he had been much loved and admired and had an almost paternal relationship with the villagers. This change had serious repercussions for the Unionists' popularity, as the officer was closely identified in the villagers' minds with the Unionist Party.

Close on the heels of the Unionist Party's defeat at the hands of the Government of India over grain requisitioning came another, this time on the issue of price control. Early in November 1943, the Punjab Assembly adopted without division an unofficial resolution to the effect that any attempt to control the price of wheat 'would result in very keen resentment and discontent amongst the agricultural classes'.[26] The new Unionist Premier, Khizr Hayat Tiwana, was, however, unable to prevent the reintroduction of price control. He was even criticized for the one concession he had gained from the Government of India that it would not come into effect until the 1944 *rabi* harvest, as it was claimed that this three months' period of grace would only benefit the large landlords.[27]

The Unionists did not only have to carry out the Government of India's unpopular policies during the war, but because of financial stringency they had to abandon many of their ambitious programmes of rural uplift. They had promised, for example, much regarding the Thal Canal Colony project but lack of funds delayed its completion. They were also unable to afford to reduce the water rates in the Canal Colonies and to introduce a sliding scale of Land Revenue charges, both of which the smaller landlords had been pressing for a long time.[28]

Fear of disrupting the war effort prevented the Unionist Party from bringing forward any further legislation which favoured the rural population at the expense of the non-agriculturalists. The dangers in pressing such 'controversial' legislation had become apparent in 1941, when the Hindu and Sikh business class had disrupted the province's commercial life for two months in protest against the passing of the General Sales Tax Act and the Agricultural Produce Markets Act.[29] The Unionists needed the Hindu and Sikhs' support in order to run the region's war effort. The Sikh community was, of course, an important source of army recruits, whilst the Hindus were influential Government contractors. Unfortunately, the Unionist Ministers' grownig ties with the urban Hindu and Sikh classes was unpopular with the cultivators. Once more, in serving British interests they were losing traditional support.

Sikhs remained reluctant to enlist in the Indian Army during the early years of the war. The British attributed this to the success of Communist anti-war propaganda in the villages of central Punjab.[30] In an endeavour to encourage greater Sikh support for the war effort, Sikander entered into an agreement with the Akali leader, Baldev Singh, in June 1942. This was mainly concerned with social and religious questions. The only purely political clause of their pact nevertheless had considerable importance. It called for the increase of Sikh representation in those Government departments in which it was below the fixed communal proportion of 20 per cent.[31] The Muslim League opposed the pact because it claimed that it would increase Sikh influence in the political life of the province. Unfortunately for the Unionists, this proved correct. Baldev Singh used his new ministerial powers to favour his community at every possible opportunity.[32] An alliance between the Unionists and the Akalis would never have occurred in a peacetime Punjab. The Akalis were the most communal and revolutionary (many of them had strong Communist sympathies) section of the Sikh community. One of their leading figures, Sampuran Singh, had become President of the Congress Legislative Party in 1937. Another, Master Tara Singh, a Hindu convert and head of the Shiromani Akali Dal, was the most outspoken critic of Pakistan in the province. He repeatedly declared that it would only come into existence in a sea of blood. Although Baldev Singh represented the moderate section of the Akalis,[33] it seemed to many Muslims that the Unionists had come to an agreement with their most deadly enemies.

Sikander agreed to the pact because of the favourable effect it would have on army recruitment. The Akalis, because they hated and feared the prospect of Pakistan, saw cooperation with the Unionists and the war effort as the best defence against it. Their close links with the Congress had first led them to adopt an attitude of non-cooperation towards the war. However, they soon realized that the maintenance of the Sikh connection with the army was vital 'for the preservation of the Sikhs as a separate entity'.[34] Although they did not openly support the Khalsa Defence of India League which was formed in January 1941 to promote Sikh army recruitment, they nevertheless promised to secretly supply *parcharaks* for propaganda work in the villages in its favour.[35] When the Akalis assumed the political leadership of the Sikh community after the death of Sir Sunder Singh Majitha in April 1941, they began to openly support the war effort.[36] Their final break with the Congress did not come over this issue but over the efforts of Rajagopalachari, the ex-Premier of Madras, to restore Hindu-Muslim unity by accepting the Muslim League's demand for Pakistan. They now looked to the Unionists as the only force which could stop Jinnah.

The growth of Sikh influence in local government which resulted from the Sikander-Bladev pact angered not only the small Muslim Government servant class. It had a far wider impact, as many of the newly appointed Sikh officials almost immediately proceeded to discriminate against the Muslims. In the Karnal district, for example, the Sikh Deputy Commissioner, Sardar Kapur Singh, reduced the magisterial powers of the Nawab families of Karnal and Kunjpura and cancelled their gun licences. No less than 80 per cent of the Muslim licensees in the district were deprived of their right to possess firearms, whilst the Deputy Commissioner indiscriminately granted fresh licences to the Hindus and Sikhs.[37] Although such actions were promoted by the desire to enable the minority communities to better defend themselves in the event of a future conflict over the issue of Pakistan, to the Muslims they appeared a deliberate attempt to undermine their predominant position within the province. They certainly added credence to the Muslim League's propaganda that the Unionists were incapable of protecting Muslim interests.

The sight of the urban population replacing them as the main beneficiary of Government patronage strained still further the landlords' loyalty to the Unionist Party. During the war, the Unionist Government controlled vast amounts of patronage in the form of contracts for supplying civilian and army stores. This soon became a more lucrative form of patronage than land. It is true that the Unionist Party still had large amounts of land in the Canal Colonies with which it could reward its supporters. In 1940, there was over 800,000 acres of unallotted land in the Colony areas.[38] Land from these areas was frequently granted as a reward for services to the war effort. The raising of army recruits became a lucrative occupation for some landlords.[39] In 1943 alone, the Government set aside 200 squares of land to reward army recruiters.[40] But the Muslim community as a whole was profiting less from the war than the Hindus and Sikhs, many of whom were involved in large-scale profiteering at the same time as receiving large amounts of Government patronage.

From April 1939, the Purchase Department of the Punjab Government replaced the central agency of the Indian Stores Department as the main purchaser of supplies. It dealt in contracts for the supply of such items as tents, hardware, textiles, leather-goods and machinery to the tune of Rs. 50 lakhs a year.[41] The Hindu and Sikh business class gained the most from the growth of lucrative government civil supply contracts. The small Muslim contractors were nearly squeezed out of existence as the Hindus and Sikhs tightened their hold on Punjab's commercial life. The presence of the leading industrialist, Baldev Singh, in the Cabinet vividly illustrated the growth in political importance which accompanied the business community's wartime bonanza.

The landlords' growing frustration with the Unionist Party boiled over during the 1943 Spring Session of the Legislative Assembly. During the course of a debate on the Irrigation Department, no less than seven hostile speeches were delivered against it by its own supporters.[42] This revealed not only the growing disquiet within the landlords' ranks at that time, but the danger of a split developing between its Muslim and Hindu wings. Virtually all the criticism concerned Chhotu Ram's management of the Irrigation Department and his alleged 'pro-Ambala' and therefore 'pro-Hindu' bias in its work.[43] It appeared possible that the Unionist Party might break up into two communal *zamindar* wings as the Agra and Oudh National Agriculturalist Parties had done shortly before the 1937 elections.[44]

There was no respite for the beleaguered Unionist ministers as economic conditions within the Punjab continued to deteriorate during the final years of the war. Whereas earlier, the countryside had escaped the worst effects of economic dislocation, by 1944 it suffered as badly as the towns from shortages of consumer goods and inflation. The Lahore Retail Price Index rose from a base of 100 in August 1939 to 371 in August 1945. It had climbed still further to 398 by the time of the 1946 elections.[45] Until 1944, the high prices which the farmers gained for their wheat and other agricultural produce largely outweighed the increased prices and shortages of consumer goods. But that autumn, a substantial and sustained fall in agricultural prices set in.[46] The Unionist Party came under increasing pressure from its supporters to alleviate this situation.[47] But its hands were tied by the Food Department's continued ban on the free movement of grain between Punjab and U.P.[48] The much higher prices which could be obtained in U.P than in Punjab, as a result of the operation of its statutory price ordinance, was a constant source of irritation in East Punjab and encouraged the growth of large-scale smuggling operations.[49]

Grain prices staged a recovery in the first few months of 1945, but as the year progressed the *zamindars* became increasingly reluctant to market their produce. Political insecurity, the unfavourable prospect for the 1946 *rabi* crop and the enticement of the black market all contributed to this. Many farmers regarded the high black market prices which they obtained for their produce as a legitimate compensation for their other economic difficulties. By December 1945, wheat, maize and gram had virtually disappeared from the open market.[50] Many towns in the province, even in the surplus grain areas of the Canal Colonies, began to experience a wheat famine.[51] West Punjab landlords with large holdings still brought at least part of their grain to the *mandis* but virtually none came from the peasant proprietors of East Punjab. The Unionist Ministry was left with no other choice but to use force to requisition grain from the villages there. This naturally aroused great opposition. Disturbances broke out as a result in the Ludhiana, Hoshiarpur and Ferozepore districts right in the middle of the 1946 elections.[52]

These disturbances highlighted the rural population's frustration as their lives becoming subject to ever increasing Government control. Direct Government intervention had been at a minimum before the outbreak of war. The peasants' main dealings were still with the *zaildar* and in many areas the *lambardar* continued to fence off the village from the central authorities, collecting the peasants' land revenue assessments and paying it for them. The need to ensure a steady supply of army recruits and wheat from the villages led the Unionist Ministry to increasingly intervene in the countryside during the war. By 1946 few areas of peasant life escaped Government regulation. The price of his agricultural produce was fixed and it was liable to be forcibly requisitioned if he did not bring it forward to market quickly enough. He could not sell a wide range of agricultural goods to anyone outside of his own district. Even if he wanted to do something as mundane as manufacture ice-cream, he had to have the permission of the District Magistrate.[53] Ration and other government control measures placed increasing power in the hands of the district officials, notably the *tehsildars* and *naib-tehsildars*. The very efficiency of the Unionist Party's contribution to the war effort thus undermined its position by arousing opposition to the growing penetration of Government into the crevices of village life.

Rationing rapidly became a communal issue. The Muslims of Lahore and the other large towns in which it was first introduced claimed that the predominantly Hindu and Sikh Civil Supply Officers[54] openly discriminated against them in the distribution of rationed goods. When rationing was introduced into the Ambala Division, there were constant complaints from the villagers that they received smaller quotas than the urban population. Most of the supplies of kerosene never in fact did find their way to the villages.[55] This so enraged the peasants of Rohtak district that they spontaneously called for the replacement of its Civil Supply Officer.[56]

The Muslim League, free from the constraints of office, was able to turn to its own advantage the communal issues involved in rationing and to exploit the growing wartime discontent. It was, however, only slowly and with great caution that the League emerged from under the Unionist Party's control and began openly to challenge its predominant position within Punjab politics.

The Punjab Muslim League: 1940–45

Once the Lahore Resolution was passed on 23 March 1940, the All-India Muslim League had to break the Unionists' hold on its Punjab organization. Jinnah could not allow the future heartland of a Pakistan state to be dominated by his main Muslim rivals. There was always the danger that the Congress would make use of this state of affairs to weaken his bargaining position in all-India politics. Jinnah had, however, learned from the failure of his previous intervention in the politics of Punjab in 1936 that it would be a mistake to move too quickly against the Unionists. The Punjab League's local workers did not however appreciate this patient approach. 'Ever since the annual meeting of the Muslim League in Lahore it is supposed to have had much greater aims and objects, but its workers are not at all active', wrote Syed Ashraf Ali Tirmizi of the Ropar (Ambala district) Muslim League, 'passing resolution after resolution does not serve any purpose. It is action that is needed.... For the last three years those people responsible for running the (Punjab) League have proved by their actions that they do not want to achieve its aims.... Do they consider it *haram* to come into the field of real action? Do they consider it *haram* even to serve their nation? Have they been placed on *gadis* for the sake of fame? ... Today those outside the League are overjoyed to see the lack of discipline we have within it.'[57]

The League's activists had become impatient because under the Unionists' control its growth had ground to a complete halt. The All-India Muslim League's investigation in October 1941 into the strength of its provincial organizations found that no Muslim League organization existed at all in the following ten districts of the Punjab: Ambala, Hoshiarpur, Shahpur, Jhelum, Mianwali, Jhang, Kangra, Dera Ghazi Khan, Rohtak and Gujranwala. The total primary League membership of the seven city and six district branches, which were able to return reasonably accurate figures, was only just under 15,000. Ferozepore had the largest number of primary members, 3,500; Montgomery was second with 3,200; next came Lahore with 2,000. Attock had the lowest district total with only 491 primary members.[58] Even more worrying for the League than the smallness of its grassroots membership was the fact that over a third of it came from the towns which were politically unimportant. Only in Sind was the League weaker in terms of the number of its primary members. Bombay had nearly double Punjab's

TABLE 1
THE Punjab MUSLIM LEAGUE'S PRIMARY MEMBERSHIP FIGURES FOR 1941

Name of District	*No. of Primary Members in District*	*No. of Primary Leagues in District*
1. Montgomery City	227	
2. Amritsar	765	22
3. Batala City	300	1
4. Montgomery	3200	20
5. Sheikhupura	500	36
6. Sialkot	1500	15
7. Rawalpindi City	1200	8
8. Attock	491	6
9. Ferozepore City	255	6
10. Rohtak City	250	3
11. Ferozepore	3515	15
12. Rewari City	620	1
13. Lahore City	2000	5
Total	14823	138

Source: Conference of the Presidents and Secretaries of the Provincial Muslim Leagues. October 1941, Vol. 326, pt. 2, p. 74, FMA.

number, U.P. eight times, whilst even the remote province of Baluchistan possessed a 1,000 more members.[59] The Punjab League's membership figures could give a misleading impression of its position in the Punjab. The possession of elite support was far more important than that of a grassroots organization. Had the League begun by 1941 to win over the support of the landlords and Pirs who had good reason to be disgruntled with the Unionist Party's wartime policies? Unfortunately, insufficient records of the League's supporters exist before 1944 to answer this question fully. Certainly, none of the leading rural families had transferred their allegiance from the Unionist Party by that time. The League's primary membership records for Amritsar do, however, indicate that a few at least of the minor Pirs and landowners were moving into its ranks.

The League's 'mass' membership in the City consisted mainly of members of the Muslim trading community, the skin merchants, the fruit merchants, and the shoe and leather workers.[60] The leaders of its primary branches were merchants, Government contractors, *rais*, honorary magistrates and Pirs. Mohammad Feroze ud-Din, the President of the Sharifpura Primary League was an honorary magistrate and Rais-e-Azam, another *rais*, Mohammad Saeed was its Vice-President. The President of the Mohullah Bulakraj Primary League was also described as a Raise-e-Azam. The President of the Darwaza Glory Primary League was Pir Ghulam Gilani, its Secretary was Pir Saeed-u-Din.[61]

The Unionist Party's control of the Punjab Muslim League severely restricted its propaganda activity in the countryside. Most of this kind of work was left to the Punjab Muslim Students Federation. It had been reorganized by Abdul Sattar Khan Niazi, Ibrahim Ali Chishti and Hameed Nizami in 1937. The majority of its members came from Islamia College, Lahore, but it soon developed close links with other Muslim social and educational organizations including the *Anjuman-i-Himayat-i-Islam*. The Federation strongly supported the demand for Pakistan and organized a Pakistan Conference at Lahore in March 1941 which was presided over by Jinnah. At this conference, a Pakistan rural Propaganda Committee was created with Niazi as its secretary. Its task was to tour the villages enlightening the Punjabi peasants about the demand for Pakistan. Towards the end of May, Niazi wrote fervently to Jinnah concerning the Committee's plans for its tour of the Sheikhupura district. 'We have fully determined', he declared, 'that to win the land of Pakistan we will launch one attack after another like Ghaznavi. . . . For a long time the Saints of Somnath[62] have been waiting for another like him'.[63] During the course of a twenty-day tour, the Committee visited fifty villages in each of which it opened a primary branch of the Muslim League.[64] Not all the members of the Punjab Muslim Students Federation were as anxious as Niazi to plunge into the fray against the Unionists. Its President, Mian Bashir Ahmed, tried to drop the idea that the Federation should hold a Pakistan Day celebration in 1942.[65] His resignation, ostensibly on health grounds,[66] paved the way, however, for greater activity. The Federation divided up the province into four zones and sent student propagandists to work full-time in each during May and July 1943.[67] This was to be a useful dress-rehearsal for the students' propaganda campaigns in the Punjab countryside during the 1946 elections.

As the Unionists' influence weakened, Jinnah tentatively encouraged the resumption of official League activities in the rural areas. In January 1943, meetings were held at Shahkot, Hoshiarpur, Qasur, Jullundur, Patti, Palwal and Ludhiana in the Ambala and Jullundur divisions.[68] A month later they were extended to Gujranwala, Wazirabad, Sialkot, Gujrat and Jhelum.[69] Emphasis was placed on the establishment of new primary Leagues and on holding district conferences which were hoped to 'galvanise' League activity throughout their surrounding areas.[70] Eight new primary Leagues were established in January and February and a district conference was also held at Fazilka.[71] In March, a further three conferences took place at Karnal, Amritsar and Chiniot (Jhang).[72] A further conference was held at Chiniot in August whilst two others took place during that month at Phillaur and Multan.[73]

These efforts were not enough to satisfy the local activists who remained dissatisfied with the progress which was being made. In January 1943, a Muslim League Workers' Conference at Lahore was chaired by Nawabzada Rashid Ali Khan, the President of the Lahore Muslim League. It was attended by leading members of the Lahore, Amritsar, Jullundur, Kasur, Sialkot, Phillaur, Sheikhupura, Campbellpur, Ludhiana, Ambala, Hissar, Rawalpindi, Karnal, Lyallpur and Mianwali district Leagues.[74] After four hours of heated discussion it was decided to establish a provincial Muslim League Workers Board, 'In view of the fact that the enemies of the League both inside and outside our ranks are asserting that there is no Muslim League in the real sense either in the province or in the Legislature.'[75]

The Muslim League Workers Board aimed to establish new district and primary Leagues and to revitalize those which already existed so that half a million two *annas* League members could be enrolled within the Punjab. It also sought to raise at least Rs. 200,000 for the Central Muslim League Fund.[76] The Conference elected the following seven permanent members of the Workers Board: Maulana Zafar Ali Khan, President; Malik Barkat Ali and Mian Nurullah, Senior Vice-Presidents; Nawabzada Rashid Ali Khan, General Secretary; Syed Mustafa Shah Gilani, Secretary; Haji Abdul Karim, Financial Secretary; and Khan Rabb Nawaz Khan, Propaganda Secretary.[77]

This unauthorized action was condemned by the Punjab League's leaders. 'I have no hesitation in saying that it is a mischievous and dangerous move', Mian Bashir Ahmed wrote to Jinnah at the end of January, 'at the moment the League in the Punjab is not half as active as it ought to be. I think the latest movement of the 'rebels' ought to be checkmated soon and *that by you*. Otherwise even the little good that is being done will be seriously affected.'[78] Nawabzada Rashid Ali Khan strenuously denied the accusation that the Workers Board was a rival to the Punjab Muslim League. 'The Board cannot by any stretch of the imagination', he declared, 'be called a parallel organisation with the Provincial League nor is there or ever has been any intention of making it such.'[79] Despite his entreaties, Jinnah was not prepared to see the League's control pass from the Unionists into any other hands except his own. He therefore telegrammed Rashid Ali Khan on 13 February and ordered him to suspend the Board's activities.[80] The Nawabzada finally complied with this on 9 March. The League Workers Board's criticism of the Punjab Muslim League did not of course cease thereafter. Khan Rabb Nawaz Khan complained to Jinnah in March that the Nawab of Mamdot was an obstacle to the League's development. How could it grow, he asked, if its leader refused to allow Primary League branches to be established on his Ferozepore estate.[81] The Nawab was certainly not an inspiring League President,[82] but apart from being the largest Muslim landowner in East Punjab, he was influential amongst the province's Pathan community.[83] Jinnah therefore wisely ignored the continued complaints about his leadership.

The Muslim League Workers Board episode nevertheless jolted Jinnah into challenging the Unionist Party. He put pressure on the new Premier, Khizr Hayat Khan Tiwana, to dissolve the Unionist Party and form a purely Muslim League Assembly Party. At the same time, the League's leaders attempted to undermine the Unionists' position by whipping up religious feeling. Plans were made to saturate the villages with Muslim League propaganda. Students once more played an important part in taking the Pakistan message to the villages but the League's star speakers were its landlord converts, Raja Ghazanfar Ali Khan, the youthful Nawab of Mamdot, Shaukat Hayat and Mian Mumtaz Daultana.[84] During June and July, they toured all the five divisions of the province and addressed Muslim League Conferences at Montgomery, Lyallpur, Sheikhupura, Sargodha, Jhang, Sialkot and Rawalpindi.[85] These attracted large audiences; over 15,000 attended the meeting at Multan and 10,000 at Montgomery.[86] For the first time ever, primary League branches were established in such rural areas as Sargodha and Mianwali. In July alone, it was reported that 7,000 members had been enrolled in these two areas.[87]

The Muslim League's message to the villagers was simple. It called on them in the name of Islam to support the Quaid-e-Azam in his struggle for Pakistan. Religious festivals such as Id were used by the League to spread its message and to 'promote unity and social solidarity amongst the Muslim of India'.[88] Mosques, because of their importance as centres of Muslim life, were used to spread League propaganda.[89] Propagandists were advised when they visited a village to join in the prayers at the local mosque and gain its Imam's permission to hold a meeting there.[90] League meetings were regularly held in mosques especially after the Friday prayers. The Quran was also frequently paraded as the League's symbol and pledges to support it being made on it.[91] Students who played an important part in the Muslim League's rural propaganda campaign[92] had been especially trained to appeal to the rural population on religious lines. The lectures which the Aligarh students attended at their League Workers Training Camp before they left for the Punjab were on such topics as the Muslim League in the Light of Islam and Islamic History and the religious background to the demand for Pakistan.[93] Students from the Punjab Muslim Students Federation were advised to follow the Prophet's example in all things during their propaganda visits to the villages. They were to join in the prayers at the mosque or better still lead them like 'Holy Warriors'. Their speeches were to be filled with emotional appeal and to always commence with a text from the Quran, invoking God's protection and praising His Wisdom.[94] Because of its importance in North Indian society, poetry, particularly Iqbal's, was to be declaimed at such meetings.[95]

Despite the intensity of the Muslim League's propaganda campaign, its unfurling of the green flag of Islam made little impact on the mass of the rural population. 'League attempts to penetrate the villages', the Governor noted in July 1944, 'have been mainly confined to the somewhat disjointed tours by peripatetic members of the Muslim Students Federation, the distribution of propaganda pamphlets and approaches to village officials. These moves in spite of the Islamic appeal behind them have so far had little effect on the Muslim masses who are concerned with tribal and economic considerations (rather) than with party politics and do not appear to have affected the communal situation adversely.'[96] The Unionists continued to win district board and provincial assembly by-elections throughout 1944. In August, for example, they defeated the Muslim League in the Sialkot district board elections;[97] they also retained the Hoshiarpur and Kangra and Jhajjar Legislative Assembly seats. The Muslim League was unable to field a rival candidate to Sardar Ghaus Mazari in the by-election which took place in its southern contituency in April 1945.[98] In the neighbouring Mianwali district, the League was still trying to establish an effective organizational base at the time of the 1946 elections.[99] In many of the western districts of the Punjab, it was faced with the same problem of having to resolve local factional rivalries which had impeded Mian Fazl-i-Husain's efforts to establish a popular base for the Unionist Party there a decade earlier. In the Gujjar Khan and Rawalpindi districts, factional rivalry was so acute that parallel Muslim Leagues competed against each other.[100] As late as May 1945, the Muslim League could still only boast of a Punjab membership of 150,000.[101]

Why had the Muslim League's rural propaganda campaign achieved such limited success? Mian Mumtaz Daultana blamed its lack of progress on the influence of the bureaucracy. 'Time is unquestionably on our side. But the Punjab is the darling of the bureaucrats', he wrote to Jinnah in June 1945, 'the people of the Punjab have never known political consciousness, are untrained to modern political ways of thought, have never experienced organised political effort. . . . For a nation to shake off the cobwebs of time takes time. In 2-3 years I can promise you a fully conscious and determined Muslim Punjab.'[102] The Muslim League could not afford, however, to wait so long as the provincial elections were approaching rapidly. Nor was the bureaucracy to blame for the League's lack of impact, but rather its over-reliance on Islamic appeals to mobilise mass support.

The Unionist Party made a similar mistake during the 1946 election campaign. Malik Khizr Hayat Khan Tiwana began to garnish with quotations from the Quran his discourses on the economic benefits which the Unionist Party had brought to the rural population. In a speech at Gujrat he used the first verse of the Sura Fatiha to prove that the Unionist Party had greater Islamic justification than the Muslim League.[103] The Unionist Party flew at its election camps an Islamic flag identical to the League's. Shortly before his death, Sir Chhotu Ram had drawn up a plan for employing the *ulema* to campaign against the demand for Pakistan.[104] Some indeed worked for the Unionist Party in 1946 but they had little political effect.

The Unionists' efforts during the elections and the Muslim League's earlier attempt in 1944 to use Islam as a mass mobilizer made little impact because their religious appeals were mediated by outsiders who lacked personal influence in the villages and because they were based on sources of Muslim authority, the Quran, the alim and the mosque which were unimportant to the illiterate 'pir-ridden' villagers. Even if they had been made through the right channels, the Sufi networks, the peasants would not have been readily moved by Islamic appeals alone. In order to have maximum impact, they would have to be accompanied by efforts to solve the villagers' immediate social and economic problems in order to overcome their fear of Government and their suspicion of outsiders. The Muslim League was only able to achieve a rural breakthrough when it had won over the support of the landlords and Pirs who possessed personal authority in the villages and when it had addressed itself to the peasants' wartime grievances. At first, however, it merely raised the cry of Islam in danger in order to win support.

The Punjab Muslim League only gradually adopted a different approach to winning support in the countryside. It was not until late in 1944 that it switched its attention from organizing local branches to winning over the rural elite. At about the same time it first linked the demand for Pakistan with the solution of the peasants' wartime difficulties. Worsening wartime dislocation, Jinnah's growing prestige in national politics and the death of Sir Chhotu Ram, the Punjab League's most redoubtable opponent, all combined to assist this new strategy.

The Communists were the first in the province to attempt to win popular support by articulating the *zamindars'* grievances about the conduct of the war effort. In November 1943 they began work in the villages of central Punjab, attacking the wartime dislocation.[105] The Congress had earlier adopted similar tactics in the North West Frontier Province against the Aurangzeb Khan Muslim League Ministry. In May 1943, it had formed an Anjuman-i-Ghurta (Council for the protection of the poor), which led the opposition to the rationing and requisitioning of grain. Its success soon earned it the displeasure of the Governor, Sir George Cunningham. 'When the history of this period comes to be written in a dispassionate atmosphere', he wrote to the Viceroy, 'Dr. Khan Sahib and the Congress Party will have to answer accusations of exploiting the poor for political ends. It will not be easy for them to plead the excuse that their sole object was to break the Muslim League Ministry on the Food Control issue.'[106] The success of these tactics did not go unnoticed by the Punjab Muslim League, particularly as large numbers of Communists who were experienced in such activity, began to enter its ranks from 1943 onwards.[107]

The Punjab League exploited the growing wartime discontent in a number of ways. Its propagandists pointed out that whilst the large landlords had gained a great deal from the Government's reforms, virtually nothing had been done for the smaller *zamindars* and *kisans*. Despite the Unionist Party's vaunted support for the Punjab Alienation of Land Act during the war, it had auctioned land in the Canal Colonies to the *mahajans* as well as to the large landlords who had already 'usurped 80 per cent of the Punjab's land surface'.[108] In the Ambala Division, the League voiced the Muslims' anger at the Unionist Party's failure to ensure that they had gained as much as the Hindus from the new irrigation facilities created by the extension of the Western Jumna Canal.[109] The League attempted to win support by leading the rural opposition to the rationing and requisitioning of grain supplies. It frequently organized protest meetings about alleged communal favouritism in rationing.[110] In May 1945, for example, it held a series of such meetings in the leading mosques of Lahore to complain about the way cloth was distributed in the city.[111] It also expressed the Muslims' increasing dissatisfaction with the Unionist Party's inability to control inflation and to curb the profiteering of the Hindu and Sikh business community. The League attempted to gain a foothold in the villages by helping the peasants in their wartime distress. League propagandists took medical supplies, which had become increasingly expensive and difficult to obtain during the war, with them to the villages.[112] They also distributed cloth there and endeavoured to obtain increased ration allowances for the villagers.[113] Wherever possible, they gained control of the rationing machinery as the first step towards setting up a parallel government in the countryside. Most importantly of all, however, they linked the solution of the peasants' economic and social problems with the successful establishment of a Pakistan State. Members of the Punjab Muslim Students Federation were directed when they visited a village to: 'Find out its social problems and difficulties to tell them (i.e., the villagers that the main cause of their problems was the Unionists (and) give them the solution—Pakistan.'[114]

The Muslim League propagandists thus attempted to win support by solving the villagers' economic problems in the same way as Mao was doing in China. He had declared in the late 1920s that the key to peasant political mobilization lay in providing the rural population with immediate material aid. Ideological appeal on its own would not be sufficient to achieve this. 'If we do no other work than simply mobilising the people to carry out the war, can we achieve the aim of defeating the enemy? Of course not. If we want to win, we still have a great deal of work. Leading the peasants in agrarian struggles and distributing land to them; arousing their labour enthusiasm so as to increase agricultural production; safeguarding the interests of the workers; establishing cooperatives; developing trade with the outside; solving the problems that face the masses problems of clothing, food and shelter, of fuel, rice, cooking oil and salt, of health and hygiene, and of marriage. In short all problems facing the masses in their actual life should claim our attention.'[115] Though the Muslim League had only taken faltering steps along this path by 1946, they were, however, to reap rich electoral dividends. The League's policy was in this respect in marked contrast to its Unionist opponents' who appeared increasingly divorced from the needs of the rural population.

The strategy of exploiting wartime discontent became even more valuable after the summer of 1945 when large numbers of demobilized soldiers began to return to the province only to face massive unemployment. Even by the end of 1946 less than 20 per cent of the ex-servicemen registered with employment exchanges had found work.[116] The speedy end of the war in Asia had taken the Unionist Government by surprise so that its plans to ease the situation of postwar unemployment by resettling servicemen on land in the Canal Colonies were not yet completed. The Muslim League gained great popularity in the major recruiting areas of Rawalpindi and Jhelum by providing work for the ex-servicemen in its organization as well as by setting up committees to look into their problems.[117] It hammered home the message that although the Unionists had given vast amounts of patronage to the 'recruit hunters' during the war, they were now offering to the returning soldiers 'a meagre bonus of Rs. 5 per head (and) 50,000 acres of land for a million soldiers in the Punjab'.[118] The Muslim League also interested itself in the soldiers' wider concerns which included such issues as the Palestine Question, the use of Muslim troops in Indonesia and, more importantly, the fate of the Punjabi members of the Indian National Army. Its decision to follow the Congress' example and establish a Defence Committee for I.N.A. (Indian National Army) members who were on trial was well received in the main recruiting districts.[119] Despite its late development in these traditionally 'loyalist' areas and the Unionist Party's considerable opposition, the Muslim League captured all six of the rural seats in the Rawalpindi and Jhelum districts in the 1946 elections. It also swept the board in the Ambala Division where rationing and requisitioning of grain had aroused the strongest opposition. In Central and South-West Punjab where there had been less wartime dislocation, war-weariness and anti-Government feeling played a smaller part in the Muslim League's rise to power. It succeeded in these areas mainly because it had won the support of the landlords and Pirs who controlled the traditional channels of political mobilization in the province.

During the summer of 1944, the Muslim League was too preoccupied with setting up primary League branches in the countryside to approach the landlords who remained loyal to the Unionist Party. Its failure to mobilize mass support in the rural areas, together with the drift back into the Unionists' ranks of some of its landlord converts,[120] forced it, however, to re-examine its approach. It launched a concerted effort early in December to win over the support of the landlords and Pirs.[121] This was a complete reversal of the League's earlier policy and marked a crucial turning-point in the history of its development within the Punjab. Its leaders had previously believed that the villagers' commitment to Islam was stronger than their *biradari* ties[122] or their loyalty to their landlords. They thus assumed that the rural elite which remained loyal to the Unionists could be bypassed by a direct religious appeal to the peasants. All that was required was for the League to mobilize sufficient resources for its rural propaganda campaign. 'It is becoming quite clear', wrote Mian Mumtaz Daultana, the Punjab League's General Secretary as late as July 1944, 'that in view of the determined government opposition our basic strength must come not from the landlords or the *Zaildar-Lambardar* class but from the masses of the Muslim people'.[123] This attitude was now reversed. The Muslim League stood at the crossroads. The future of Pakistan hinged on its ability to undermine the Unionists' elite support in the countryside. This task was made easier by the disunity within the Unionist Party's ranks which followed Sikander's sudden death on 26 December 1942.

Factional Realignment with the Unionist Party

Sikander's death was a severe blow to the Unionist Party. No plans had been drawn up for choosing his successor and it was doubtful if anyone else could weld together the rural Assembly members as well as he had done. Chhotu Ram was now the senior member of the Unionist Party but he knew that it would be impossible for a Hindu to become Premier. The Governor was faced with a tricky problem in choosing Sikander's successor. It was almost impossible to pick a candidate who could command the support of all the rival factions within the party. The two major groupings, the Khattars and the Noon-Tiwanas had worked well together under Sikander's leadership but almost as soon as he had died they began to plot against each other.[124] Each put forward rival claimants for the vacant Premiership. The three Khattar candidates were Muzaffar Khan, Mir Maqbool Mahmood, Sikander's brother-in-law, whose daughter had recently married Sikander's eldest son; Nawab Sir Liaqat Hayat Khan, Sikander's cousin and brother-in-law who had been a member of the Punjab Legislature for many years. The Noon-Tiwanas pinned their hopes on Malik Khizr Hayat Khan Tiwana who had been the Minister of Public Works in Sikander's cabinet.[125]

Glancy considered that the only serious candidates were Muzaffar Khan and Khizr.[126] Before making his final decision he consulted Sikander's former ministerial colleagues. He attached particular weight to Chhotu Ram's advice as the inter-communal unity of the Unionist Party was so important to Punjab's stability. The ministers confirmed Glancy's own preference for Khizr who was duly appointed as Premier.

Although Khizr was relatively inexperienced, Glancy felt sure that his social background suited him for the major task of running the Punjab's war effort and maintaining the Unionist Party's unity. The Tiwanas had strong martial traditions, having furnished successive Punjab governments with military recruits. During the Ranjit Singh period, the Tiwana Cavalry troop had formed an important part of the army. The Tiwanas transferred their allegiance to the British during the Sikh Wars and thereafter remained their most loyal supporters, even during the troubled times of the Mutiny. Khizr, true to this tradition, had broken off his studies at Government College, Lahore to serve in the army during the First World War. He was commissioned in 1918 at the tender age of 19.[127] The Tiwanas were highly respected by the other landlords of West Punjab and were the leading tribe in the Shahpur district. Khizr's father, Nawab Malik Sir Umar Hayat Khan Tiwana was head of the tribe's leading section, the Mitha Tiwana branch. The Kalra estate on which Khizr had been brought up in feudal splendour[128] was acknowledged as one of the finest properties in the Rawalpindi Division and had the largest stud in the province.

Although all these social advantages made Khizr appear a pre-determined successor to Sikander, when Glancy appointed him as Premier he was taking a considerable risk. The Khattars were extremely disappointed that Sikander's mantle had not fallen to one of them.[129] The fact that he had been succeeded by one of their Tiwana rivals rubbed salt into the wound. Because the Tiwanas intermarried mainly with the neighbouring Noon tribe, they did not have the widespread *biradari* links which formed the nucleus of Sikander's support within the Unionist Party. In the absense from the Punjab of Firoz Khan Noon, who was a member of the Viceroy's Council and the Noon's leading representative, Khizr had only five members of the Noon-Tiwana family to call on for support in the Legislature.[130] Sikander had been advised by such experienced politicians as Mir Maqbool Mahmood and Ahmad Yar Khan Daultana. Khizr, on the other hand, had only his uncle, Allah Bakhsh Khan, as a close family adviser after his father died in 1944. He, therefore, came to rely increasingly on Chhotu Ram and thus played into the hands of the Muslim League propagandists who claimed that the Hindus were using the Unionist Party to deprive the Muslims of their rightful predominance within the province.

Immediately after Khizr was appointed, rumours began to circulate about a split within the Unionist Party. They were not dispelled until a Party meeting held on 23 January unanimously elected Khizr to succeed Sikander as its leader. Earlier that same day, sixty-nine Muslim members of the Unionist Party had met at Khizr's residence and endorsed the vote of confidence in his leadership which they had earlier passed as the Unionist/ Muslim League members of the Assembly. The only important group which did not attend was the Gilani faction from the Multan division.[131]

Despite this assurance of loyalty, Khizr was faced with the thorny problem of recommending who should become the sixth member of his cabinet. All the rival factions put forward their candidates. The ideal solution for ensuring Party unity seemed to have been reached when they all agreed to step down in favour of Sikander's eldest son, Shaukat Hayat, who until his father's death had been on active army service. From the outset, however, there was considerable personal rivalry between the Premier and his young minister who was out to prove that he was as capable as his father had been. Shaukat did not possess

Sikander's patience and diplomacy and he soon found himself in trouble with both the Governor and Khizr. In August 1943, a serious disagreement arose between him and the Premier over his embarrassing declarations in favour of Pakistan.[132] The rivalry between Khizr and Shaukat would not have been so serious if the Muslim League had not been anxiously waiting for the first opportunity to split the landlords' ranks.

The difficulties with Shaukat were not the only problem which faced Khizr during his first year in office. Jinnah attempted to take advantage of his inexperience by stepping up his efforts to extend Muslim League influence within the Punjab. Khizr faced a torrid time at the March 1943 Session of the All-India Muslim League Council, although he pointed out that:

> We in the Punjab feel proud of the great services rendered by the All India Muslim League under the leadership and guidance of the Quad-e-Azam to the cause of the Muslims. You will never find me and my Muslim colleagues failing in our loyalty to the cause of the Mussalmans and to their sole representative body—the All India Muslim League.[133]

Jinnah would not recommend the withdrawal of a resolution advocating more active intereference by the League in Punjab until Khizr gave a definite assurance to 'make the (Punjab Muslim League) party worthy of the prestige and honour of the sole authority and representative body of the Mussalmans'.[134]

Glancy grew increasingly concerned about the ambiguous nature of the Jinnah-Sikander pact upon which Khizr and the Unionist Party based their independence from the Muslim League in provincial politics.[135] He was horrified by the fact that:

> A pre-eminently Muslim Government, which, whatever its defects, has carried on for so many years with reasonable efficiency should now collapse through the machinations of the Quaid-e-Azam and be replaced by a system of administration set up under Section 93 of the (Government of India) Act.[136]

Such a possibility did not, however, worry Jinnah. He realized that the establishment of a Muslim League Ministry in the

Punjab could provoke such strong Hindu and Sikh opposition that Governor's Rule would have to be introduced. But he believed that this might well help to rally the Muslim to its support. Anyway his sights were set on a far higher goal than merely running an effective administration in the Punjab.

The All-India Muslim League's pressure on the Unionist Party increased throughout the summer months of 1943. Khizr had an inconclusive meeting with Jinnah in September, during which the latter claimed that the Unionist Party had ceased to exist as soon as the Jinnah-Sikander Pact had been drawn up. 'It seems fairly clear that Jinnah will stage an attack on the Punjab Ministry before very long, but the precise moment which he will choose is still obscure'. Glancy wrote immediately afterwards to the Viceroy. Khizr, however, forestalled such an attack by establishing a Muslim League Assembly Party early in November. The following two provisions in its constitution made it appear that Jinnah's demands had been fully met.

(i) The Muslim League Assembly Party shall be subject to the control and discipline of the central and provincial Muslim League Parliamentary Boards.

(ii) In all matters relating to Muslim interests the members of the Party shall vote in accordance with the decisions arrived at in the Party meetings, or when no such decision has been arrived at in regard to a matter, in accordance with the directions of the leader given through a whip.... (Only) in matters of common interest the members of the Party will vote in accordance with the Ship issued by the larger combination, namely by Unionist Party.[137]

In actual fact, Khizr had gone little more than halfway towards meeting them. A separate Muslim League Assembly Party had been formed in accordance with Jinnah's wishes, but it was still tied to the leading strings of the Unionist Party. The meeting of the Muslim Unionists at which the League Assembly Party was established had only decided on its constitution after more than four hours of discussions. The provision that it should be under the Parliamentary Boards' control and discipline had only been adopted as an amendment to the original constitution. The meeting had unanimously ratified the Jinnah-Sikander pact and decided by a majority vote to incorporate it in the Assembly Party's Constitution. The way was, therefore, still at least partly open for the Unionists to continue to claim autonomy from the Muslim League in the provincial political sphere. Jinnah would not, however, be able to rest content with such a state of affairs for long. The *Eastern Times* warned of the difficulties created by the inclusion of the Jinnah-Sikander Pact in the new Muslim League Assembly Party's Constitution:

> The Pact will make itself a nuisance to everybody and then they shall be glad to get rid of it. It is never right in principle to live under the tyranny of a dead hand.[138]

Jinnah efforts the following spring to repudiate the pact led to the collapse of the seven-year old agreement between the Unionist Party and the Muslim League. Its repercussions were to be felt far beyond the Punjab.

Jinnah came to Lahore in March 1944 for talks with Khizr, determined to settle the issue once and for all. He aimed to repudiate the Jinnah-Sikander pact and to replace the Unionist Ministry with a Muslim League Government similar to those which existed in Sind, Bengal and the North-West Frontier Province. Although Khizr did not want open conflict with the Muslim League, he was unable to meet Jinnah's demand to abolish the pact as it symbolized the guarantees of the Muslim members of the Unionist Party to their Hindu and Sikh colleagues.[139] Their talks continued into April and at one stage it looked as if a compromise solution would be cobbled together.[140] However, on 27 April, the negotiations finally collapsd. Khizr issued a statement explaining that the repudiation of the Jinnah-Sikander pact would amount to a breach of faith and that he could not accept Jinnah's demand, 'involving interference in provincial affairs and the inner working of the Ministerial Party formed under the Jinnah-Sikander Pact as this would be contrary to the accepted democratic principle that the wishes of the electorate and legislature should prevail' [141] He went on to declare that he was prepared to extend his whole-hearted and fullest support to the Quaid-e-Azam in all questions which related to the Muslim community and also promised to strengthen the Punjab Muslim League. Khizr concluded his statement, however, by warning that 'the disunity of different communities (can) only spell disaster, embitter non-Muslims and intensify communal hatred leading to bloodshed and disorder and serious interference with the war effort at a time when the Japanese aggressor (is) on the soil of India'.[142] Jinnah retorted at the Sialkot Punjab Muslim League Conference that an assurance of non-interference in Punjabi politics had never existed in his pact with Sikander and that in accordance with it, it was open to the League Party in the Assembly to terminate any coalition arrangement.[143] The breach was widened between the Unionists and the Muslim League the following month when Khizr was expelled from membership of the All-India Muslim League.

The demands of the war effort had put the landlords' loyalty to the Unionist Party. under severe strain. Khizr therefore attempted to steady the situation immediately after his split with Jinnah by appointing two new Muslim ministers, both of whom came from the Multan Division of the Punjab in which the largest number of rural seats were situated.[144] Sir Mohammad Jamal Khan Leghari, the representative of the Tumandar Constituency, replaced Shaukat Hayat[145] as Minister of Public Works and Nawab Ashiq Hussain became Minister of War Planning. They both wielded immense authority in the western districts of the province. Sir Mohammad Jamal Khan Leghari was a great tribal leader with large landholdings in the Dera Ghazi Khan district.[146] Nawab Ashiq Hussain was a member of the leading Qureshi Pir family of Multan and was also the son-in-law of Sir Liaqat Hayat Khan, the late Sir Sikander's elder brother. Khizr hoped that his appointment would prevent the Khattar faction transferring its allegiance to the Muslim League. The Khattars would not, however, allow the opportunity to pass of revenging themselves on their Tiwana rivals. They formed the majority of the earliest and most active landlord converts to the Muslim League.[147] In December 1944, for example, members of the Khattar faction made up nearly a third of the Punjab League Assembly Party.[148]

The Muslim League made maximum use of local rivalries and family loyalties in its efforts to drive a wedge in the Unionist Party's landlord ranks. It approached those landlords who remained loyal to the Government through their relatives. In the Lyallpur district, for example, the League attempted to win over the support of the Nawab of Kamalia by persuading his close relatives, Khan Bahawal Khan, Saadat Yar Khan and Nawazish Ali Khan to publicly move a resolution calling for his resignation from the Unionist Party. If he failed to do so, he would have placed his family's *izzat* at stake.[149]

A further blow was dealt to the Unionist Party's crumbling unity by Chhotu Ram's death at the end of 1944. The Hindu Jat peasant proprietors of East Punjab were as divided about who should succeed him as the Muslim landlords had been over Sikander's successor. It was only after arbitration that a small town pleader named Chaudhri Tikka Ram was finally selected as the new Jat leader. 'Things may go badly with the Unionists in the Eastern Punjab', Wavell noted presciently to Amery in January 1945, 'unless the Jats manage to sink their differences and follow Tikka Ram.'[150]

In East Punjab, the Congress, and in West Punjab the Muslim League eagerly took advantage of the growing divisions within the Unionists' ranks. The Unionist Party had never been an organised, disciplined political organization. It had functioned more as an uneasy coalition of the rural faction leaders. The impact of war, together with the deaths of Sikander and Chhotu Ram, strained its members' loyalty to the breaking point. The fragile bonds which held it together were finally snapped by the political changes which the war brought at the all-India level of politics. However much they might have wished, neither Sikander nor Khizr could isolate the Punjab from all-India political developments which increasingly threatened the Unionist Party's continued existence.

Notes

1. Linlithgow to Glancy, 17 Augut 1943. Linlithgow Papers Mss. EUR. F. 125, File 92, IOR.
2. As a result of the efforts of the 'grow more food' campaigns, the area under food crops in the Punjab in 1942–3 was nearly half a million acres more than the previous record of 1933–4. Punjab FR, 24 June 1944, L/P&J/5/247, IOR.
3. Craik to Linlithgow, 16 September 1939. War Staff Department File L/WS/1/136 W.S. 1680, IOR.
4. R. S. Nakra, *Punjab Villages in the Ludhiana District during the War*, Punjab Board of Economic Enquiry, No. 91 (Lahore, 1946), p. 8.
5. R. S. Nakra, *op.cit.*, p. 22.
6. R. S. Nakra, *op.cit.*, p. 1.
7. G. Rai, *Agricultural Statistics of the Punjab 1940–41 to 1943–44*, Punjab Board of Economic Enquiry, No. 52 (Lahore, 1945), Table 54, p. 21.
8. An example of the wartime price rise of agricultural products can be seen in the price increase of the following five products sold at the market of Jagraon in the Ludhiana district. From a prewar index of 100, wheat had risen to 368 by 1944; gram to 281; maize to 273; *bajra* to 262; ghee to 329. Nakra, *op.cit.*, p. 15.
9. Nakra, *op.cit.*, p. 28.
10. During the war, the urban moneylenders created a loophole in the Restitution of Mortgaged Lands Act by transferring their land to friends or relatives who were on active military service. Such persons were exempt, on the receipt of a letter from their Commanding Officer, from having their land returned until the end of the war. *Eastern Times* (Lahore), 11 February 1944.
11. Punjab FR for the second half of January 1943, L/P&J/5/246, IOR.
12. From May 1942 to January 1943, the number of deserters more than doubled. In January 1943, there were still some sixty armed deserters at large. Punjab FR for the second half of January 1943, L/P&J/5/246, IOR.
13. From 1942 onwards, it was a common sight in the major recruiting areas of the North-West Punjab to see only women and children at work in the fields, all the men of military age having enlisted in the army. The impressive recruitment figures of the Rawalpindi and Jhelum districts during the First World War in which one man in every four who was eligible enlisted, were even bettered. It was estimated during the Second World War in the leading recruiting district of Rawalpindi, two men out of every five of military age enlisted. No less than 1,420 persons in the district sent three or more sons to the armed services. File 16 Khizr Papers, Chicago.

14. *The Army Quarterly*, Vol. 11, No. 2 (1921), p. 261.
15. Tour-Note of Biggs-Davidson Assistant Commissioner Amritsar, 19 January 1945. Biggs-Davidson Papers Mss. Eur. D. 844, IOR.
16. Punjab FR for the first half of December 1942, L/P&J/5/245, IOR.
17. *Ibid.*, (16) above.
18. *Civil and Military Gazette* (Lahore), 14 March 1942.
19. Linlithgow to Glancy, 27 September 1943, Linlithgow Papers, Mss. Eur. F. 125, File 92, IOR.
20. Linlithgow to Glancy, 19 June 1943. Linlithgow Papers Mss. Eur. F. 125, File 92, IOR.
21. Linlithgow to Glancy, 17 May 1943. Linlithgow Papers Mss. Eur. F. 125, File 92, IOR.
22. Glancy to Linlithgow, 21 July 1943. Linlithgow Papers Mss. Eur. F. 125, File 92, IOR.
23. Linlithgow to Amery, 21 September 1943. *Transfer of Power*, Vol. 4 (London, 1973), p. 301.
24. I am under the very strongest pressure from the cabinet, in this matter and I am gravely concerned, less about the future of your ministry, though that of course is very much in my mind than about the good name of the Punjab. We are rapidly reaching a point at which the whole force of public criticism here and at home is going to concentrate on the Punjab ... that the Punjab Ministers are engaged in blackmailing the starving peasants of Bengal so as to make inordinate profits at a time when they have already made very substantial profits indeed. I should find it impossible to stand against that criticism. Linlithgow to Glancy, 27 September 1943. Linlithgow Papers Mss. Eur. F. 125, File 92, IOR.
25. Linlithgow to Glancy, 17 August 1943. Linlithgow Papers, Mss. Eur. F. 125, File 92, IOR.
26. *Civil and Military Gazette* (Lahore), 6 November 1943.
27. *Ibid.*, (26) above, 19 December 1943.
28. Mian Nurullah who claimed to represent the smaller landlords' and tenants' interests had for some years been agitating that the *abiana* rates should be reduced. By 1943 he was going so far as to advocate that a system of collective farming should be introduced by the Government. Such a system would, he declared, result in economies in the use of water and increase production. *Civil and Military Gazette* (Lahore), 16 March 1943.
29. The General Sales Tax Act which aimed to distribute the burden of taxation more evenly between the urban and rural population aroused the greatest opposition. It taxed all traders who had an annual turnover of over Rs. 5,000. The traders formed a *beopari mandal* to fight this and the Marketing Act. It organised hartals in the region's main towns. Punjab FR, 28 April 1941, L/P&J/5/244, IOR.

30. It was in fact more the result of the Sikhs' Canal Colony prosperity. Military service had lost its economic attraction for many Sikh cultivators.
31. *Civil and Military Gazette* (Lahore), 5 June 1942.
32. 'Though not a professed Akali himself, he owes his seat in the cabinet to the support of the Akali Party and he is seldom able to stand up against the dictation of Master Tara Singh and his henchmen, even when he knows that their injunctions are ill-advised. In consequence, he is in effect the most communally minded of all the Ministers; he allows communal considerations to obtrude themselves when no kind of regard should be paid to them'. Glancy to Linlithgow, 21 July 1943. Linlithgow Papers, Mss. Eur. F. 125, File 92, IOR.
33. The Communalist Akali leader, Master Tara Singh adopted a vacillating attitude towards the Pact prompted by his uneasiness over the Hindu Mahasabha's opposition to it. Although Baldev Singh relied upon Akali support, he officially entered the Government as leader of the United Punjab Party which contained some Muslim and Hindu members as well as Sikhs.
34. Craik wrote to the Viceroy in June 1941 describing the Akalis' changed attitude towards the war effort. 'Even the Akalis have come to realise that a decline in the Sikh military quota must result in a serious setback to the community and it is obvious that any Sikh aspiring to the position of a leader may land himself in difficulties if he preaches non-cooperation with the Government in the war.' Craik to Linlithgow, 23 June 1941. Linlithgow Papers, Mss. Eur. F. 125, File 90, IOR.
35. Craik to Linlithgow, 10 February 1941. Linlithgow Papers Mss. Eur. F. 125, File 90, IOR.
36. Glancy to Linlithgow, 22 November 1941. Linlithgow Papers, Mss. Eur. F. 125, File 90, IOR.
37. QEAP File 1090/60, NAP.
38. *Annual Report on Punjab Colonies* (Lahore, 1942), Statement No. 2. Unallotted Land in the Canal Colonies 1939–40, p. 18 & ff.
39. Particularly as the declining levels in recruitment from the end of 1942 onwards led the British to increase the rewards for raising recruits.
40. This area was approximately 6,000 acres in extent.
41. *Tribune* (Ambala), 27 September 1940.
42. *The Civil and Military Gazette* noted at the close of the session, the growing 'slackness in party discipline'. *Civil and Military Gazette* (Lahore), 28 March 1943.
43. Jagjit Singh Bedi for example strongly criticized Chhotu Ram for his 'pro-Ambala' bias. The Revenue Minister, he declared, paid no attention to the interest of the *zamindars* of West Punjab. Syed Mubarik Ali Shah pleaded with the Government to provide better irrigation facilities for the people of the Jhang district.

44. The Agra NAP split into a Hindu wing led by Sir Jivala Prasad Srivastava and a Muslim wing led by Muhammad Yusuf. During May 1935, the Hindu *taluqdar* members of the Oudh NAP reorganized the Oudh Liberal League as an organization to represent their communal interests. A large number of *taluqdars* deserted the NAPs immediately before the elections to join communal parties. Amongst them was the Raja of Mahmudabad who was to play an influential role in the UP Muslim League. P. D. Reeves, 'Landlords and Party Politics in the UP 1934–7' in D.A. Low (ed.), *Soundings in Modern South Asia History* (London, 1968), p. 275 & ff.
45. Punjab Board of Economic Enquiry, No. 90, *Annual Review of Economic Conditions in the Punjab* (Lahore, 1946), p. 62, Table XII.
46. Punjab FR, 20 September 1944, L/P&J/5/247, IOR.
47. Punjab FR, 25 October 1944, L/P&J/5/247, IOR. See also *Tribune* (Ambala), 8 October 1944.
48. This was in spite of the representations made by the deputation led by Baldev Singh which discussed the food situation with the Central Food Department in October 1944.
49. Punjab FR for the first half of November 1945, L/P&J/5/248, IOR.
50. *Ibid.*, Punjab Board of Economic Enquiry, No. 90, p. 6 & ff.
51. Punjab FR for the second half of February 1946. L/P&J/5/249, IOR.
52. *Ibid.*, Punjab FR for the second half of February 1946.
53. *Ibid.*, Punjab Board of Economic Enquiry, No. 90, p. 4.
54. The Civil Supply Department of the Punjab Government grew larger during the war than any other department. By the end of hostilities it exceeded in size the entire prewar Civil Secretariat. Muslims held only three of the twenty-one highest posts within it. Only four of its eighteen foodgrains clearing agents were Muslim. *Eastern Times* (Lahore), 1 May 1945.
55. Punjab FR, 15 August 1946, L/P&J/5/249, IOR.
56. *Mawa-e-Waqt* (Lahore), 23 March 1945.
57. Punjab Muslim League 1940, Vol. 132, pt. 5, p. 36, FMA.
58. Conference of the Presidents and Secretaries of the Provincial Muslim Leagues October 1941, Vol. 326, pt. 2, p. 74, FMA.
59. The Baluchistan Muslim League possessed 16,000 primary members enrolled in 44 primary Leagues; the Bombay League had 24,564 enrolled in 48 primary Leagues; the Sind Muslim League had 264 primary Leagues but only 3,599 primary members; the UP Muslim League had 120,560 primary members enrolled in 351 primary Leagues. *Ibid.*. Conference of the Presidents and Secretaries of the Provincial Muslim Leagues October 1941, pp. 4, 32, 87 and 95.
60. Mohammad Amin to the Chairman of the Provincial Muslim League Parliamentary Board, 19 December 1945. Shamsul Hasan Collection, Vol. 1, Punjab General Correspondence.

61. Punjab Muslim League 1940, Vol. 132, pt. 5, p. 69 & ff, FMA.
62. Mahmud of Ghaznavi's sacking of Somnath Temple was a famous episode in Indian Muslim history. Mahmud sacked the temple dedicated to Shiva amid terrible bloodshed in January 1025 A.D. The temple situated on the coast of Kathiawar was a major Hindu religious centre. A thousand Brahmins daily attended the huge *lingam* shrine which had the revenues of 10,000 villages attached to it. The idol was daily washed with water brought from the Ganges 750 miles away and the temple's jewels were famed throughout India. Mahmud Ghaznavi's sacking of the temple became a by-word amongst Muslims for unyielding resistance to idolatry; to the Hindus it symbolized Muslim intolerance and ferocity. W. Haig (ed.), *The Cambridge History of India*, Vol. 3, Turks and Afghans (Cambridge, 1928), p. 23.
63. Punjab Muslim Students Federation, Vol. 230, p. 16, FMA.
64. Report of Mohammad Sadiq: Sheikhupura Student Deputation 22 July 1941, QEAP File 1099/84, NAP.
65. S.Q.H. Jafri and S.A. Bukhari (eds.), *Quaid-i-Azam's Correspondence with Punjab Muslim Leaders* (Lahore, 1977), p. 105 & ff.
66. Jafri and Bukhari, *op. cit.*, p. 109.
67. *Ibid.*, p. 211.
68. *Ibid.*, Conference of the Presidents and Secretaries of the Provincial Muslim Leagues, p. 77.
69. *Ibid.*, p. 79.
70. *Ibid.*, p. 77 & ff.
71. *Ibid.*, p. 77.
72. *Ibid.*, p. 80.
73. *Ibid.*, p. 83.
74. Punjab Provincial Muslim League, Vol. 162, pt. 7, p. 2, FMA.
75. *Ibid.*, Punjab Provincial Muslim League, Vol. 162, pt. 7.
76. *Ibid.*
77. *Ibid.*
78. Mian Bashir Ahmad to Jinnah, 30 January 1943. QEAP File 1701/29, NAP.
79. Punjab Provincial Muslim League, Vol. 162, pt. 7, p. 13, FMA.
80. Jafri and Bukhari, *op. cit.*, p. 318.
81. The Mamdot Estate is situated in the Ferozepore district. I was the General Secretary of the Ferozepore District League from 1939 to 1943. I wrote letters and approached the Nawabzada, now Nawab, Iftikhar Hussain Khan at Jallalabad the headquarters of his estate. He did not allow me to form Leagues in his estate. After Nawab Iftikhar Hussain Khan became President of the Punjab Provincial Muslim League I again requested him to establish Leagues in his estate and he again refrained. By this time there is no League at Jallalabad Memdot or any other place in the precincts of his estate. Khan Rabb Nawaz Khan to Jinnah, 25

March 1943. QEAP File 579/46, NAP.

82. Glancy was of the opinion that he 'was very far from being bright'. Glancy to Linlithgow, 6 July 1943. Linlithgow Papers, Mss. Eur. F. 125, File 92, IOR.
83. L. Griffin, *Chiefs and Families of Note in the Punjab*, Vol. 1 (Lahore, 1910), p. 205.
84. This trio of new generation landlord Muslim Leaguers became known as the three musketeers.
85. *Ibid.*, Report of the Punjab Provincial Muslim League's Work for June and July 1944.
86. *Ibid.*
87. Report of the Organizing Secretary, Rawalpindi Division Muslim League, Vol. 162, pt. 7, Punjab Muslim League 1943–44, p. 74 & ff. FMA.
88. Muslim League Council Meetings, Vol. 253, pt. 2, p. 60, FMA.
89. A grandiose proposal was once placed before the All-India Muslim League Working Committee to use 5,000 mosques in the Pakistan areas as League missionary sub-centres. Muslim League Working Committee Meetings, 1943–47, Vol. 142, p. 23, FMA.
90. Translation of an Urdu pamphlet issued by the Election Board of the Punjab Muslim Students Federation, Vol. 230, Punjab Muslim Students Federation, FMA.
91. Hussain Bakhsh, Propaganda Secretary, Anjuman Islah-ul-Muslemeen Miancharri (Khanewal Tehsil Multan District) to Jinnah, 21 January 1946. Shamsul Hasan Collection, Punjab, Vol. 1, General Correspondence.
92. See Punjab FR for the first half of July 1944, L/P&J/5/247, IOR. The peak of student activity on the Muslim League's behalf however was not in 1944 but during the 1945 Christmas vacation when there were 1550 members of the Punjab Muslim Students Federation and 250 Aligarh Students working on the League's behalf, mainly in the East Punjab constituencies.
93. Muslim University Union Aligarh and Muslim University Muslim League, Vol. 237, p. 71.
94. *Ibid.*, Punjab Muslim Students Federation Election Board Pamphlet.
95. *Ibid.*, The Unionist Party responded employing *mirasis* to work on its behalf during the provincial elections, *Eastern Times* (Lahore), 30 December 1945.
96. Punjab FR for the first half of July 1944, L/,P&J/5/247/, IOR.
97. Punjab FR, 23 August 1944, L/P&J/5/247, IOR
98. This by-election took place as a result of the death of Khan Bahadur Muhammad Hasan Khan Gurmani. The league was unable to find anyone to oppose Sardar Ghaus Bakhsh, a leading member of the Mazari

Baloch tribe which maintained its wild, nomadic way of life even into the twentieth century.

99. Mumtaz Daultana to Mian Amiruddin 16 January 1945. QEAP File 588/143, NAP.
100. *Nawa-e-Waqt* (Lahore), 30 April 1945.
101. *Eastern Times* (Lahore), 23 May 1945.
102. Daultana to Jinnah, 15 June 1945. Shamsul Hasan Collection, Punjab, Vol. 3.
103. Khizr's point was that Allah is described in the Quran as Rabb-ul-Alameen, that is, Lord of everything and everyone, not just of the Muslims. In this light, the Unionist Party's principle of non-communalism was, he maintained, more Islamic than the Muslim League's communalism.
104. M. Gopal, *Sir Chhotu Ram, A Political Biography* (New Delhi, 1977), p. 146.
105. Punjab FR for the second half of October 1943 and the first half of November 1943, L/P&J/5/246, IOR.
106. N.W.F.P. FR for the first half of May 1944, L/P&J/5/221, IOR.
107. Their entry into the League resulted from the decision reached at the October 1943 Bombay meeting of the Central Committee of the Communist Party of India to make special efforts to approach the Muslim population. Punjab FR for the first half of October 1943, L/P&J/5/246, IOR. The most vivid example of the Communists' growing influence came in July 1944 when the prominent Communist Daniel Latifi became the League's Office Secretary. Punjab FR for the second half of July 1944, L/P&J/5/247, IOR.
108. Speech of Mian Mumtaz Daultana. *Civil and Military Gazette* (Lahore), 19 March 1946.
109. *Eastern Times* (Lahore), 9 March 1946.
110. *Nawa-e-Waqt* (Lahore) 19 April 1945.
111. *Eastern Times* (Lahore), 27 May 1945.
112. *Ibid.*, 28 December 1945.
113. As for example in the Khanewal district. *Eastern Times* (Lahore), 28 August 1945.
114. *Ibid.*, Punjab Muslim Students Federation Election Board Pamphlet.
115. Mao Tse-tung, *Mind the Living Conditions of the Masses and Attend to the Methods of Work* (Peking, 1953), p. 2.
116. Punjab FR, 14 December 1946. L/P&J/5/249, IOR.
117. *Dawn* (Delhi), 8 October 1945.
118. *Eastern Times* (Lahore), 29 September 1945.
119. This decision was the result of pressure from local League branches in the recruiting areas. See Resolution of the Montgomery District Muslim League, Shamsul Hasan Collection, Punjab, Vol. 2, General Correspondence.

120. The Muslim League's Assembly strength which had been at twenty-six shortly after the collapse of the Jinnah-Khizr talks in April 1944 had fallen a year later to twenty-two as a result of Rai Faiz Khan, Talib Hussain, Rai Shahadat Khan and Syed Nawazish Ali Shah temporarily rejoining the Unionist Party. *Civil and Military Gazette* (Lahore), 16 and 20 March 1945.
121. Punjab FR for the first half of December 1944, L/P&J/5/247, IOR.
122. The Muslim League had attacked the existence of 'tribalism' in the Punjab, it had appealed in the name of Islam to the Muslim peasants of the Lyallpur district to boycott the 1944 Jat Mahasabha Conference which was held there.
123. Report of the Punjab Provincial Muslim League's Work for June and July 1944. Shamsul Hasan Collection, Punjab, Vol. 1, General Correspondence.
124. Glancy to Linlithgow, 2 January 1943. Linlithgow Papers, Mss. Eur. F. 125, File 92, IOR.
125. Glancy interviewed Firoz Khan Noon, the most experienced politician of the Noon-Tiwana group to ascertain if he wished to give up his seat on the Viceroy's Executive Council for the Punjab Premiership. Firoz made it plain that he had no desire for the Premiership himself but pressed strongly for the appointment of his less-experienced kinsman.
126. Glancy to Linlithgow, 2 January 1943. Linlithgow Papers, Mss. Eur. F. 125, File 92, IOR.
127. Griffin, *op. cit.*, Vol. 2, p. 167 & ff.
128. Khizr's opponents declared that his feudal background and temperament made him unsuited for the wheeling and dealing which was necessary to maintain the Unionist Party. QEAP File 1101/156, NAP.
129. Mir Maqbool Mahmood and Nawab Muzaffar Khan were both ambitious to become Premier and viewed Khizr's appointment with 'not a little disappointment and heartburning'.
130. They were, Nawab Malik Sir Umar Hayat Khan Tiwana, Malik Sardar Noon, Malik Muhammad Habibullah Khan, Nawab Sir Muhammad Hayat Khan Noon and Allah Bakhsh Khan Tiwana.
131. The Gilanis' loyalty to the Unionist Party had been tenuous for some time; they had, moreover, unsuccessfully aspired to the sixth seat in Khizr's cabinet. Khizr who was well aware of their spiritual and political influence in the Multan district made it his business in December 1943 to attend the *Urs* at the Gilani shrine of Abdul Qadir so that he could pay his respects to Pir Mahomed Sadr-ud-Din Shah Gilani, head of the Musa Pak Shahid branch of the Gilani family. *Civil and Military Gazette* (Lahore), 21 December 1943.
132. 'Captain Shaukat Hyat Khan's unpardonably indiscreet references to 'Pakistan' in the course of his recent tour came near to bringing matters to a head.... He has not entirely made up his mind whether to pose as

the repentant sinner or the injured innocent; in the latter role he is sadly unconvincing.... League newspapers incited by Shaukat's vagaries clamour more loudly than ever for a declaration that the Unionist Party is at an end, and a mischievous and unedifying controversy has been raging round the question whether the party in power is a creation of the League or a combination or merely a union.'

133. *Civil and Military Gazette* (Lahore), 9 March 1943.
134. *Ibid.*
135. He wrote:

> One of the difficulties as I have mentioned in my last letter is the loose wording of the Sikander-Jinnah Pact; the more I study this document the less I like it. Unfortunately it is easier for Jinnah to twist the Pact to suit his own convenience than for the Unionist Party; it contains no satisfactory annunciation of the doctrine that the Central Muslim League authorities are expected to refrain from interference in Punjab politics.

Punjab FR, 17 April 1943, L/P&J/5/246, IOR.

136. Punjab FR, 6 August 1943. L/P&J/5/246, IOR.
137. *Eastern Times* (Lahore), 10 November 1943.
138. *Ibid.*, 11 November 1943.
139. Sir Chhotu Ram led the opposition to any abolition of the Jinnah-Sikander pact. He forcefully expressed his views on this issue both to Khizr and to the Quaid-e-Azam when they met for discussions during the latter's visit to Lahore.
140. A draft agreement was drawn up at one stage which represented a considerable concession on Jinnah's part. It read: (a) The League Party is to be accepted as the primary (Muslim) Party in the Provincial Assembly. Members of the Party owe allegiance to no other party and do not belong to the Unionist Party. (b) The Muslim League in conjunction with other parties in the Assembly will carry out the programme of the Unionist Party as contained in the rules and regulations framed originally in 1936. (c) The existing combination shall maintain its present name—the Unionist Coalition. (d) The Muslim members of the Legislature who constitute the Muslim League Assembly Party will be governed by the rules and regulations already published with the exception of rule 11 (relating to the Jinnah-Sikander Pact) which is being replaced by the present agreement. (e) Malik Khizr Hayat Khan Tiwana as leader of the Muslim League Assembly Party will select his ministerial colleagues in the Ministry from among the members of the Assembly in whom he has confidence. (f) The Punjab Provincial Muslim League will hereafter not raise any matter about the workinig of the League Assembly Party and its proposed coordination with the Punjab Provincial League. Khizr Papers, Chicago, File 21.
141. Punjab FR for the second half of April 1944, L/P&J/5/247, IOR.

142. *Ibid.*
143. *Ibid.*
144. Twenty-three of the seventy-five Muslim rural seats were situated in the Multan Division. Rawalpindi had the next largest with twenty, followed by Lahore with eighteen, then Jullundur and Ambala with eight and six respectively.
145. Shaukat Hayat had been dismissed by Khizr on the alleged charge of corruption. He vehemently pleaded his innocence, however, declaring that it was a political move prompted by his forthright support for Pakistan. Khizr's decision embittered the Khattars still further and formed the background to his split with Jinnah in April 1944.
146. The Leghari Estate was 155,000 acres in extent. The Nawab's total income from all sources aggregated in 1940 to Rs. 10,10,000. G. L. Chopra, *Chiefs and Families of Note in the Punjab*, Vol. 2 (Lahore, 1940), p. 421.
147. Mir Maqbool Mahmood and Mian Allah Yar Khan Daultana both resigned as Parliamentary Secretary on the day the Jinnah-Khizr talks broke down.
148. Eight of the twenty-seven members of the Muslim League Assembly Party in December 1944 were members of the Khattar faction. They were, Shaukat Hayat, Sheikh Sadiq Hassan, Mian Mumtaz and Allah Yar Khan Daultana, Mian Abdul Aziz, Mian Amiruddin, Sheikh Mohammad Amin Khan and Mian Nurullah. *Dawn* (Delhi), 6 December 1944.
149. *Dawn* (Delhi), 13 February 1946.
150. Wavell to Amery, 30 January 1945. N. Mansergh (ed.), *The Transfer of Power 1942–1947*, Vol. 5 (London, 1974), p. 489.

CHAPTER 8

The British Desert their Allies

> After the war was declared, the Viceroy naturally wanted help from the Muslim League. It was only then that he realised that he Muslim League was a power. For it will be remembered that up to the time of the declaration of war, the Viceroy never thought of me but of Gandhi and Gandhi alone.[1]

The pressing needs of war led the British to order their Unionist allies to adopt unpopular policies within the Punjab. Their interests were also increasingly ignored at the all-India level. They lost the influence which Mian Fazl-i-Hussain had once possessed in constitutional negotiations. Instead, Jinnah was recognized as the spokesman of Muslim India. The war's acceleration of the British withdrawal from India made this a crippling blow for the Unionist Party whose *raison d'etre* was loyalty to imperial interests in return for protection and patronage. Jinnah's elevation in national politics enabled the Muslim League to capture power within the Punjab. By the end of 1945, large numbers of the Unionist Party's rural supporters had deserted it for the League.

THE IMPACT OF THE WAR ON THE BRITISH

The war caused the British to reconsider their plans for India's constitutional development. Before it began, the leisurely progress towards self-government seemed set for perhaps another quarter of a century.[2] The 1935 Government of India Act had established responsible government in eleven Indian provinces and provided for a federation of India, comprising both provinces and Indian states, with a federal central Government and legislature which would control all central subjects of administration except foreign affairs and defence. It thus represented a further important step along the gradual road to self-government. The outbreak of war, however blocked this avenue of advance. The Viceroy, Lord Linlithgow, was forced to halt his protracted efforts to gain the Princes' accession to the federal scheme, which was shelved. Thereafter, he opposed all proposals for constitutional reform on the basis that this would divert energy from India's assistance to the British war effort.

The Viceroy's efforts to maintain the status quo were however, frustrated by the Congress' attitude to the war. It demanded that the British should give India the same freedom and democracy for which they claimed to be fighting elsewhere. It asked for an immediate demonstration of their goodwill by enabling it to participate in the war effort through representatioon in the Viceroy's executive. Linlithgow was opposed to meeting these demands and advocated the policy of 'lying back' and waiting on events. As early as 1940, however, he found this position impossible to maintain as 'things (had) . . . advanced at a far more rapid pace than anyone had imagined' six months previously.[3] The pace quickened still further in March 1940 when within four days of each other the Congress demanded 'complete independence' and the Muslim League adopted the Pakistan resolution.[4] Linlithgow's response to this new situation was surprising in the light of his previous attitude. He placed before the cabinet the 'somewhat revolutionary' proposal that the British Government should declare that it 'would spare no effort to bring about Dominion Status within a year after the conclusion of the war, 'and (would) set up whatever machinery those concerned agreed upon as appropriate to work out (a) new constitution immediately on (the) conclusion of the war'.[5] This proposal was considerably watered down as a result of

Churchill's opposition and the draft which finally emerged as Linlithgow's August Offer was an imprecise and long-winded document. The Congress rejected it and two months later, under Gandhi's leadership, launched the Civil Disobedience Campaign. By the end of November 1940 it had spread to all of India's provinces.

The arrest of many of its top leaders severely weakened the Congress and enabled the Non-Party Conference, which met at Bombay in March 1941 under Tej Bahadur Sapru's Presidentship, to momentarily set the pace for reform. The Conference, which consisted mainly of Indian Liberals, called for a new Viceroy's Executive Council that would have an Indian non-official majority and would control all portfolios including finance and defence. The Viceroy and the Secretary of State both regarded this proposal as being completely out of the question during the war. Linlithgow, however, did reconstitute his Executive Council in July so that for the first time there was an Indian non-official majority. Nevertheless, the British still retained control of defence and finance. Linlithgow also created a new thirty member national defence council. These moves did not, however, go far enough to gain the Congress' support and it continued to adopt an attitude of non-cooperation towards the war effort.

As the Japanese advanced rapidly in early 1942, the British were forced to adopt a bolder approach to break the stalemate between the Congress and the Government. For a short time, following the fall of Singapore and Rangoon, there appeared to be a serious threat of invasion.[6] In such circumstances, the British needed the whole-hearted support of the major political party in India. Even so, Linlithgow was against doing a deal with the Congress. 'I shall not have an easy hand to play here if we stand firm', he telegraphed Churchill on 21 January, 'but I think I can hold the position well enough. Vital thing is that people should stand firm out here.'[7] This 'defeatist' approach came in for some severe criticism from Clement Attlee, the Lord Privy Seal.[8] He attacked the 'fatally short sighted' and 'crude imperialism' of the Viceroy and called someone to be sent out to India to negotiate a political settlement which could save India for the Empire as Lord Durham had earlier saved Canada.[9]

The situation appeared so grave by the end of the February that the Indian War Cabinet Committee which was chaired by Attlee met for three days in succession. It produced a Draft Declaration which declared that 'immediately on the cessation of hostilities there should be set up in India an elected body with the power to frame a new constitution for India'.[10] On 9 March the Cabinet accepted Sir Stafford Cripps' offer to go to India to negotiate on the basis of the Declaration. Churchill sent a telegram to explain the situation to Linlithgow who had threatened to resign in protest against this new initiative. 'The document on which we have agreed represents our united policy', declared, 'if that is rejected by the Indian politicians for whose benefit it has been devised, our sincerity will be proved to the world and we shall stand together and fight on it here should that ever be necessary. It would be impossible owing to unfortunate rumours and publicity, and the general American outlook, to stand on a purely negative attitude and the Cripps Mission was indispensable to prove our honesty of purpose and to gain time for the necessary consultations.'[11] Churchill and Amery, the Secretary of State, both breathed huge sighs of relief when the Cripps Mission broke down early in April. (The Congress accepted the proposed post-war arrangements but refused to back down on its demand that defence should be under Indian control for the remainder of the war). As far as Amery was concerned, once the Congress had rejected the British offer, 'everything in India was now subordinate to getting ahead with the war'.[12] The British could not, however, behave as though nothing had happened. Things could never be the same again following their promise of Dominion Status at the end of the war. That the British were about to leave India was further underlined by the Simla Conference which Linlithgow's successor as Viceroy, Lord Wavell, convened in June 1945 to discuss the transfer of power and to set up an Interim Government. When the conference collapsed, Wavell announced the holding of provincial and central assembly elections in preparation for the convention of a consitution-making body for British India.

What the British Decision to Leave Meant to the Unionists

The British decision to leave India was a bitter blow to the Unionists.[13] The Unionist approach to politics had always been based on loyalty to the British and had looked to their continued presence at the Centre. In the light of their impending departure, a growing number of Punjabi Muslims came to believe that the Unionist approach to politics had outlived its *raison d'etre*. Firoz Khan Noon, for example, declared in September 1945 that the Unionist Party no longer served its original purpose. When the Party was founded, he maintained, the transfer of power appeared remote, but now that it was going to take place the Unionist Party was 'positively harmful to the Muslim community's interests'.[14] The knowledge that the British would soon be leaving reopened the Centre-State question for Punjabi Muslims. Throughout the 1930s, the Unionist-dominated Muslim Conference had frequently asked for the delay of reforms at the Centre because of the fear that they would undermine provincial Muslim interests. 'Provincial Governments would prefer being under an irresponsible Home Department at the Centre', Mian Fazl-i-Hussain, for example, wrote in 1930, 'an irresponsible Home Department cannot set itself against the responsible Home Department in the province; but a responsible Home Department can claim to represent the Legislature, and through the Legislature, the country, quite as much, if not to a larger extent than the provincial Government. Again, there is a tendency in all deliberate bodies of an all India nature to kill provincial bodies'.[15] His worry was thus that with a Hindu majority in the Cental Legislature, the Muslim majority in the Punjab would be given 'short shrift'. Such anxieties were resurrected by the impending British departure; the Punjab might one day be relegated 'to the position of a backward province tied to the chariot wheels of Hindu India'.[16]

Despite these anxieties, the Unionists did not, as David Page suggests, go over to the Muslim League's support because the Pakistan demand offered a chance to create a Centre of their own.[17] Most Punjabi Muslims realized that such freedom from possible Congress interference from the Centre was heavily outweighed by the economic and communal drawbacks of a Pakistan state. Sikander and Khizr were not alone in fearing widespared communal unrest if Pakistan was created. Its appeal remained strongest amongst the Muslim populations of the minority areas. To the Muslim businessmen of Bombay, for example, it presented an opportunity to gain financially from the removal of Hindu commercial competition; the Government service class of the UP saw in its creation an opportunity not only to revive the past glories of Mughal rule and to safeguard the Urdu language and culture, but also to protect their own livelihood. The Muslim *zamindars* of the Punjab did not, however, share this enthusiasm for Pakistan. They were not threatened by the Hindu and Sikh communities and indeed recognized that their own prosperity was dependent on co-operation with the Hindu and Sikh Jats. They feared that the Sikhs might use force to oppose the creation of Pakistan. They stood to lose their considerable possessions in the West Punjab Canal Colonies and had pledged themselves to never again submit to Muslim rule, so bitter were their memories of Mughal oppression. Sikander prophetically feared that, if Pakistan was created, there would be widespread bloodshed within the Punjab. In fact, he put forward his plan in 1939 for a loose Indian Federation[18] only in order to head off the demands for a 'crude.' Pakistan state. Again in 1941, he attempted to distance himself from the Pakistan demand. 'We do not ask for freedom, that there may be a Muslim Raj here and a Hindu Raj elsewhere', he declared during the course of a debate in the Legislative Assembly on Pakistan, 'If this is what Pakistan means I will have nothing to do with it.... If you want real freedom for the Punjab ... then that Punjab will not be Pakistan, but just Punjab, the land of the five rivers; Punjab is Punjab and will always remain Punjab whatever anybody may say. This then, briefly is the political future which I visualise for my province and for my country under the new Constitution.'[19] Sikander and his followers viewed the Pakistan Scheme with such distrust because they feared that it would disrupt Punjab's vital war effort.[20] In the long term they had even more reason to be wary of it because of the possibility that it would lead to the partition of their province. Sikander, along with many other Punjabis, believed that this would be a complete disaster for its population. Even those Punjabi political leaders who finally joined the Muslim League desired close collaboration between a future Pakistan and India. Many of them hoped that the concession of Pakistan in name would be the means of 'approximating most nearly to a united India in fact'.[21] They had entered its ranks not out of any positive enthusiasm for Pakistan but in order to accommodate themselves with the League which was growing rapidly in power and influence at the Centre.

The War's Effect on the Muslim League

The war not only accelerated the British departure from India, but boosted the Muslim League's importance in all-India politics. Its rapid wartime increase in status led many of the Unionist Party's landed supporters to consider whether their interests might not be served better by entering its ranks. This question was raised most starkly at the time of the 1945 Simla Conference although, as early as 1941, the Unionist Party had found itself under pressure from a revitalized All-India Muslim League organization.

The Muslim League's status had been transformed literally overnight as a result of the outbreak of the war. Just one day after the Viceroy had announced that India was at war with Germany, Jinnah was summoned to see Lord Linlithgow on an equal footing with Gandhi. When Linlithgow made his statement on war aims on 18 October 1939, he dubbed the Congress a Hindu organization whilst implicitly accepting the claim of the Muslim League's Working Committee that its organization spoke for all the Muslims of India. The League was given a further boost following Linlithgow's discussions in November with Gandhi, Rajendra Prasad and Jinnah, when the Viceroy made any further constitutional advance dependent on the Muslim League and the Congress coming to an agreement.[22] The League's veto on further constitutional reform was finally made explicit by the Viceroy's 1940 August Offer which declared that the British Government 'could not contemplate the transfer of their present responsibility for the peace and welfare of India to any system of Government whose authority is directly denied by large and powerful elements in India's national life'.[23] The Cripps Mission, which arrived in India in March 1942, went even further to meet the Muslim League's demands. Its declaration included an option clause which 'gave the right of any province of British India that is not prepared to accept the new constitution to retain its present constitutional position, provision being made for its subsequent accession if it so decides'.[24] Although the actual operation of the option clause made secession from the all-India Union a remote possibility,[25] it conceded in theory the partition of India. The Cripps Mission ended in failure but the Muslim League gained considerably from it as the British had gone a long way towards accepting its demand for Pakistan. Indeed, Jinnah at the time of his interview with Sir Stafford Cripps had been 'rather surprised' to see how far the declaration went 'to meeting the Pakistan case'[26]

The Muslim League's rise in importance owed its existence not only to the genuine British desire to secure communal co-operation before they embarked on further constitutional reform but also to the need for 'lying back' during the war and for creating a counterweight to the non-cooperating Congress. Jinnah adroitly exploited to the full the fortuitous circumstances in which the Muslim League now found itself. The League grew in the 'sunshine of official favour' following the resignation of the Congress Ministries in October 1939 and the Congress' eventual slide towards the 1942 Quit India movement.

The rise in the Muslim League's prestige during the war weakened the Unionists' influence in all-India Muslim politics. Sikander became increasingly isolated within the League Council and Working Committee. Jinnah no longer supported him in the face of the often hostile criticism of its other members.[27] Sikander was so upset by this that he threatened to resign from the League first in August 1940 and then later again in March 1941.[28] It was not, however, until March 1942 that he finally withdrew from the League Council and the Working Committee. If he had done this earlier it would have posed a serious threat to Jinnah; by this time, however, it was merely a recognition of defeat. It brought to an end a period of nearly twenty years in which the Unionist Party had played an influential role in all-India Muslim politics.

The Punjab Muslim League's growth was directly linked to the strength of its parent body. Only when the All-India Muslim League had undermined the Unionists' influence at the Centre could it successfully challenge their power within the Punjab. The 1937 elections had clearly revealed that the provincial League organization was unable to win over a sufficient number of the Unionist Party's landlord and Pir supporters to develop a rival power-base unaided by the resources and prestige of a strong national party; but during the war this is what the All-India Muslim League had become.

The struggle between the Muslim League and the Unionist Party at first centred not on the workings of the Jinnah-Sikander pact nor on the issue of Pakistan, but on the Unionists' attitude to the war. As it progressed, Jinnah's desire to demonstrate his new authority in Muslim politics increasingly conflicted with their unconditional commitment to the war effort. In July 1940 a clash occurred over the Unionist Party's defiance of the Muslim League ban on membership of the provincial war boards which the British had just created. The Unionists stood firm in this dispute. Only the Nawab of Mamdot, the President of the Punjab Muslim League, resigned from among the thirty-eight Unionist members of the provincial war board.[29] His action was no more than a token gesture as he had earlier personally written to Jinnah asking him to change his mind over this issue[30] and had led the deputation which had gone to Bombay in order to argue the case for exemption from the ban.[31] Jinnah could scarcely have picked a worse issue on which to test his new authority. His demand went completely against the Punjabi landlords' long-established loyalty to the British. If he had not lifted the ban less than a month after its introduction he would have undoubtedly encountered serious opposition over this issue.[32] It was reopened during the summer of 1941 when Jinnah successfully persuaded Sikander to resign from the Viceroy's National Defence Council. The reasons for Sikander's climb-down are still not fully clear.[33] His action, however, constituted a major defeat and damaged the Unionist Party's standing in the eyes of the rural elite. If it could not stand up to the Muslim League on this issue in which it had the landlords' unanimous support, what hope would it have on others? 'The Premier has, I am afraid become more vulnerable since he yielded to Jinnah at Bombay', the Punjab Governor wrote anxiously to the Viceroy in October 1941, 'the more intelligent amongst the Muslims are obviously doubtful as to whether the Unionist Party can remain indefinitely in the ascendant if it is tied to the wheels of the Muslim League'.[34]

Sikander's new vulnerability was clearly visible during Jinnah's visit to the Punjab the following month. Sikander had made no effort to meet him at the time of his previous visit to the province in March 1941, and leading members of the Unionist Party had been conspicuously absent from the major meeting which Jinnah had addressed in Lahore.[35] During this second visit, however, Sikander, almost visibly squirming in embarrassment, had attended the Muslim League Lyallpur Conference over which Jinnah was presiding. At this conference he not only effusively described Jinnah as India's greatest Muslim leader, but reversed his earlier attitude to Pakistan. He explained that he 'fully subscribed to the Lahore Resolution of the League which provided for territorial readjustment'.[36] Sikander had been forced to reluctantly adopt this attitude. It further weakened his position, however, as it not only encouraged the Muslim League to redouble its efforts in the Punjab but also destroyed the effect of his earlier reassurance to the Hindus and Sikhs.[37]

As the war progressed and it appeared more certain that the

British would transfer power jointly to the Congress and the Muslim League, the Punjabi landlords' enthusiasm for the Unionist Party waned. However, they remained uneasily in its ranks until Khizr's open break with Jinnah in April 1944 ended their ability to 'sail in two boats'. At first, only the Tiwanas' Khattar opponents joined the Muslim League, but within a year most other leading landlords and Pirs had followed suit. In many cases they did so simply because they wanted to be on the winning side. They had looked to the Unionist Party for patronage and to safeguard their local interests. When it became uncertain whether it would be able to continue to discharge these functions, they deserted, revealing once more their traditional opportunism.[38]

Khizr himself shared many of the Punjabi landlords' anxieties concerning future political developments. In September 1944 he wrote a long letter to the Secretary of State for War pleading that in any future constitutional negotiations 'the interests and desires of those Indians who had played the most prominent part in winning victory (should not be passed over in favour of) those who had played no part or a very minor one'.[39] He repeatedly expressed the fear to Glancy that the British would let down their friends and that he and his supporters would suffer for opposing the Muslim League.[40] He aired his intention to retire to his estate at the end of the war and made it plain that he was only remaining in office in order to serve the war effort. '(Khizr) would not mind taking risks for himself alone', Glancy wrote to Wavell, 'but he does not like the idea of jeopardising his followers. He believes that there will only be two parties of importance in India in the near future—the Congress and the Muslim League; if he defies Jinnah and persuades his staunch adherents to adopt this course, he fears that in a comparatively short time they will all be relegated to political oblivion'.[41] In order to protect himself from future recriminations Khizr pleaded with Glancy to give him an 'order' to stand up to Jinnah in the interests of the war effort. The Punjab Governor naturally rejected this appeal although he was forced to admit that 'there is a good deal of force in Khizr's apprehensions'.[42]

The Muslim League did everything possible to increase Unionist fears about opposing its growing influence. It resorted to threats[43] and aroused agitations in the villages of Unionist landlords. The Rajput Unionist members for the Rawalpindi East and Gujjar Khan constituencies, Major Farman Ali and Raja Fateh Khan, were both put under pressure in this way to join the League.[44] The Muslim League press launched a series of bitter attacks on Khizr and called him a traitor to the Muslim nation. They compared his future with the fate that had already befallen Fazlul Haq in Bengal and reminded him 'that no reliance could be placed on British imperialism which had no hesitation in letting down its supporters'.[45]

The Unionist Party, because it had never commanded great loyalty,[46] found it almost impossible to overcome the pressures on its landed supporters to join the Muslim League. Their entry into its ranks was paralleled in other provinces by the loyalist Hindus' movement into the Congress. Wavell greeted such political opportunism philosophically: 'I have talked to a number of good sensible and influential Indians who have hitherto supported us', he wrote to Pethick-Lawrence in November 1945, 'but who are now doubtful of our willingness or ability to protect them and are therefore considering going over to the Congress side.... Many of them are quite frank in their attitude and say that it is the habit of Indians to worship the rising and never the setting sun; and that as our sun seems definitely on the decline in India, we can hardly expect much support—not an heroic attitude but an understandable one in view of the Indian character and not very easy to give stiffening or comfort to in the present conditions!'[47]

The Muslim League's capture of the elite's support in the Punjab was not, however, an inexorable process. By 1945, some of the League's landlord converts had drifted back into the Unionist Party's ranks. The largest contingent of these came from the Jhang district and included Rai Faiz Khan, Talib Hussain, Rai Shahadat Khan and Syed Nawazish Ali Shah. The fact that a Unionist Ministry still existed and was supported by the majority of the Muslim Assembly members represented a setback for Jinnah. Indeed, some Punjabi Hindu leaders even hoped that Jinnah's failure to upset the Unionist Government would be followed by the breakdown of the Muslim League Coalition Ministries in Sind and the NWFP.[48] 'Jinnah's shares in the political market had begun to deteriorate'.[49] But fortunately for the League's position in the Punjab, the Gandhi-Jinnah Talks of August 1944 and the Simla Conference some eleven months later intervened to restore Jinnah's prestige.

Officials, Congress and Mahasabha leaders all agreed that the Gandhi-Jinnah Talks wiped out the effects of the Quaid-e-Azam's failure to destroy the Unionist Ministry. 'It is a tragedy that Gandhi should have given the League a new lease of life', wrote Shyama Prashad Mukherji, the Bengali Mahasabha leader, 'just when it was dying and that Jinnah should be gloating over the fact that Gandhi had accepted the principle of the Partition of India'.[50] His judgment was echoed by Sir Bertrand Glancy who also declared that Gandhi's acceptance of the Pakistan principle made up for the setback to Jinnah's prestige which followed his failure to impose a Muslim League Ministry on the Punjab.[51]

Gandhi, following his release from prison in May 1944, had attempted to break the communal deadlock by initiating discussions with Jinnah on the basis of what was known as the Rajagopalachari Award. Although Gandhi still rejected the Two-Nation Theory, he agreed that after India was free from British rule, a boundary commission should demarcate contiguous Muslim majority districts in north-west and north-east India and that all the inhabitants of these areas should be permitted to decide through a plebiscite whether they wished to form a separate state. If the vote was in favour, a treaty of separation should be drawn up between the successor states in the subcontinent. However, such matters of common concern as foreign affairs, defence, communications, customs and commerce would be the subject to 'efficient and satisfactory administration' under a central authority[52] made up of boards of representatives of both the states. Despite this provision, Gandhi had nevertheless recognized the principle of partition which he had branded in 1940 'as a patent untruth with which he believed there could be no compromise'.[53] Jinnah, having allowed Gandhi to commit this 'Himalayan blunder', promptly rejected the offer on four counts: that he would accept nothing less than the 'full' six Muslim provinces for Pakistan, that any plebiscite on the issue of separatism must be confined to the Muslim population, that there should be no common ties between India and Pakistan and finally that Partition should come before, not after, the British departure from India. Although these conversations came to nothing, they did give an immense boost to Jinnah's prestige. Gandhi had not only recognized the principle of partition, but had suggested a mechanism for it.[54] The Mahatma had also sought out Jinnah in order to come to a communal agreement, following the British example in dealing with the Muslim League on equal terms. The view that the Muslim League was the only Muslim political party to which either the British or the Congress attached any importance thus gained further ground.

It was to prevent the spread of this idea that Glancy expressed his opposition to the Viceroy in October 1944 to any attempt to set up a Congress-Muslim League Transitional Government at the Centre.[55] He advocated instead the calling of a representative conference to discuss further constitutional reform. This took place at Simla in July 1945. Throughout its proceedings, both Glancy and Khizr fought hard to ensure that a Punjabi Unionist should be a member of the new Executive Council. Khizr told the Viceroy that he was abandoning his supporters and declared that 'if we faced him with a Congress-League Coalition at the Centre, he would be in a most difficult position'.[56] His fears, however, were groundless as Wavell was as determined as either Glancy or Khizr that one of the five Muslim seats should go to a Punjab Unionist, although he was prepared to risk alienating the Congress by excluding any Nationalist Muslims. On 11 July, Jinnah refused to cooperate further in the conference unless all Muslim Council members were chosen from the Muslim League and the Governor-General's power of veto was reinforced by a provision that any measure to which the

Muslims objected could only be carried by a clear majority.[57] Lord Wavell would not accept either of these conditions which he considered signalled the collpase of the Conference. After first informing Azad, Khizr and Gandhi, in an attempt to prevent communal recriminations, he publicly called the conference to an end on 14 July, taking full responsibility himself for its breakdown.

The effects of Jinnah's wrecking of the conference were almost as disastrous from the Unionist point of view as the creation of a Congress-League Executive Council would have been. Not only was the Muslim League press provided with plenty of ammunition to attack Khizr as the main culprit for its failure, but Lord Wavell's capitulation to Jinnah without so much as a fight increased still further the Quaid-e-Azam's prestige. Many Punjabi Unionists as a result felt badly let down by the Viceroy's handling of Jinnah. 'There is still a feeling of considerable resentment among the loyal section of the public', Glancy wrote to Wavell some weeks after the end of the conference, 'which is summed up in the following quotation heard in one district 'The enemies of England have nothing to fear, and her friends have nothing to hope for'.[58] The wrecking of the Simla Conference was especially damaging to the Unionist Party because it brought home the fact that the Punjabi landlords' future access to high office would be cut off if they remained outside the Muslim League's ranks. It was this fear rather than the Muslim League's depiction of Khizr and his supporters as traitors to Islam and their *millat*[59] which sparked off the rural elite's large scale exodus from the Unionist Party's ranks in the weeks which followed the Simla Conference.

The Landlords' and Pirs' Entry into the Muslim League

By the end of 1945, the Muslim League had captured the support of a third of the Unionist Party's Assembly members. This was a major breakthrough. It included in its ranks the leading landlords and Pirs. The Hayats, Noons and Daultanas, from whom the Unionist Party had traditionally drawn its leaders, had joined, as had the influential Naru Rajputs of Hoshiarpur, the Pirachas of Bhera, the Dastis of Muzaffargarh and the Arain Mians of Baghbanpura, Lahore. Moreover, the Pirs of Jalalpur, Jahanian Shah, Rajoa, and Shah Jiwana, who had represented the Unionist Party in the Legislature since 1923, had also joined along with the Chishti Revivalist Pirs and the Gilani Pirs of Multan. In two districts, Jhang and Sheikhupura, all seven of the sitting Muslim members had joined the League.[60] Khizr was even deserted by his Parliamentary Provate Secretary, Syed Amjad Ali, and his kinsmen, Malik Sardar Noon, Firoz Khan Noon[61] and Major Mohammad Mumtaz Khan Tiwana.[62]

The Muslim League had also gained the support of a large number of Muslim Congressmen. Two former Punjab Congress leaders, Malik Lal Khan and Mian Iftikhar-ud-Din joined its ranks at this time as well as many local officials and leaders. Their defection wiped out what remained of the Congress' influence amongst the Muslim community and was greeted with great jubilation by the Muslim League. When the Khateeb of the Mosque of the Sadar Bazaar Lahore announced his resignation from the Congress, he was led in triumphant procession through the bazaar garlanded in currency notes.[63]

The extent of the Muslim League's breakthrough even surprised its own leaders. 'The League is spreading even to the rural areas with what is seen to the League leaders here (as) *unexpected* rapidity', Mian Bashir Ahmed wrote to Jinnah in November 1945, 'our workers have not yet reached the villages in adequate numbers and yet one hears sensational stories of conversions to the League. Some say the League will capture sixty seats out of eighty-four, others put it even higher at seventy.'[64] The League's local workers sent numerous jubilant reports to its Lahore headquarters describing the transformation which had taken place. Typical of these was the report received in January 1945 from Nazir Ahmad Khan, a local organizer in Montgomery. He hailed the presence of large numbers of landlords and Pirs at a recent Shergarh Muslim League rally as a landmark in the Muslim League movement in the province, particularly as 'several of them (were) *Zaildars* and *Lambardars*, the class that is generally under the Unionist thumb'.[65]

The landlords and Pirs entered the Muslim League's ranks in large numbers against the background of increasing political uncertainty which followed the collapse of the Simla Conference. The exodus gained further momentum from the aftermath of bitterness between the Congress and the Muslim League. The Unionist Party found it increasingly difficult to maintain its non-communal stance as Hindu-Muslim relations progressively deteriorated. Nehru's declaration, for example, at the September 1945 Bombay All-India Congress Committee meeting that he would have 'no truck' in future with Jinnah and the Muslim League[66] provoked a further reaction in the Punjab in favour of the Muslim League.[67]

Events at Delhi, Bombay and Simla played an even more important role than local factional rivalries in the landlords' and Pirs' dramatic transfer of political allegiance. Their entry into the Muslim League transformed its position. The League's influence had previously been confined to the towns. Its efforts to expand into the countryside, wherein lay the key to political power, had been frequently frustrated by the elite's support for the Unionist Party. Although the Muslim League increasingly used religious appeals in an attempt to bypass the Unionist Party's landed supporters, they remained firmly in control in the rural areas. The League was thus unable to recover from its humiliating election defeat of 1937 and was excluded from power in the future heartland of Pakistan. Even in 1944, it appeared unlikely to defeat the Unionist Party. The landlords' and Pirs' movement into its ranks, however, completely altered the situation. The tables were turned on the Unionist Party which had never before encountered serious opposition in the countryside. The Muslim League was now able to rival it in fielding candidates who possessed personal influence in the villages. Its converts all controlled large numbers of votes which were placed for the first time in 1946 at the Muslim League's disposal. Thus, even before the electioneering began, the League was in a strong position. This resulted not from the popular support for Pakistan but from wartime developments at the Centre which had transformed its position in the Punjab.

Notes

1. Muhammad Ali Jinnah's speech in March 1940 as reported in *Speeches and Writings of Mr Jinnah*, Vol. 1, (ed.), Jamal-ud-Din Ahmad (Lahore, 1968), p. 154.
2. C. H. Philips and M. D. Wainwright (eds.), *The Partition of India* (London, 1970), p. 18.
3. Philips and Wainwright, *ibid.*, p. 93.
4. The 53rd session of the Congress which met at Ramgarh 19–20 March 1940 demanded complete independence and carried by a large majority the Congress Working Committee Resolution which had been passed at Patna on 1 March and had contained the determination to resort to civil disobedience as soon as the organization was strong enough. The Muslim League's Pakistan Resolution was passed on 23 March during its 27th session at Lahore.
5. Philips and Wainwright, *op. cit.*, p. 90.
6. The rapid Japanese advance threatened all the north-eastern provinces of British India. The arrival of evacuees from Burma increased the general uneasiness in Orissa which had close connections with Burma. The Japanese air raids in April on Madras City, Vizagapatnam and Kakinada created widespread panic. The Governor of Madras evacuated all government offices inland from Madras City after the Southern Command warned him of a possible Japanese invasion any day after 15 April. Sir A. Hope to Linlithgow, 18 April 1942 in N. Mansergh (ed.), *The Transfer of Power, 1942–1947*, Vol. 1 (London, 1970), p. 801.
7. Linlithgow to Churchill, 21 January 1942, *Transfer of Power 1942–47*, Vol. 1, *op. cit.*, p. 54.
8. Attlee to Amery, 24 January 1942. *Transfer of Power 1942–47*, Vol. 1, *op. cit.*, p. 75.
9. 'The Indian Political Situation', memorandum by the Lord Privy Seal, 2 February 1942, *Transfer of Power, 1942–47*, Vol. 1, *op. cit.*, p. 112.
10. Third Meeting of the War Cabinet Committee on India, 28 February 1942, *Transfer of Power*, Vol. 1, *op.cit.*, p. 266.
11. Churchill to Linlithgow, 10 March 1942, *Transfer of Power, 1942–47*, Vol. 1, *op. cit.*, p. 395.
12. Amery to Linlithgow, 10 June 1942 in N. Mansergh (ed.), *The Transfer of Power, 1942–1947*, Vol. 2 (London, 1971), p. 197.
13. Khizr repeatedly expressed the view that the British were abandoning their friends to 'the more vocal groupings who have stood apart from the Allies and who claim to be the sole representatives of India'. Khizr to Sir James Grigg, 18 September 1944 in N. Mansergh (ed.), *The Transfer of Power, 1942–1947*, Vol. 5 (London, 1974), p. 222.
14. *Eastern Times* (Lahore), 18 September 1945.

15. D. Page, 'Prelude to Partition: All India Moslem Politics 1920–1932', Oxford D. Phil. Thesis 1974, p. 213.
16. Page, *op.cit.*, p. 221.
17. Page, *op.cit.*, p. 262.
18. Sikander's plan was for a three-tier system of provinces, regions and a Centre. The scheme envisaged a loose federation, with maximum powers residing at the provincial level. In March 1939, the Muslim League set up a committee to examine and report on the various draft schemes 'already provided by those who are fully versed in the constitutional developments of India and other countries', Sikander was a member of this committee and drafted the resolution which went before the League's Working Committee and emerged as the Lahore Resolution. The Committee however radically amended it and removed the latter part of his resolution which related to the Centre and the coordination of the various units. K. B. Sayeed, *Pakistan: The Formative Phase, 1857–1948*, 2nd edn., (London, 1968), p. 193.
19. H. V. Hodson, *The Great Divide* (London, 1969), p. 89.
20. The rural Hindu and Sikh communities provided a large number of army recruits and both were violently opposed to the Pakistan demand as also, of course, was the important Hindu commercial class.
21. Memorandum by E. P. Moon, January 1946 in N. Mansergh (ed.), *The Transfer of Power, 1942–1947*, Vol. 6 (London, 1976), p. 773.
22. Philips and Wainwright, *op.cit.*, p. 86.
23. Philips and Wainwright, *op.cit.*, p. 212.
24. G. Rizvi, *Linlithgow and India. A Study of British Policy and the Political Impasse in India, 1936–1943* (London, 1978), p. 183.
25. Over 40 per cent of the Members of a provincial legislature needed to vote in favour of secession in order to throw the issue open to a plebiscite of the entire population. Because of the large number of non-Muslims in the Punjab and Bengal Assemblies and their large minority populations, it was unlikely that 'Pakistan' would be achieved by this method of constitution-making.
26. Interview with Jinnah 25.3.1942. P&J/10/4, *Transfer of Power Records*, Departmental Papers, IOR.
27. Raja Ghazanfar Ali Khan wrote to Jinnah on Sikander's behalf in October 1941 to complain about the increasing attacks on the Punjab Premier in the Working Committee. 'There has not been a single meeting of the Working Committee when . . . some members have not indulged in personal attacks on him and were it not for the great personal regard which he has for you, he would have abstained from attending those meetings. As you are perhaps aware Malik Barkat Ali's nomination on the Working Committee caused a good deal of surprise and resentment in League circles within the province. It gave a handle to Sir Sikander's

political opponents to carry on a vicious propaganda that the Quaid-e-Azam has no faith in the provincial Muslim League.' S. Q. H. Jafri and S. A. Bukhari (eds), *Quaid-i-Azam's Correspondence with Punjab Muslim Leaders* (Lahore, 1977), p. 193 & ff.

28. Craik to Linlithgow, 18 August 1940. Linlithgow Papers, Mss. Eur. F. 125, File 89. Linlithgow to Craik 1 March 1941. Linlithgow Papers, Mss. Eur. F. 125, File 90, IOR.
29. Craik to Linlithgow, 24 September 1940. Linlithgow Papers, Mss. Eur. F. 125, File 89, IOR.
30. Jafri and Bukhari, *op.cit.*, p. 193 & ff.
31. *Tribune (Ambala)*, 11 August 1940.
32. In August 1940, Sikander attempted to win support for a resolution which he intended to move in the Muslim League Council to the effect that: 'The Council of the All India Muslim League considers it necessary in the best interests of the Mussalmans as well as of India that instructions should forthwith be issued to the Muslim Leagues all over the country that they should participate fully in the provincial and district war boards and committees and in their war activities.' Punjab Muslim League 1940, Vol. 132, pt. 5, p. 48, FMA.
33. The Muslim League was preparing to expel Sikander before his climb-down but in view of his earlier thoughts about resigning, this hardly seems sufficient cause for his action which totally perplexed the Governor and many leading politicians in the province. 'Sikander left for Bombay confident of his ability to maintain his position, and he certainly had the dice heavily loaded in his favour. He proceeded however, to strike his flag without a struggle on being confronted at the League meeting with the message sent to Jinnah by the Governor of Bombay which Jinnah professed to interpret as meaning that the Muslim Premiers had been invited to serve on the Council merely as Muslims and not in their official capacity. As you are aware, Sikander had been shown this letter at Bombay well in advance of the actual meeting, and he should have had sufficient time to collect his thoughts and realise that Jinnah's interpretation was manifestly dubious.... The Premier returned here in an uneasy frame of mind with his personal dislike and distrust of Jinnah strongly intensified. Since then he has been at pains to explain his surrender and though his arguments have carried little conviction to critical minds, he has exhibited a considerable degree of political agility. He has prudently placed the war in the forefront and stressed the paramount necessity of maintaining at full pressure the war efforts of the province. His Muhammadan followers he has reminded of the importance of ensuring Muslim solidarity, the non-Muslims of the Unionist Party he has invited to accept the proposition that the Premier's continuation on the National Defence Council as a purely Muhammadan representative would be unfair to all other communities.' Punjab FR, 10 September 1941, L/P&J/5/244, IOR.

34. Punjab FR, 21 October 1941, L/P&J/5/244, IOR.
35. Punjab FR for the first half of March 1941, L/P&J/5/244, IOR.
36. *Civil and Military Gazette* (Lahore), 19 November 1941.
37. Glancy to Linlithgow, 28 November 1942. Linlithgow Papers, Mss. Eur. F. 125, File 91, IOR.
38. The Noons and Tiwanas, for example, served in Ranjit Singh's army for which they were rewarded with *jagirs* in the Shahpur district. They perceptively switched to the British side, however, during the Sikh Wars. The Punjabi landlords' political opportunism however has been displayed and taxed even more in this century than the last. In the 1970 Pakistan elections, Zulfiqar Ali Bhutto's Pakistan People's Party did not attract the support of many of the large landlord families with the exception of the Multan Qureshis and a branch of the Noons in Sargodha. Just a year after its victory, however, the landlords had flocked to it in large numbers. They eventually dominated the party's list of electoral candidates so that in the March 1977 elections, many dedicated party officials were passed over for tickets. M. G. Weinbaum, 'The March 1977 Elections in Pakistan', *Asian Survey* 7 (1977), p. 602.
39. Khizr to Sir James Grigg, 18 September 1944, *Transfer of Power 1942–47*, Vol. 5, *op.cit.*, p. 222.
40. Wavell to Amery, 13 April 1944 in N. Mansergh (ed.), *The Transfer of Power, 1942–1947*, Vol. 4 (London, 1973), p. 898.
41. Glancy to Wavell, 14 April 1944, *Transfer of Power, 1942–47*, Vol. 4, *op.cit.*, p. 880 & ff.
42. *Ibid.*, p. 881.
43. *Civil and Military Gazette* (Lahore), 23 October 1945.
44. Report of the Organizing Secretary, Rawalpindi Division, Muslim League, Vol. 162, pt. 7. Punjab Muslim League 1943–44, p. 74 & ff. FMA.
45. Punjab FR for the first half of June 1944, L/P&J/5/247, IOR.
46. Craik to Linlithgow, 1 May 1939. Linlithgow Papers, Mss. Eur. F. 125, File 88, IOR.
47. Wavel to Pethick-Lawrence, 16 November 1945. *The Transfer of Power, 1942–1947*, Vol. 6, *op.cit.*, p. 488.
48. Punjab FR for the first half of August 1944, L/P&J/5/247, IOR.
49. Glancy to Wavell, 23 August 1944. *The Transfer of Power, 1942–1947*, Vol. 4, *op.cit.*, p. 1224.
50. Punjab FR for the first half of September 1944, L/P&J/5/247, IOR.
51. Punjab FR for the first half of August 1944, L/P&J/5/247, IOR.
52. Philips and Wainwright, *op.cit.*, p. 215.
53. Gandhi wrote in April 1940: 'As a man of non-violence, I cannot forcibly resist the proposed partition if the Muslims of India really insist upon it. But I can never be a willing party to the vivisection. . . . For it means the undoing of centuries of work done by numberless Hindus and Muslims

to live together as one nation. Partition means a patent untruth. My whole soul rebels against the idea that Hinduism and Islam represent two antagonistic cultures and doctrines.' Philips and Wainwright, *op.cit.*, p. 210.

54. Philips and Wainwright, *op. cit.*, p. 174.
55. Note by Sir Bertrand Glancy, 26 October 1944. *The Transfer of Power, 1942–1947*, Vol. 5, *op.cit.*, p. 141.
56. Wavell to Amery, 24 June 1945. *The Transfer of Power, 1942–1947*, Vol. 5, *op.cit.*, p. 1151.
57. Wavell to Amery, 11 July 1945. *The Transfer of Power, 1942–1947*, Vol. 5, *op.cit.*, p. 1225.
58. Punjab FR for the second half of July 1945, L/P&J/5/248, IOR.
59. Several Muslim Leaguers issued press statements attacking Khizr's 'traitorous' behaviour at Simla. See *Dawn* (Delhi), 21 July 1945.
60. *Eastern Times* (Lahore), 13 September 1945.
61. Firoz Khan Noon had resigned from the Viceroy's Council in September 1945 in order to return to the Punjab and work for the Muslim League. He had been showing signs of interest in Punjabi politics for some time and was reported to have been intriguing with the Muslim League throughout the Simla Conference. Khizr publicly attacked his kinsman's entry into Punjabi politics as opportunistic and cynical. It certainly does not appear to have been prompted purely by disinterested support for Pakistan demand as Firoz frankly admitted to Glancy during an interview in October 'that he did not believe in Pakistan as preached by the Muslim League and heartily wished that the term Pakistan had never been invented'. Punjab FR 27 October 1945. L/P&J/5/248, IOR.
62. *Dawn* (Delhi), 4 October 1945.
63. *Eastern Times* (Lahore), 11 January 1946.
64. Mian Bashir Ahmed to Jinnah, 14 November 1945. Shamsul Hasan Collection, Punjab, Vol. 3.
65. Nazir Ahmed Khan, 'Thoughts on Muslim League Speakers' Tour of Montgomery', 10 January 1945. Shamsul Hasan Collection, Punjab, Vol. 3.
66. *Indian Annual Register*, July-December 1945 (Calcutta, 1945), p. 98.
67. Punjab FR, 29 September 1945, L/P&J/5/248, IOR.

Chapter 9

The Muslim League Wins

> In giving its allegiance to the Pakistan movement the Muslim community was not merely seeking to escape the domination of the Hindus. What filled the masses with the urge for action was the desire to recreate a truly Islamic society in which the justice, the democratic equality, the freedom from want and the devotion to social welfare that had characterised the earliest Muslim community should again prevail. It was the appeal of this idea which transformed the Muslim League from a body representing the upper classes of Muslims into a mass organisation.[1]

> The extent to which the Muslim League will be able to exploit the influence of families and clans in the service of its main election slogan in the individual constituencies will determine not only the future course of politics in this province, but also to a large extent the future of India.[2]

The 1946 provincial elections formed the most crucial period in the Punjab Muslim League's history. It had to destroy the Unionist Party's traditional influence in the rural constituencies in order to prove that the demand for Pakistan was popular in this key Muslim area. There could be no Pakistan without Punjab's support. This chapter is concerned with how the Muslim League achieved its vital breakthrough in the region.

Its explanation will have significant bearing on our understanding of political mobilization in Muslim peasant societies.

As in previous elections, in most of Punjab's rural constituencies, the selection of candidates was more important than the electioneering itself. 'The parties have yet to choose their respective candidates and much thought and study will be needed for this important step in electioneering', the Editor of the *Civil and Military Gazette* declared on 4 September 1945, 'the party which chooses a better set of candidates, keeping in view the local alliances and clannish feelings will, of course, have a tremendous advantage'.[3] Although it had earlier criticized the Unionist Party for using 'tribalism' and the villagers' superstitious reverence for Pirs to win political support, the Muslim League did not quibble about adopting these same methods when it was in a position to do so. Indeed, it was so determined to field candidates who possessed personal influence in the villages, that it passed over many of its loyal workers in order to run 'convert' landlords and Pirs on its ticket. Sardar Barkat Hayat, Sikander's younger brother, was, for example, selected as the League candidate for the North Punjab Labour Seat instead of the President of the Rawalpindi Artisans Union who was also Vice-President of the Rawalpindi Muslim League.[4] Despite the unpopularity of this policy with its activists, it was vital to the League's success in many of the West Punjab constituencies. Its failure to pursue a similar course of action in the North-West Frontier Province was in part responsible for its embarrassing defeats there.[5] The League's organization and popular base of support was, if anything, even weaker in the Frontier Province than the Punjab.[6]

During the 1946 elections, the Pirs issued *fatwas* to their disciples to support the Muslim League; landlords marshalled their tenants and labourers in its support and the clan networks were used to mobilize the rural voters. In addition, the Muslim League exploited the growing anti-Government feeling amongst the peasant proprietors of East Punjab and the ex-servicemen of its north-western districts.

As in 1937, the *biradari* played an important part in mobilizing the peasant proprietor voters. The Meos' support in the Gurgaon district was assured for the League when it won over the *biradari*'s two main leaders, Sardar Muhammad and Sapat Khan, who openly agitated for the inclusion of Mewat in Pakistan.[7] Just before the elections, the Punjab League persuaded Jinnah to remove the ban on Begum Shah Nawaz's membership so that her influence as the Vice-President of the Punjab Arain Anjuman could be utilized in those constituencies of the Lahore, Jullundur and Ferozepore districts in which most voters were Arains.[8] Mian Nurullah used his influence amongst his fellow Arains in the Lyallpur district on the Muslim League's behalf. He devoted the biggest part of his electioneering effort to the registering of voters rather than popularizing the League's message, as he knew that if he increased the number of voters from his *biradari*, he would almost certainly secure election.[9]

Wherever strong *biradaris* existed, the Muslim League endeavoured to choose their leaders as its candidate. An interesting case in point was the Wazirabad constituency in which most of the voters were Jats. The Muslim League Parliamentary Board had to choose between two applicants for the League ticket for this seat. One was Mohammad Salah-ud-Din, the son of Mohammad Nasir Din, the sitting Unionist member; their family was one of the most influential Jat families in the district. Mohammad Salah-ud-Din was, however, a very recent convert to the Muslim League in 1946, although he had almost immediately been made its district organizer. The other applicant was Captain Raja Mohammad Abdullah Khan whose father had been Chairman of the Gujranwala District Board and President of the Wazirabad Municipal Committee until his death. Raja Mohammad Abdullah Khan had been active in League politics ever since 1936, first as President of the Gujranwala District League and then as President of the Wazirabad City League. He was, however, a member of the small Rajput community. The Parliamentary Board could not risk losing the Jat vote, and so gave the ticket to Mohammad Salah-ud-Din, despite his rival's longer service in its cause.[10]

The Muslim League went to considerable lengths to gain the cooperation of the leading *biradaris*. In January 1946, for example, it organized a special Gujar Conference at Lahore which was presided over by Captain Chaudhri Shamshir Ali. The conference appealed to the Muslim Gujars, not only of the Punjab, but of the whole of India to 'sacrifice body, heart and wealth for Pakistan', so that 'like every other *biradari* our *biradari* should gain a Divine Reward'.[11] It condemned Mohammad Shafi who was the Unionist candidate for Ludhiana and declared that he and his supporters were not really Gujars. 'They were the people who were going to give the *biradari* a bad name when Pakistan was formed'.[12] In order to counter the influence of Mohammad Shafi's paper, the *Gujar Gazette*, it was proposed to start a new pro-League Gujar paper.

The landlords who had joined the Muslim League used their influence over their tenants and their wealth to mobilize political support. 'Treating' the electorate baulked as large in the 1946 Indian elections as in any eighteenth century British election. 'In Bannu where I spent 3 days recently, the result in the voting for the Muslim seats seem likely to be decided by the number of sheep each candidate can kill to feast his supporters', the Governor of the North-West Frontier Province wrote to the Viceroy, 'one was said to have killed 93 sheep already and the general estimate is 10 votes per sheep'.[13] In Sind, it was estimated that the average cost to a candidate was around Rs. 50,000.[14] In contrast, in the Punjab the votes of whole villages were bought up for a thousand or two thousand rupees with 'a few goats and bottles of country liquor ... thrown in for good luck'.[15] However, inflation so took its toll during the course of the week's polling that quotations for a vote in some constituencies soared to twenty times the original price.[16]

The Muslim Leage realized how vital it was to obtain the Pirs' support, not only in the Punjab but in the other Muslim areas of India. It had therefore proposed in 1943 to 'respectfully (request) the Muslim religious heads, pirs and sufis to help the Muslim Nation of India in its present life and death struggle, by their sincere prayers and by exhorting their followers to sacrifice their all in the cause of the attainment of a free and independent Muslim India'.[17] In the period immediatley preceding the provincial elections, the Punjab League created a committee of men of religious influence known as the *Masheikh* Committee in order to marshal Sufi support behind its cause.[18] As in the North-West Frontier Province, where League propagandists were sent into the countryside disguised as Pirs in an attempt to win the Pathans' support,[19] so in the Punjab many landlords adopted the garb of Pirs during the course of the elections. Among the members of the *Masheikh* Committee were such unlikely Sufis as Pir Mamdot Sharif (Khan Iftikhar Husain Khan of Mamdot), *sajjada nashin* of Wah Sharif (Shaukat Hayat) and *sajjada nashin* of Darbar Sargodha Sharif (Firoz Khan Noon).[20] The Pirs were not easy to organize, few attending the Jamiat-u-Ulema-i-Islam Conference which the Muslim League held in the grounds of Islamia College, Lahore in January 1946 and so most of its dealings with them had to be done at the local level.[21] It approached individual Pirs and asked them to issue *fatwas* in its support. These were disseminated by means of small leaflets and wall-posters as well as by publication in such newspapers as *Nawa-e-Waqt* and *Inqilab*. In them, appeals to vote for the Muslim League were often couched solely in terms of loyalty to the *piri-mureedi* relationship. The following *fatwa* issued by Syed Fazal Ahmed Shah, *sajjada nashin* of the shrine of Hazrat Shah Nur Jamal is a good illustration of this.

> An announcement from the Dargah of Hazrat Shah Nur Jamal. I command all those people who are in my Silsilah to do everything possible to help the Muslim League and give their votes to it. All those people who do not act according to this announcement should consider themselves no longer members of my Silsilah.
> Signed Fazal Ahmad Shah, Sajjada Nashin Hazrat Shah Nur Jamal.[22]

Even *fatwas* such as that issued by the Qadiri *dargah* of Hazrat Shah Muqim Mujravi at Hujra which appealed for the restoration of the glories of Mughal rule were still firmly set within the framework of the *piri-mureedi* institution.

> Brothers in unity, many of my friends, brother sufis and my murids have asked my help as to whom they should give their votes in the Provincial Elections. I'm not only making an announcement but a

compassionate appeal to my brothers in unity that they should give every vote to the nominated candidates of the Muslim League and prove their solidarity. The bold struggle of the Muslim League against a well organised party like the Congress has given it an immense respect as also has its provincial success. God willing after it had captured political power in the provinces, the Sun of glory of the Muslim Government that has ruled India for 800 years and which set in 1857 in the Red Fort at Delhi with its last rays of glory, will rise again from the land of India. We can see the harbingers in the dawning light of the sky of slavery and cruelty. God's promise that He made in the Sura 'Nur' in the Quran will be fulfilled, If you are in love with Islam you should do things in the way Iqbal asked you to do it. Syed Imdad Ali Shah Gilani, Sajjada Nashin Dargah Hazrat Shah Muqim Mujravi. 1-1-1946.[23]

Most of the leading Sufi shrines issued similar *fatwas* to support the Muslim League.

The Pirs of the Chishti revivalist shrines were among the most active on the Muslim League's behalf. Pir Jamiat Ali Shah toured the Jhelum tehsil issuing *fatwas* and contacting his followers to support the League. Pir Golra worked for the League in the Rawalpindi tehsil and Pir Fazl Shah 'tipped the scales against (the Unionsts) in the Gujar Khan tehsil'.[24] Pir Golra also issued the following *firman* in favour of the League candidate Raja Said Akbar Khan at Gujar Khan. 'To oppose the Muslim League at this moment is in fact to harm the whole Muslim Nation. Therefore I hope that nobody will take any step against the League at this stage. As you all knew the League has given a ticket to Raja Said Akbar Khan in Tehsil Gujar Khan. I hope that nobody will be careless in supporting him.'[25] Pir Qamaruddin, *sajjada nashin* of Sial Sharif and his son Sahibzada Karam Shah Makervi attended a Muslim League meeting at Shahpur at the end of December less than two miles distant from the Kalra estate. Pir Qamaruddin publicly challenged the Tiwanas to reverse their opposition to the Muslim League. 'I have never begged for anything in my life before', he declare, 'but today I have come out of my home to beg for votes, believing God is present here (the meeting was being held in a mosque), it is Islamic to ask for votes and 'religious' to give them. The Muslim

League is purely a religious movement in which all the rich, poor, sufis and scholars are participating. Not as a pir but even as a Muslim, I have repeatedly advised Nawab Allah Bakhsh Khan Tiwana who is my *murid* not to desert the Muslims at this critical time.... Pir Mehr Ali Shah *sajjada nashin* of Golra Sharif who is also my *murid* has told Khizr Hayat Khan that he should not separate himself from the Islamic movement and become a fiend in hell but Khizr does not accept his advice.'[26] He was interrupted at this point in his speech by some Tiwana supporters who had infiltrated the meeting.[27] Although Pir Sial was unable to break the Tiwanas' stranglehold in Shahpur, he, like the other Chisti revivalists, did valuable propaganda work for the Muslim League elsewhere in the Punjab. For example, he spoke in favour of his brother Sufi Muslim League candidate at Jhang, Syed Mubarik Ali Shah.[28]

The Chishti revivalist Pirs were prompted to join the Muslim League due more to religious than political considerations unlike the Pirs of the older established shrines. The Chishti revivalist shrines had never been fully integrated into the Unionist political system. Their *sajjadas* had been waiting for a long time to put politics in the province on a firmer religious footing. The desire to achieve this had led Pir Jamiat Ali Shah to uncomfortably assume the leadership of the Shahidgunj Agitation in 1935.[29] Pir Fazl Shah of Jalalpur had formed his own political party to avoid entanglement with the Unionists. This party, known as the Hizbullah, 'Party of God' provided him 'with a platform for the political expression of an independent religious view'.[30] The prospect of a future Pakistan controlled by Muslim rural politicians held none of the misgivings for the Chishti revivalists which it did for many of the Deoband Ulema. 'The idea of a state in the hands of such leaders was for them perfectly natural, for in the establishment of such a state, based on the Shariat, they could see the projection of their local religious concerns into a larger political arena.... The thrust of their concern had always been to influence the political leaders and followers to regulate their lives according to religious injunctions'.[31]

The Chishti revivalist Pirs were not alone, however, in

rendering valuable support to the Punjab Muslim League during the 1946 elections. The *sajjada* of the older established Chishti shrine of Sharfu'd-Din Bu Ali Qalandar at Panipat appealed to his *murids*, 'to give their votes only to the Muslim League in the present election and not to be deceived by the false propaganda of the enemy'.[32] The *sajjada nashin* of the Naqshbandi shrine at Leiah in the Muzaffargarh district, 'prayed for the success of the Muslim League', and urged his *murids* to support it.[33] The *sajjada nashin* of the Qadiri shrine of Pir Syed Mohammad Ghaus intervened on the League's behalf in the Shakargarh constituency and thus enabled Chaudhri Abdul Ghafoor to defeat the Unionist Chaudhri Abdul Rahim who had been its representative since 1937.[34] Sahibzada Syed Mohammad Abbas, the son of the *sajjada nashin* of the Shergarh shrine which had extensive influence in the Lower Bari Doab Canal Colony, was the Divisional Organizer of the Montgomery Muslim League.[35] The shrine of Mian Mir, the founder of the Miyan Khel section of the Qadiri order, issued *fatwas* for the League.[36] Makkdum Syed Mohammad Nazar Hussain Shah, *sajjada nashin* of Koranga Sharif in the Multan district, was largely instrumental in the defeat of his brother Syed Nasir-ud-Din Shah as the Unionist candidate for the Toba Tek Singh constituency.[37] Finally, the Gilani Pirs of Multan supporting the Muslim Leauge did much to counter the influence of the Qureshis on behalf of the Unionists. Mohammad Reza Shah Gilani in fact defeated Nawab Ashiq Hussain at Shujabad, although he was subsequently returned as the Unionist member for Multan.

What made the activities of the Chishti revivalist Pirs significant in 1946 was not so much that they were more important than other Pirs in gathering votes for the Muslim League, but that for some of them this was the first occasion on which they had taken an active part in politics, unlike for example, the Gilanis who had been active in provincial politics since 1919.

The Gilanis, like many of the Pirs of the older established shrines, had been prompted to join the Muslim League primarily by political considerations. They saw entry into its ranks as an opportunity to gain advantage over their traditional rivals in Multan politics, the Qureshis who remained closely linked to the Unionists. However, most of the Pirs of the older established shrines deserted the Unionist Party not due to local factional squabbles, but because of the Muslim League's rise in status in all-India politics. Like the landlords, they wanted to protect their local influence by being on the winning side. They realized that if they unsuccessfully opposed Pakistan, they would be vulnerable to renewed attack from the reformist *ulema* who were critical of the practices at their shrines.

Whether a shrine derived its wealth and status mainly from Government patronage or spiritual influence was another important factor in determining its *sajjada's* response to calls to join the Muslim League. *Sajjadas* of small shrines who owed their status more to their political loyalty than to their religious influence were less likely to join the Muslim League than those of large and influential shrines whose reliance on Government patronage was much smaller. An interesting example of a Pir from the first category was Pir Mian Syed Badr Mohy-ud-Din who was narrowly defeated as the Unionist candidate for the Batala constituency in 1946. He was the son of the *sajjada nashin* of the Qadiri *dargah* at Batala. The *dargah* was small and the family's high social status stemmed not from its sanctity but rather its long tradition of loyalty to the British. This dated to before the Mutiny, after which the shrine's *sajjada* was rewarded by being granting a *jagir* for life and being made a provincial *darbari*. The *sajjada nashin* in 1946, Khan Bahadur Syed Nazar Mohy-ud-Din, held a hereditary seat in the *darbar*, whilst Mian Syed Badr Mohy-ud-Din was himself a honorary magistrate and Sub-Registrar besides holding the title of Khan Bahadur.[38]

Other syed families which had a similar tradition of Government loyalty but whose status ultimately derived from their religious influence were far more responsive to calls to join the Muslim League. One such family was the Pir family of Jahanian Shah. Their Bukhari Syed ancestors had migrated to India about the beginning of the eleventh century. The shrine at

Jahanian Shah had large landholdings attached to it (around 7,000 acres) and its spiritual influence was great throughout West Punjab. The Pirs of Jahanian Shah were loyal supporters of the British and had played an active part during the First World War, enlisting sixty-five recruits and raising over Rs. 6,000 for the Provincial War Fund. In reward for this, Pir Sultan Ali Shah was made a provincial *darbari* and one of his sons, Pir Naibahar Shah was granted five squares of Canal Colony land. When Pir Sultan Ali Shah died in 1929, his eldest son, Pir Ghulam Muhammad Shah, succeeded him as *sajjada*. He was not only a provincial *darbari* but was also an honorary magistrate, *zaildar* of Jahanian Shah and a Unionist Legislative Council member. Despite his close links with the Unionist Party, Pir Ghulam Muhammad Shah joined the Muslim League along with Major Mubarik Ali Shah of the neighbouring Shah Jiwana Pir family. Both subsequently secured election as Muslim League candidates for the Jhang constituencis.[39]

The older established Chishti shrines, like the revivalist shrines, has been influenced to support the Muslim League by the Ajmer *dargah* of Hazrat Moinuddin Chishti. The Unionist Party had approached the *dargah* for support in the 1937 elections. During the 1940s, however, this shrine of India's premier Sufi Saint had become closely connected with the Muslim League. Mirza Abdul Qadir Beg, the Vice-President of the *dargah* Committee which administered its affairs, was the President of the Ajmer Muslim League. He claimed that although only a third of Ajmer's population was Muslim, the *dargah*'s spiritual influence was so great that it should be included in the future state of Pakistan. Muslim League meetings were regularly held at the shrine.[40] A huge assembly of over 20,000 gathered there in January 1946 to celebrate the Muslim League's 'Election Victory Day'. At the time of the *Urs* the League's message was spread amongst the vast numbers of pilgrims which flocked to the shrine. Included amongst them were the *sajjada nashins* of many of Punjab's leading shrines as well as those from U.P and the rest of India.[41] In November 1945, the *dargah*'s *sajjada nashin* Maulana Syed Shah Diwan Rasul Ali Khan announced his fullest possible support for the pro-League Jamiyat-ul-ulema-i-Islam organization and called on the *mashaikh* and *sajjada nashins* of the different *dargahs* and *khanqahs* of India and the *ulema* to come out in open support of the Muslim League.[42] This leadership from Ajmer was an important factor in the Chishti Pirs' support for the Muslim League in the Punjab.

The Pirs played a crucial role in the Muslim League's success in Punjab. It received its greatest number of votes in such areas as Jhang, Multan, Jhelum and Karnal where it had won over the leading Pirs. Khalid Saifullah, the editor of the Muslim paper the *Eastern Times* recognized their importance when analyzing the League's victory soon after the elections.

> What are the factors that have brought about the revolution in the Pakistani lands? What has made the great change possible? In my view the greatest praise must be levished, as far as the Punjab is concerned on the Pirs ... who when they saw the Pakistani nation in mortal danger emerged from their cells and enjoined upon their followers to resist evil and vote for the League and Pakistan.[43]

It is particularly interesting to note that the Pirs played an important part in the Muslim League's success in the Canal Colony areas. These were the most prosperous and economically advanced districts in the whole province, but thanks to British social engineering, there had been no weakening of the Pirs' spiritual and temporal influence in the Colonies. The Muslim League gained its high level of support in the Colony constituencies in the 1946 elections,[44] not because of the social mobilization of their Muslim inhabitants, but because of the work on its behalf of the landlords and Pirs who had retained their traditional authority in these new areas. Two of its candidates for the Jhang constituencies came, for example, from leading Pir families, as also its candidates in such other colony seats as Khanewal.

Although the Muslim League's capture of the rural elite's support stacked the odds heavily against the Unionist Party, it also contributed to its own defeat. Instead of pacing out its impressive programme of agricultural reforms it had packed them all into 1938 and 1939, with the result that its legislative programme had run out of steam long before the elections. To offset its wartime loss of support, it had opened the doors of the Zamindara League of non-agriculturalists[45] and had moved closer to the Congress,[46] thus proving to many Muslims the truth behind the Muslim League's allegations that it was a treacherous and quisling party. Moreover, through no fault of its own, it had to bear the brunt of the unpopularity created by the wartime controls and restrictions. Its complete preoccupation with the war effort had led it to neglect the interests of its rural supporters and it had become 'an aloof body seasonally resident in Lahore or Simla remote and for all practical purposes out of touch with the people'.[47] This point was forcibly brought home to Khizr during his election tour of the Jhelum district, when he unsuccessfully interviewed 120 people in an attempt to find someone willing to oppose Raja Ghazanfar Ali Khan in the Pind Dadan Khan constituency.[48] Faced with the disruption of its rural support, the Unionist Party relied heavily on its control of the machinery of government to mobilize voters.[49] Attempts to coerce the village voters proved disastrous. They did irreparable damage to the reputation which the Party had gained during its early years of office and compared badly with the Muslim League's efforts to help the peasants in their wartime difficulties.

The Results

The election results revealed the Muslim League's rapid advance since 1944. The Unionist Party was reduced to a rump of eighteen members in the 175 strong Assembly. The Muslim League had captured seventy-five of the eighty-six Muslim seats, winning all eleven of the urban and sixty-four of the seventy-five rural constituencies. Its greatest success had been achieved in the eastern Divisions (Ambala and Jullundur), where it had captured all but one of the seventeen Muslim seats in the areas which on partition would go to India. In the Multan and Lahore Divisions, the League had captured twenty-one

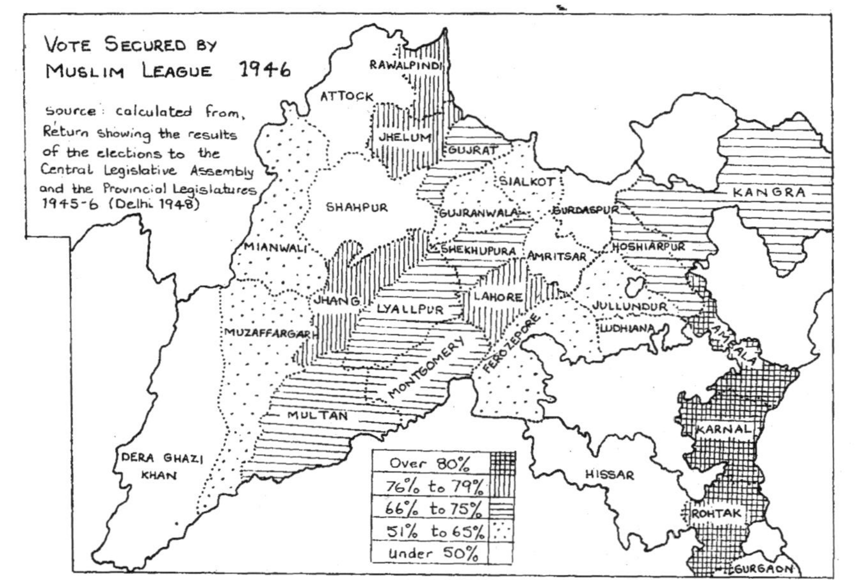

PERCENTAGE OF THE MUSLIM LEAGUE VOTE IN THE 1946 PUNJAB PROVINCIAL ELECTIONS

SOURCE: Calculated from, Return showing the *Results of the elections to the Central Legislative Assembly and the Provincial Legislatures 1945–46* (Delhi 1948)

and twenty-two respectively of the twenty-four rural seats. Only in the Rawalpindi Division where it had won fourteen of the twenty-one seats, had its progress been slightly checked.

The elections also highlighted the consolidation of opinion in the minority communities in the face of the Pakistan threat. The Congress' success was unprecedented. It had eclipsed all competitors for the Hindu vote, including the Unionist Party, and won fifty-one seats in the Assembly under the leadership of Bhim Sen Sachar. The Sikhs had formed a Panthic Pratinidhi Board representing all groups except the Communists in order to present a common front in the elections.[50] In all, the Panthic Sikhs won twenty-two seats.

Despite the Hindus' and Sikhs' common opposition to Pakistan, the rift which had opened up between their communities during the Gurdwara Reform movement had been widened during the war. There had been growing friction between the Akalis and the Congress over Sikh army recruitment; the Sikhs had viewed with alarm the apparent softening attitude towards Pakistan of such leading Congress figures as C.R. Rajagopalachari and Gandhi himself. Finally, the Punjabi Hindus viewed with disquiet the Azad Punjab demand raised by Master Tara Singh,[51] especially as it was opposed by such respected Sikh 'nationalists' as Baba Kharak Singh and Udham Singh Nagoke. The prospects for united action against Pakistan thus did not appear favourable early in 1946.

Notes

1. Chaudhri Muhammad Ali, *The Emergence of Pakistan* (London, 1967), p. 40 & ff.
2. The Editor, *Eastern Times* (Lahore), 6 September 1945.
3. *Civil and Military Gazette* (Lahore), 4 September 1945.
4. M. Haqil Bukhsh to Jinnah, 14 January 1946. Shamsul Hasan Collection, Punjab, Vol. 1, General Correspondence.
5. *Khyber Mail* (Peshawar), 15 February 1946.
6. As late as 1944, a Committee of Action Enquiry Report into the N.W.F.P Muslim League reported to Jinnah that its ramshackle organization was confined to the Hazara district alone.
7. P. C. Aggarwal, 'The Meos of Rajasthan and Haryana' in I. Ahmad (ed.),

Caste and Social Stratification among the Muslims (New Delhi, 1973), p. 27.
8. Vicky Noon to Jinnah, 18 October 1945, Shamsul Hasan Collection, Punjab, Vol. 4.
9. The Unionist candidate Pir Nasir-ud-Din exerted influence mainly over the *jangli* section of the population. He endeavoured to enrol 10,000 new *jangli* voters, whilst Mian Nurullah submitted about 8,000 fresh applications for the constituency's Arain community. Abdul Bari, President, Lyallpur District Muslim League to Jinnah, 23 January 1946. Shamsul Hasan Collection, Punjab, Vol. 1.
10. *Eastern Times* (Lahore), 27 October 1945.
11. *Nawa-e-Waqt* (Lahore), 19 January 1946.
12. *Ibid.*
13. NWFP FR, 24 January 1946, L/P&J/5/223, IOR.
14. Sind FR, 5 October 1945, L/P&J/5/261, IOR.
15. *Civil and Military Gazette* (Lahore), 7 February 1946.
16. *Ibid.*
17. G. F. Ansari to Jinnah, 25 April 1943, QEAP File 1101/105, NAP.
18. Interview with Abu Saeed Enver (Propaganda Secretary of the Punjab Muslim League in this period), Lahore, 10 April 1978.
19. *Pioneer* (Lucknow), 24 November 1945.
20. K. B. Sayeed, *Pakistan, The Formative Phase 1857–1948*, 2nd end., (London, 1968), p. 203.
21. *Ibid.*, Interview with Abu Saeed Enver.
22. *Nawa-e-Waqt*, 19 January 1946.
23. *Ibid.*, 3 January 1946.
24. D. Gilmartin, 'Religious Leadership and the Pakistan Movement in the Punjab', *Modern Asian Studies*, 13, 3 (1979), p. 514.
25. *Nawa-e-Waqt*, 19 January 1946.
26. *Ibid.*, 5 January 1946.
27. *Ibid.*
28. *Ibid.*, 23 January 1946.
29. Punjab FR for the first half of November 1935 18/11/1953–Poll., NAI.
30. D. Gilmartin, *op.cit.*, p. 497.
31. Gilmartin, *op.cit.*, p. 509.
32. *Nawa-e-Waqt*, 23 January 1946.
33. *Ibid.*, 18 January 1946.
34. *Ibid.*
35. *Dawn*, 14 January 1945.
36. *Inqilab* (Lahore), 8 November 1945.
37. Apart from using his personal influence amongst the voters, he donated Rs. 5,000 to the provincial Muslim League's election fund. *Eastern Times* (Lahore), 29 September 1945.

38. Information compiled from G. L. Chopra, *Chiefs and Families of Note in the Punjab*, Vol. 2 (Lahore, 1940), p. 52, and *Gurdaspur District Gazetteer* (Lahore, 1915), p. 74.
39. Pir Ghulam Muhammad Shah was unopposed in the Jhang East constituency. Mubarik Ali Shah defeated Khan Inayat Ullah by over 7,000 votes in the Jhang Central seat.
40. See the Fortnightly Reports for Ajmer in the 1940s, L/P&J/5/280–86, IOR.
41. The *Urs* of leading saints were great meeting places not only for the ordinary *murids* but also for fellow Sufis. It was also common for Pirs to be *murids* themselves of other Pirs. Pir Taunsa and Pir Golra were just two of the leading Pirs who attended Baba Farid's *Urs* at Pakpattan for example.
42. *Star of India* (Calcutta), 13 November 1945.
43. *Eastern Times*, 15 March 1946.
44. The Muslim League gained 80 per cent of the popular vote in the Jhang district, 77 per cent in the Montgomery district, and 70 per cent in the Lyallpur district, the three main colony areas.
45. In July 1944 the Unionist Party opened the doors of the Zamindara League for the first time ever to urban Hindus and Sikhs who soon played an important part in its organization. Over 30 per cent of its donations in Multan came from these groups. Baldev Singh himself contributed Rs. 25,000 to the Zamindara League's Central Fund. In the Gurdaspur district, Hindus and Sikhs made up six of its ten-man committee. *Dawn* (Delhi), 21 July 1944, *Tribune* (Ambala), 26 July 1944.
46. Chhotu Ram in a speech to a joint meeting of the Jat Sabha and the National War Front in January 1944 declared that the Unionist Party in the Punjab had imbibed the true spirit of the Congress and lived up to it. The Unionist Party was in fact a 'real Congress'. His successor Chaudhri Tikka Ram in a speech at Sonepat shortly after the failure of the Simla Conference declared that 'the Unionist Party is really carrying out the constructive part of the Congress programme'. *Civil and Military Gazette*, 26 January 1944 and 24 July 1945.
47. *Civil and Military Gazette*, 14 July 1945.
48. *Dawn*, 28 October 1925.
49. In both the Toba Tek Singh and Lyallpur constituencies, for example, individual voters were contacted by the police and Government officials and persuaded to support the Unionist Party. In the neighbouring Samundri seat, the Police Superintendent, Waryam Singh, was particularly open in his support for the Unionists. Influential supporters of the Muslim League were entangled in legal cases in the hope that this would frighten off voters from supporting it. The Samundri *tehsildar* called a meeting of all the *lambardas*, *sufedposhes* and *zaildars* of the *tehsil* on 3 January and warned them that they would be instantly dismissed and

prosecuted, their grants confiscated and their supplies of canal water withheld if they opposed the Unionist Party. On the other hand, four squares of land and *jagirs* carrying recurring cash awards of several hundred rupees had been set apart for persons who did the 'best work' in the elections. The proceedings reached comic proportions when a *lambardar* who was a member of influential Baloch family and a zealous supporter of the Mulsim League was lifted bodily into the car of the Baloch Unionist candidate, Raja Ali and driven at breakneck speed to the surrounding Baloch villages in an endeavour to hoodwink the voters into believing that he had switched his allegiance to the Unionist Party. Abdul Bari to Jinnah, 23 January 1946, Shamsul Hasan Collection, Punjab, Vol. 1.

50. This was to be shortlived. Major differences of opinion over the issue of Partition surfaced between the West and East Punjab leaders. This failure to achieve a united approach was a major weakness in the negotiations of 1946–47.
51. The Sikhs were to hold the balance between equal Muslim and Hindu populations in a new state comprising of Ambala, Jullundur, Lahore Divisions, Lyallpur district and portions of Montgomery and Multan districts.

CHAPTER 10

The Collapse of Collaboration

> Two steps rendered the partition of the Indian Subcontinent an entirely unsuccessful exercise in averting (communal) tragedy. First, the hurried and premature transfer of power, and second, the division of the services, especially the police and the army, on communal lines.... It is now evident that antedating the transfer of power was a 'bargain' to secure India's accession to the British Commonwealth.[1]

> Every British official in the ICS and IP including myself, would be very glad to leave (the Punjab) tomorrow. Six months ago the position was quite different, but we feel now that we are dealing with people who are out to destroy themselves and that in the absense of some agreement between them the average official will have to spend his life in a communal civil war. The Punjab is not now in a constitutional but in a revolutionary situation.[2]

The Second World War had buckled the system of local British control in the Punjab. The deteriorating communal situation in 1946 finally shattered it. British officials stood by helplessly as the Punjab slid into civil war. The region which had been a major pillar of British power in India became a source of growing danger and anxiety. The fear that its violence would spread to other regions and sap the loyalty of the Indian Army was a major factor in Mountbatten's controversial decision to divide and quit as early as August 1947. A decade of political developments and worsening relations led to this situation and yet one cannot help asking why the century-old webs of alliance between the British and the landowners unravelled so suddenly and disastrously in 1946–7?

The Collapse of British Rule

British authority received a setback from the results of the 1946 Punjab elections. The Unionist Party's collapse was seen by many Indian politicians as a defeat for the colonial regime. British officials had undeniably had close links with the Unionists. These had received much publicity during the long years of war. Firoz Khan Noon and Mumtaz Daultana had lent their considerable influence to accusations during the election campaign that the Punjab Governor and his senior officials were doing all in their power to secure a Unionist victory. Although these claims were unfounded, many Muslims believed them. It certainly appeared to them that the British were at best lukewarm towards the demand for Pakistan. Nevertheless, many of the Muslim League's recent converts were landowners who had previously worked hand-in-glove with the colonial regime. They might well have done so again, if the British had not precipitately encouraged Khizr to form a precarious coalition government consisting of the rump of the Unionist Party, the Akalis and the Congress. The incensed Muslim landowners of West Punjab withdrew their cooperation. Thus, the century-old system of local control collapsed at the very moment it was most needed. When the scattered Sikh communities of West Punjab were attacked by Muslim tribesmen in March 1947, the British found themselves helplessly isolated. By the time they rushed in troops, it was too late to prevent a massacre which set off a chain reaction of retaliatory killings, wrenching the region out of British control. Events in the Punjab overtook the constitutional deliberations in New Delhi and accelerated the British departure from India.

Sir Bertrand Glancy's ill-advised attempt to resurrect the Unionist Party stemmed from the shock he felt at its defeat,[3] and his personal distaste for the polarization of communal opinion. The Muslim League's success had been matched by the Akalis who remained implacably opposed to the Pakistan scheme. The Muslim League's failure to secure an absolute majority in the Assembly opened the way for Glancy to attempt to restore the Unionists as a bridge between the communities. Glancy greeted with relief the Muslim League's failure to form a ministry and encouraged Khizr to do so. Shortly after he was installed in office, Glancy retired, leaving the hot seat to Sir Even Jenkins, the Viceroy's former Private Secretary. The coalition government appeared, superficially, to have restored the traditional pattern of inter-communal cooperation. In reality, it stood in the way of lasting agreement. The Muslim League hardened its attitude towards the Hindus and Sikhs and scarcely concealed its hostility towards the British as well. Their ability to counter any future Muslim League disruption had been seriously undermined by the wartime neglect of the Indian Police and Indian Civil Service.[4]

An uneasy peace reigned in the Punjab during the summer of 1946. Khizr found himself increasingly isolated as the Muslim members of his government bowed to intense Muslim League pressure and abandoned him. The Punjab, however, escaped the violence which broke out elsewhere in India following the collapse of the Cabinet Mission proposals. At a Governor's Conference held in the wake of the 'Great Calcutta Killing' of August 1946, Jenkins assured the Viceroy, Lord Wavell, that all the villages which he had recently toured remained 'as friendly as ever' and that the rural population appeared unconcerned with politics. The Governor of Bengal brought far less comforting news. He maintained that his police force had degenerated into an ill-disciplined rabble and that he could not 'carry Bengal for another 12 months' because 'after that there would be no Bengal to carry'.[5]

Wavell responded to the deteriorating situation in Bengal and other parts of India by drawing up his celebrated Breakdown Plan. This envisaged a phased withdrawal from India by 31 March 1948. It met with an icy reception in London. Wavell's repeated efforts to win support for it played a large part in his dismissal and the decision to send Mountbatten to India to replace him. Ironically, Mountbatten agreed to accept the post of Viceroy only if he was armed with a similar deadline for British departure. This was fixed as June 1948.

The announcement that the British would quit India by June 1948 had a disastrous effect on the situation in the Punjab. Khizr's immediate response was that it 'is the work of lunatics'.[6] He was well aware that the Muslim League would step up its pressure on him in order to hold office in the region before the British departed. The pretext for the League's launching a campaign of direct action against the coalition government was its banning, on 24 January 1947, the para-military Muslim League National Guards organization along with the Hindu Rashtriya Swayam Sevak Sangh (RSS). Muslim League leaders courted arrest by taking out illegal processions and there were strikes in Lahore and other leading towns. Khizr was forced to come to terms with the League by lifting his ban on processions and meetings, but by now thoroughly unnerved, he tendered his resignation on 3 March. Whilst Evan Jenkins held negotiations with the Nawab of Mamdot over the formation of a Muslim League Ministry, Tara Singh appeared outside the Legislative Assembly brandishing a sword and shouting 'Pakistan Murdabad'. Within it, the Panthic Party passed a resolution declaring that it would fight Pakistan to the last drop of its blood. The following day, an anti-Pakistan demonstration by Hindu and Sikh students in the Anarkali bazaar sparked off widespread rioting. During the course of the week, this spread from Lahore to Amritsar. Four thousand Muslim shops and businesses were burned down within the walled area of the city.[7] These sufferings were savagely revenged when the shock waves of the disturbances reached the outlying districts of West Punjab. In the Multan, Mianwali, Jhelum, Attock and Rawalpindi districts, the Muslims launched vicious attacks on the scattered Hindu and Sikh communities. Whole villages were put to the sword. Muslim raids on larger centres of Hindu and Sikh population such as Murree were organized and in some instances led by retired army officers.[8] The low morale of the predominantly Muslim police force and the unreliability of some of the officers and men of the Indian 7th Division which had been sent to the disturbed region, hampered British efforts to halt the attacks.[9] They claimed nearly 3,000 Hindu and Sikh victims. Another 40,000, mainly Sikhs, had to take refuge in hurriedly-established refugee camps. The riots left a legacy of hatred and distrust. Barricades went up in some of the Punjab's towns. Muslim villagers stockpiled weapons smuggled in from the Frontier, whilst the Sikhs acquired weapons from the neighbouring princely States. They harboured a burning desire for revenge and began to form raiding parties of armed horsemen.

The Muslim League made little effort to improve relations with the Sikhs. One prominent leader, during a tour of the riot-torn Attock district, even promised protection for those Muslims who had been arrested and threatened recriminations against the district officials who had attempted to maintain law and order.[10] The British instituted an enquiry into the worst cases of official negligence and threatened to relieve all those who were found guilty of their titles and Government grants of land.[11] This was an empty threat because of their imminent departure. All it did was to declare publicly that the system of political control in the countryside had finally collapsed.

The British had barely restored order in the north-west of Punjab before violence flared up between the Muslim Meos and Hindu Jats in the south-eastern Gurgaon district. More than fifty villages were destroyed in the disorders which swept over 1,000 square miles of countryside.[12] At first, only 365 troops could be spared to quell the trouble, with the result that the British lost control of several areas for a few days in May.[13] Communal violence was not unknown in this region. But two novel features disturbed British officials considerably. The first was the extensive use of firearms and even mortars, instead of the more usual clubs and knives. The second was the fact that the trouble was no longer confined to the towns in which the authorities could easily muster forces to quell them, but had spread to the vast rural tracts.

Mountbatten reacted to the serious situation which had developed within the vicinity of New Delhi by touring Gurgaon with Evan Jenkins early in June. By this date, Jinnah and Nehru were also becoming concerned about the drift towards civil war in the Punjab. Nehru complained to Mountbatten that not enough was being done to maintain law and order and suggested that the British impose martial law on Lahore. Beginning in April, a concerted Muslim effort had been made in Lahore to burn the Hindus and Sikhs out of the city. By mid-July, over 700 non-Muslim houses had been burned down.[14] The Hindus and Sikhs retaliated by waging urban guerilla warfare. Bombs were thrown into the crowded alleyways of the Muslim quarters. One such attack on 21 June claimed close to fifty victims.[15] As reports of such incidents steadily mounted, Jinnah also grew concerned about the havoc which was being wreaked in the future capital of West Punjab. He begged Mountbatten to be utterly ruthless in stamping out violence even if it meant shooting Muslims.[16] This was desperate advice indeed from the future ruler of Pakistan.

Both Jenkins and Mountbatten believed, however, that the use of troops would not prevent violence in Lahore. After 'a very difficult' cabinet meeting with his Indian colleagues, Mountbatten persuaded the Muslim League and Congress members to agree to an alternative policy of calling on the local community and political leaders to help restore order. They heartily disliked it since it implied that their supporters were at least partially responsible for the violence. Jenkins, in fact, possessed evidence that the arson attacks in Lahore were not spontaneous, but were the work of fire-raisers who were organized and paid for their activities. The Punjab Governor was of the opinion that the local leaders of both the Muslim League and the para-military Hindu force, the RSS movement, were abetting murder and arson, although the provincial and all-India leadership were not directly implicated.

An inter-communal political organization called the Punjab Security Council was established and met daily to review events and suggest steps for the maintenance of law and order. Muslim, Hindu and Sikh leaders issued statements in which they condemned communal violence. Areas of Lahore were sealed off by troops and thoroughly searched for weapons and explosives. Local protests about one such search in the northern Muslim suburb of Misri Shah lay behind the Punjab Muslim League President's sudden resignation from the Security Council on 3 July.[17] His action put paid to any lingering hopes of containing the escalating communal violence. British control of the province grew weaker and weaker during the spring and early summer of 1947. Jenkins had the disquieting experience of having his telephone tapped and confidential information passed on to the Muslim League politicians.[18] Muslim officials became increasingly reluctant to carry out any duties which might displease them. The landowners who had once been the linchpin of British control in the localities were also no longer reliable. Finally, the police, particularly in the major cities of Amritsar and Lahore, became unreliable when called upon to take action against members of their own community.[19]

At the end of the Second World War, British morale had been higher in the Punjab than in those provinces in which officials had been subject to constant Congress attacks.[20] But this slumped in the wake of the March 1947 disturbances. 'Every British official in the ICS and IP including myself', Jenkins wrote to Mountbatten in April 1947, 'would be very glad to leave (the Punjab) tomorrow. Six months ago the position was quite different, but we feel now that we are dealing with people who are out to destroy themselves and that in the absence of some reasonable agreement between them the average official will have to spend his life in a communal civil war. The Punjab is not now in a constitutional but in a revolutionary situation.'[21] In the light of such reports, Mountbatten pushed forward with his plan for Partition and a speedy British withdrawal from India.

Partition

Mountbatten realized shortly after his arrival in India that it would be impossible to resurrect the Cabinet Mission proposals. The only alternative was Partition. But Evan Jenkins and other British officials in the Punjab opposed this idea because they believed that it was impractical. Early in April 1947, Jenkins advised Giani Kartur Singh, the powerful Sikh Jat leader from Lyallpur, that the Sikhs should not rule out a local settlement with the Muslim League in order to maintain the Punjab's unity.[22] Jenkins also wrote to Mountbatten warning him of the difficulties facing Partition because of the conflicting territorial claims of the Muslims and the Sikhs, with the former, 'hoping to stretch their tentacles as far east as Ambala' and the latter demanding the Chenab as 'the western boundry'.[23] 'No leader seems yet to have considered', the Punjab Governor wrote, 'the implications and difficulties of partition'.[24] His warnings to Mountbatten lost much of their weight because he was unable to put forward a realistic alternative. His advocacy of a local settlement ignored the fact that the Punjab's fate was tied up with the wider issue of Pakistan. The Punjab Muslim League leaders were under express orders from the League Council to avoid any negotiations which might undermine the Pakistan demand. Jinnah was not prepared to risk this in order to secure peace in the Punjab. Its problems could only be solved by 'a political detente at the Centre'.[25] Mountbatten believed that in the circumstances the best policy was to secure the all-India leaderships' agreement to Partition. This was finally obtained on 3 June 1947. Nehru and Patel had accepted the proposals on behalf of the Congress because they did not want the Pakistan issue to delay independence any further. They certainly did not want to inherit a country in the throes of civil war. Moreover, Patel harboured doubts about the survival of Pakistan. Gandhi agreed with a heavy heart to the 'vivisection' of the subcontinent, as it repudiated his lifetime works and aims. He called partition a 'wooden loaf'. Jinnah was also unhappy. He had been claiming the whole of Bengal and the Punjab for Pakistan, but all he received from the 3rd June Plan was a 'moth-eaten' Pakistan. Both regions were to be partitioned, the exact lines of demarcation to be drawn up by a boundary commission under the chairmanship of the British legal expert, Sir Cyril Radcliffe. A Punjab Boundary Force was also to be established to maintain law and order during Partition.

At a press conference on 4 June, Mountbatten dramatically brought forward the date of the transfer of power to 15 August 1947. Leonard Mosley[26] and more recently Y. Krishan[27] have called this an ill-judged decision which contributed considerably to the communal massacres which accompanied partition. The course of events in the Punjab following the publication of the plan for the transfer of power in fact fully justified Mountbatten's decision to press on as quickly as possible.

The statement of 3 June was greeted in the province with sullen fatalism. It did nothing to improve communal relations. Within days of its acceptance on behalf of the Sikh community by Baldev Singh, local Sikh leaders were urging him to repudiate it, as it increasingly dawned on them that Partition could leave the Sikh's Canal Colony holdings and major shrines stranded in Pakistan. They resurrected the demand for Khalistan, despite its rejection by the Cabinet Mission. It seemed even less convincing than it had appeared earlier, because of their erstwhile enthusiasm for Partition.[28] Moreover, the Sikhs were so divided, and their demand so obviously a response to the Pakistan scheme, that the British did not take it seriously. The West Punjab Sikh leader, Kartar Singh, urged Baldev Singh to publish the letter in which he accepted the Plan of 3rd June and make it clear that although the Sikhs agreed to the principle of Partition, they would not accept a decision arrived at strictly on a population basis.[29] Kartar Singh emotionally pointed out to Jenkins that the Sikhs would be obliged to fight if the boundary award went against them.[30] Although he subsequently retracted this threat, it added substance to Muslim claims that the Sikhs were planning a major attack on the Muslim population of east Punjab.

'Ungraded' intelligence reports were in fact filtering through to the Punjab Governor linking the neighbouring Sikh princely States with plans for a terror campaign in East Punjab.[31] The almost total collapse of the provincial services and their infection with communalism made it imposible for Jenkins to assess the authenticity of such reports. Baldev Singh, however, was adamant that they were the fabrications of Muslim CID Officers who wanted to discredit the Sikhs.[32]

These unsubstantiated reports worried the British particularly because of the continued growth of para-military organizations within the province. By June 1947, the RSS had over 58,000 members, the Muslim League National Guards 39,000, and the Sikh Akali Fauj 8,000 members. Large Sikh *jathas* were also being formed in the countryside.[33] During the final days before the publication of the Radcliffe Boundary Award, Sikh raiding parties were launching heavy attacks on Muslim villages in the areas disputed by both communities.[34] The Muslims retaliated on a smaller and less well-organized scale.

Such violence before the issuing of the Boundary Award questions Krishan's view that the hasty decisions of the Boundary Commission were partly responsible for the 'failure to implement the partition agreement in peaceful circumstances'.[35] However long Radcliffe had taken over his deliberations, it would have been extremely difficult to satisfy the claims of both the Muslims and the Sikhs. The Partition massacres were not the result of Radcliffe's 'unjudicial procedure, but of the politically-inspired communal hatred which necessitated his labours. He produced his report on the assumption that the difficulties raised by Partition would be overcome by goodwill and co-operation. It was not his fault that this was unfounded.

Trust and goodwill were conspicuously lacking at all levels of Punjabi society as British rule drew to a close. Typical of the animosity were the proceedings of the Provincial Partition Committee set up in Lahore under Sir Evan Jenkins' chairmanship. Its task was to ensure a smooth transfer of power by determining the division of assets, personnel and liabilities before partition. In the Punjab Governor's words, it set about this task 'very slowly indeed', the Committee's meetings resembling 'a Peace Conference with a new war in sight'.[36]

The British divided and quit India on 15 August 1947. Whilst huge crowds in New Delhi joined in the Independence Day celebrations, less than 250 miles away in the Punjab, Muslims, Hindus and Sikhs were rounding on each other in frenzied fury. During the next two months the violence spread to every corner of the Punjab. Despite repeated appeals by the Sikh leaders, the *jathas* set about their bloody business in East Punjab. In Lahore and elsewhere in West Punjab, Muslims rounded on the remaining Hindu and Sikh inhabitants, putting paid to their leaders' smug assurance that the violence would cease as soon as the British had departed.[37]

The Sikhs were the aggressors in East Punjab. Their attacks resulted not from a plan to drive out the Muslims as some Pakistani writers have claimed but from a pent-up feeling or revenge. The publication of the Boundary Award added desperation to their anger, caused by the loss of the rich farmlands of Lyallpur[38] and of Nankana Saheb to Pakistan. Their victims were the Muslim villagers of Amritsar, Hoshiarpur and Jullundur and the Muslim refugees packing the trains from Delhi to Lahore. *Jathas* operating from the Sikh princely States preyed mercilessly[39] on the trains travelling west, until Tara Singh issued a statement[40] appealing for their operations to cease.

There were immediate calls for revenge when survivors reached Lahore.[41] The *Zemindar* published in verse the overwhelming Muslim feeling.

Strange are the ways of the justice of
    the government of the Hindus
The mosques have become desolate while
    the Gurdwaras stand intact
May the Almighty keep us from this
    time of trial!
Lo, our chests are exposed to their bullets,
The hour has arrived for the extinction
    of the new civilization
About to fall are the stams from the skies,
Destruction must befall the Sikhs and
    their allies![42]

Innocent Hindus and Sikhs still living in Lahore or travelling east became the targets for Muslim reprisals.[43]

When it was not standing by helplessly, the Punjab Boundary Force of Major-General Rees[44] actually added to the carnage.[45] The force, despite Mountbatten's assertions to the contrary,[46] was woefully inadequate to maintain order in the 37,500 square mile area[47] which it patrolled. The disintegration of Punjab's police force and the deliberate efforts to subvert its troops[48] made an already hopeless task impossible.

The violence spread throughout the region hitting even the backwater of Simla.[49] Mountbatten himself was personally affected by the tragedy as his Muslim treasurer and his wife were dragged from a train and killed while on the way down from Simla to New Delhi.[50] The juggernaut of communal violence rolled on out of control, until sheer exhaustion halted the communal killings early in October. The floodwaters of the swollen Beas and Ravi subsequently spilled over and washed away the blood which stained the land of the five rivers.

NOTES

1. Y. Krishan, 'Mountbatten and the Partition of India', *History*, 68, 222 (February 1983), pp. 22 and 38.
2. The Governor of the Punjab to the Viceroy, 16 April 1947.
3. The run-down of the intelligence gathering agencies had misled Glancy into seriously underestimating the Muslim League's strength.
4. Sir Evan Jenkins on his installation as Governor was appalled by the administrative deterioration. P. Moon (ed.), *Wavell: The Viceroy's Journal* (London, 1973), p. 319.
5. *Ibid.*, p. 370.
6. Punjab FR, 28 February 1947, L/P&J/250.
7. *Civil and Military Gazette*, 16 March 1947.
8. Jenkins to Wavell, 17 March 1947, R/3/1/176, IOR.
9. *Ibid.*
10. Jenkins to Mountbatten, 30 April 1947, N. Mansergh (ed.), *The Transfer of Power 1942–1947*, Vol. 10 (London, 1981), p. 506.
11. *Civil and Military Gazette*, 18 March 1947.
12. Punjab Governor to the Viceroy and the Governors of the U.P, Sind and N.W.F.P, 1 June 1947, R/3/1/90, IOR.
13. Punjab FR for the second half of May 1947, L/P&J/5/250, IOR.
14. Report by John Eustace, Deputy Commissioner, Lahore n.d., R/3/1/9, IOR.

15. Governor's Report, 25.6.47, R/3/1/91, IOR.
16. Mountbatten to Jenkins, 24 June 1947, R/3/1/91, IOR.
17. In public, the Nawab of Mamdot maintained that his action was prompted by two other issues: the refusal to include another Muslim on the Security Council and the communal composition of the Special Police. Jenkins to Mountbatten, 3 July 1947, R/3/1/91, IOR.
18. Punjab FR, 14 March 1947, L/P&J/5/250, IOR.
19. Punjab FR, 13 August 1947, L/P&J/2/250, IOR.
20. See e.g., S. Epstein, 'District Officers in Decline: the erosion of British control in the Bombay Countryside 1919–1947', *Modern Asian Studies*, 16, 3 (1982), p. 517.
21. Note by Sir Evan Jenkins, 16 April 1947, *ibid.*, p. 282.
22. Note by Jenkins, 10 April 1947, *ibid.*, (9) above, p. 185.
23. Jenkins to Mountbatten, 10 July 1947, R/3/1/176, IOR.
24. Jenkins to Mountbatten, 30 April 1947, *ibid.*, (9) above, p. 506.
25. Secretary of State to the Viceroy, 14 March 1947, R/3/1/89, IOR.
26. L. Mosley, *The Last Days of the British Raj* (London, 1961), p. 247.
27. Y. Krishan, 'Mountbatten and the Partition of India', *History*, 68, 222 (February 1983).
28. Such West Punjab Sikh leaders as Sampuran Singh, Kartar Singh Dewana and Buta Singh, had not, it is true, espoused Partition as enthusiastically as Tara Singh and Baldev Singh.
29. Jenkins to Mountbatten, 10 July 1947, Report of an interview with Giani Kartar Singh, R/3/1/176, IOR.
30. *Ibid.*, (28) above.
31. Abott to Brockman, n.d., Ungraded Intelligence Report, R/3/1/145, IOR.
32. Statement of Baldev Singh on Present Situation, n.d., R/3/1/174, IOR.
33. Punjab FR for the second half of May 1947, L/P&J/5/250, IOR.
34. Punjab FR, 30 July 1947 and 13 August 1947, L/P&J/5/250, IOR.
35. *Ibid.*, (27) above, p. 38.
36. Note by Jenkins, 11 July 1947, R/3/1/176, IOR.
37. Jenkins to Mountbatten, 13 August 1947, R/3/1/91, IOR.
38. On 13 September a convoy of 40,000 Sikhs left the Lyallpur Canal Colony taking with them all they could load on to bullock carts. *Civil and Military Gazette*, 14 September 1947.
39. An attack on a train just outside Khalsa College, Amritsar, resulted in the massacre for example of 1,200 Muslims. *Civil and Military Gazette*, 19 September 1947.
40. Major Short, a long-time liaison officer between the British and the Sikhs, had been instrumental in Tara Singh making this statement.
41. Young men appeared in the streets of Lahore wearing small red cloth badges on which was emblazoned the single word, 'revenge'. *Shabaz* (Lahore), 19 September 1947, R/3/1/174, IOR.

42. *Zemindar*, 13 September 1947, R/3/1/174, IOR.
43. There were 3,000 casualties after one such attack on Hindu and Sikh refugees fleeing from Sialkot.
44. Attached to Rees as advisors were, from the Indian side, Brigadier Dhigambir Singh and from Pakistan Brigadier Mohammad Ayub Khan (later President of Pakistan). No British troops were used.
45. For details see, M. K. Sinha, Report of the Deputy Director Intelligence Bureau n.d., R/3/1/173, IOR.
46. Lord Mountbatten's 'Conclusions' appended to his 'Report on the Last Viceroyalty', submitted to His Majesty's Government in September 1948. H. V. Hodson, *The Great Divide* (London, 1969), p. 548 & ff.
47. This included seventeen towns, nearly 17,000 villages and 14.5 million population in the twelve districts of Central Punjab.
48. C. Auchinleck, Note on the Situation in the Punjab Boundary Force Area for the Joint Defence Council. 15 August 1947, R/3/1/171, IOR.
49. Memorandum Government of India, Ministry of Home Affairs, 10 September 1947, R/3/1/171, IOR.
50. Thereafter, Mountbatten decided to transport his Muslim staff in his own York Aircraft from Ambala to Delhi. Viceroy to the Minister of Defence, 2 September 1947, R/3/1/172, IOR.

Conclusion

British rule exerted a profound impact on all areas of Punjab's life. Economically, it transformed the Punjab from a poor region into the richest farming area in India; religiously, it inadvertently quickened the processes of revivalism which had begun with the collapse of Mughal rule; socially, it conservatively sustained the power of the large landowners; politically, it encouraged cross-communal cooperation amongst the landowning groups. Finally, and this was important for all the other areas of change, it made the Punjab the major centre of recruitment for the Indian Army. The loyalty of its rural population thus became of crucial importance to imperial interests.

The informal political alliances which had existed between the British and the landowners since their annexation of the region in 1849 became institutionalized in 1923 with the creation of the Unionist Party. During the years 1923–39, it dominated provincial politics and was an important stabilizing influence, helping to maintain social control in the countryside and reduce communal tension. The Muslim League's eventual eclipse of the Unionist Party has been frequently explained in terms of the Two-Nation Theory. This study has revealed it to be a myth.

Punjabi Muslims did not flock to the Muslim League's banner from 1944 onwards either because of a sense of separatism or because it offered them Pakistan. They entered its ranks because of local factional rivalries and the changes brought about by the Second World War. The strains of the war effort forced the Government of India to desert its allies in the Punjab. The Unionist Party's political interests were sacrificed to the requirements of raising army recruits and exporting foodgrains from the province. The British thus destroyed the political system which they had so carefully built up in their earlier years in Punjab. At the same time, the war shifted the focus of politics away from the provincial to the national level. The Muslim League became a crucial counterbalance to the non-cooperating Congress. The Unionist Party lost much of its influence and was pushed into the background. Its members decided that the best method of maintaining their local power in the changed national political context was to seek accommodation with the Muslim League.[1] A similar process occurred in the other 'Pakistan' regions. In Bengal, too, many members of the Krishak Praja Party defected to the Muslim League after Jinnah's deadlocking of the July 1945 Simla Conference.

Jinnah allowed his former opponents to enter the Muslim League, as he needed their influence in mobilizing support for Pakistan. It meant disappointing loyal activists who had struggled for years against the odds by passing them over for office and election tickets in favour of their erstwhile enemies. On the whole, they accepted this with good grace because of their commitment to the League's ideals. Jinnah's action was vindicated by the Muslim League's sweeping victories in the 1946 elections and the 1947 referendum on Pakistan in the North-West Frontier Province, though its position on the eve of independence was far weaker in the 'Pakistan' regions than the Two-Nation Theory trumpeted. Its predominant position rested not on a firm ideological or organizational footing,[2] but on the ephemeral loyalty of the landowners whose local allegiances had been temporarily subordinated to the crisis of the all-India political struggle. Herein lay the seeds of the Muslim League's decline and disintegration during the 1950s which so severely weakened the State it had helped to form.

In addition to shedding light on the Two-Nation Theory, this study suggests why collaboration succeeded or failed as the basis of colonial rule. Colonial governments gained the support of influential local allies by offering them access to the benefits of the wider world. The more commercial, capital and technological inputs they fed in, the more local allies they were able to acquire. The British system of rule worked so well in the Punjab precisely because so much effort was expended in its agricultural development. The British not only launched the massive Canal Colony development, but directed all their administrative, economic and constitutional policies in favour of the rural population. Until the outbreak of the Second World War, there was never any danger that they would lose rural support by not having enough patronage to go round. They were not in so fortunate a position elsewhere in India. In Madras, the Justice Party played a similar role to the Unionists. Unfortunately it could only call on patronage in local government to secure political support. By 1937, this had practically dried up, with the result that it sufferred a major defeat in the Madras provincial elections.[3]

An imperial regime had not only to ensure that it possessed sufficient patronage to draw local allies to its side, but that it did not undermine their traditional authority by forcing them to make one-sided 'bargains' with their clients. The Unionists lost their authority during the Second World War because they were forced to make demands on the villagers which far exceeded the benefits they were able to win for them from the colonial administration.

Finally, a colonial regime had to be flexible in order to secure its control by gaining the support of powerful native allies. Its officials had to be 'up to their eyes in the politics of their so-called subjects'.[4] They had to be continually casting around for new allies and drawing them to their side. Only in this way was a colonial administration able to preserve its freedom of action. If it associated itself too closely with the fortunes of one particular groups of allies, it endangered the whole basis of its rule. This was the situation which occurred in the Punjab in 1946 when the British attempted to restore the defeated Unionist Party to office. It enabled the Muslim League to form a united front of non-collaboration against them, bringing to an end over ninety years of Punjabi accommodation with British rule.

NOTES

1. This is not to argue that political opportunism was the sole factor in the 'Pakistan' area regional elites' late entry into the Muslim League. Their sense of Muslim community and brotherhood was strengthened by reports of the sufferings of the Muslim minorities living in such areas as Bombay and Bihar. The Sind Muslim League's 'Bihar Day' on 15 November 1946 brought all business to a halt in a region where the League had previously been weak. The North-West Frontier League sent medical missions to Bihar which gave aid and reported back on the Hindu violence. Members returned to Peshawar clutching blood-stained Muslim clothing, torn pages from the Quran and even in one case the skull of a Muslim victim. One leading historian of the region has explained the massive swing in public opinion away from the Frontier Congress in 1946–7 largely in terms of the feeling of solidarity with the victims of Bihar.
2. The Sind Muslim League had just 3,500 members. A Committee of Action Enquiry Report into the N.W.F.P League in 1944 reported to Jinnah that there was widespread corruption, financial weaknesses and a ramshackle organization confined to those areas inhabited by the minority non-Pathan Muslim population. In Sind, the Muslim League was split into a baloch 'mir' and Sindhi 'syed' grouping. Little evidence here for the Two-Nation Theory.
3. D. Washbrook, 'Country Politics: Madras 1880 to 1930', *Modern Asian Studies* 7 (1973), p. 525.
4. R. Robinson, 'Non-European Foundations of European Imperialism: Sketch for a Theory of Collaboration' in R. Owen & B. Sutcliffe (eds.), *Studies in the Theory of Imperialism* (London, 1978), p. 135.

Glossary

Ahl-i-hadith	Reformist Muslim sect wishing to return to the authority of the Prophetic tradition.
Ahmadis	Followers of the heterodox nineteenth century Muslim religious leader in the Pujab, Mirza Ghulam Ahmad, who claimed to be the awaited Mahdi.
Ahrar	'The Free'. Islamic Party founded in the Punjab in 1931 by Mazhar Ali Azhar and Maulana Shah Bukhari.
Alim	Singular to *ulema*, a person trained in Islamic religious sciences.
Anjuman	Assembly, council, committee, meeting of Muslims. The term used similarly for Hindus and Sikhs was Sabha.
Bania	Hindu trading caste, the term was often used pejoratively to mean moneylender.
Baraka	Charismatic power believed to flow from Sufi Saints to their disciples. This power could also be invested in their tombs and relics.
Biradari	Literally 'brotherhood', used to refer to patrilineal kinship groups.
Charpoy	A wooden bed, the frame of which was covered by netted string.
Crore	100 lakhs or ten million.

Durbar	The court or levee of a ruler.
Dargah	Tomb, shrine of a Sufi Saint.
Gaddi	Literally seat or chair, usually used in the context of possession of a religious or political office.
Hartal	Strike, usually the closing of shops as a political protest.
Izzat	Prestige, honour, reputation.
Jagir	An assignment of land revenue.
Khanqah	Hospice, alms-house of the early Sufi Saints.
Kharif	The autumn harvest.
Khatri	Hindu and Sikh commercial caste.
Kisan	Landless agricultural labourer.
Lakh	One hundred thousand.
Lambardar	Village headman.
Madrassa	Islamic Secondary School or College.
Murid	Disciple of a Pir.
Panchayat	Ruling council, especially for settling village disputes.
Patwari	Village Official, at the lowest rung of the British Revenue administration.
Pir	Persian word for elder. A term used for a Sufi spiritual guide.
Piri-Mureedi	The relationship of loyalty and obedience between a Pir and his disciple.
Rais	An important or honourable man.
Sajjada-Nashin	Literally one who sits on the prayer carpet; the custodian of a Sufi shrine.
Settlement	The periodic revision of British land revenue assessments.
Sharia	The divinely revealed Muslim law.
Shuddhi	Purification. Movement launched in the Punjab by the Arya Samaj to reconvert apostates to Hinduism.
Silsilah	Literally chain. Members of a Sufi Order who are mystically linked to their Pir and his spiritual descendants.

Square	A unit of land in the Canal Colonies of 25 acres.
Sufi	Muslim mystic. The word derives from the coarse woollen cloth worn by the early Muslim mystics.
Taluqdar	Name given in the U.P to a superior zamindar who engaged with the State to collect the revenue from his own and other zamindari estates. After the Mutiny, Oudh *taluqdars* were given proprietary rights over the area from which they had collected revenue.
Tehsildar	Officer in charge of a revenue sub-division of a district.
Zamindar	Term used loosely in the Punjab to refer to both large and small landholders.

Sources and Bibliography

Private Papers

INDIA OFFICE LIBRARY, LONDON (IOL)

Biggs-Davidson Papers Mss. Eur. D. 844.
Hailey Papers Mss. Eur. E. 220.
Mian Fazl-i-Husain Papers Mss. Eur. E. 352.
Linlithgow Papers Mss. Eur. F. 125.

KARACHI

Shamsul Hasan Papers. This collection contains the correspondence of the All-India Muslim League and the Provincial Leagues with its President Mohammad Ali Jinnah during the years when Syed Shamsul Hasan was Honorary Secretary. The collection is in the possession of his son Khalid Shamsul Hasan who kindly allowed me to consult the Punjab files for the years 1937–1946.

NATIONAL ARCHIVES OF PAKISTAN, ISLAMABAD (NAP)

Quaid-e-Azam Papers. Microfilm copy.

Unpublished Government Records

The general headings under which government files and proceedings were kept are listed below. Specific references will be found in the text.

INDIA OFFICE RECORDS (IOR)

Economic and Overseas Department Files, Financial Department Collections.

Information Department Files; Political and Judicial Department Files.

Governors' Report for Punjab, Bengal, North West Frontier Province and Ajmer.

Transfer of Power Papers; Punjab Revenue and Agricultural Proceedings.

War Staff Department.

NATIONAL ARCHIVES OF INDIA (NAI)

Records of the Home Department of the Government of India; Home Political (Pol.) Home Judicial. Reforms Office of the Government of India.

RECORDS, PUBLISHED AND UNPUBLISHED OF POLITICAL AND STUDENT ORGANIZATIONS

THE MUSLIM LEAGUE

Pirzada, Syed Sharifuddin (ed.), *Foundations of Pakistan: All India Muslim League Documents: 1906–1947*, 2 vols., (Karachi, 1970).

The following Muslim League Papers are all held in the Freedom Movement Archives (FMA) of Karachi University:

All-India Muslim League Working Committee Meetings 1932, 1933 & 1938; 1941; 1943–47. All-India Muslim League Council Meetings 1939 and 1940.

Conference of the Presidents and Secretaries of the Provincial Muslim Leagues, October 1941.

Punjab Provincial Muslim League 1938–9; 1940; 1943–44.

MUSLIM STUDENTS FEDERATION

The following records were consulted in the Freedom Movement Archives:

Punjab Muslim Students Federation (1937–46). Muslim University Union Aligarh and Muslim University Muslim League (1944–45).

INTERVIEWS

The following three interviews yielded important information:

10 April 1978, Lahore, Abu Saeed Enver (Propaganda Secretary of the Punjab Muslim League in 1945–46).

28 March 1978, Islamabad, Shaukhat Hayat.

On several occasions in April 1978, Lahore, with Zia-ul-Islam (President of the Punjab Muslim Students Federation from 1944 onwards).

NEWSPAPERS

The years given with each newspapers mark the period within which references to it have been made.

Civil and Military Gazette (Lahore, 1936–47). British Library Newspaper Section.

Dawn (Delhi, 1945–48), Microfilm, Seeley Library, Cambridge.

Eastern Times (Lahore, 1943–46), Punjab Public Library, Lahore and the Library of Congress Newspaper Section, Washington D.C.

Hindustan Times (Delhi, 1937 and 1944), microfilm, Centre of South Asian Studies, Cambridge.

Inqilab (Lahore, 1945), Research Society of Pakistan, Lahore.

Khyber Mail (Peshawar, 1946), Office of the Khyber Mail, Peshawar.

Leader (Allahabad, 1937), India Office Library, Newspaper Section.

Nawa-e-Waqt (Lahore, 1945–46), Office of Nawa-e-Waqt, Lahore.

Pioneer (Lucknow, 1937), India Office Library, Newspaper Section.

Star of India (Calcutta, 1945–46), British Library, Newspaper Section.

Tribune (Ambala, 1936–1944), microfilm, Centre of South Asian Studies, Cambridge, and microfilm, Nehru Memorial Museum and Library, New Delhi.

Official Publications

The frequency of publication is stated, as well as the period within which references have been made to the publication.

Board of Economic Inquiry, Punjab. *Annual Review of Economic Conditions in the Punjab 1945–6* (Lahore, 1946).

Census Reports and Tables. Decennial series. Punjab Reports 1881–1941.

District Gazetteers of the Punjab published in the years stated and for the following districts: Ferozepore (1916); Rawalpindi (1895); Attock (1909); Jhang (1930); Shahpur (1918); Montgomery (1933); Rohtak (1884); Muzaffargarh (1884); Dera Ghazi Khan (1898); Gurgaon (1911); Ambala (1925); Jullundur (1904); Amritsar (1914); Karnal (1919); Amritsar (1894).

Annual Report of Punjab Canal Colonies (1942).

Punjab Legislature Assembly Debates (1937, 1939 and 1940).

Punjab Press Abstract. Annual Series (1923).

Punjab Settlement Reports published in the years stated and for the following district:
Gujrat (1916); Rawalpindi (1909); Rohtak (1911); Gurgaon (1944); Attock (1928); Jhang (1907); Jhelum (1902); Ferozepore (1915); Amritsar (1914); Lower Bari Doab Canal Colony (1935); Chenab Canal Colony (1915).

Report of the Punjab Provincial Banking Enqiury Committee (1942).

Report on the Administration of Estates under the Charge of the Punjab Court of Wards. Annual Series (1893, 1910, 1911, 1921 & 1928).

Published Works

Only those works cited in the notes to the text are listed below.

Afzal, M. R., *Malik Barkat Ali: His Life and Writings* (Lahore, 1969).

Aggarwal, P. C., 'The Meos of Rajasthan and Haryana' in I. Ahmad (ed.), *Caste and Social Stratification among Muslims* (Delhi, 1973).

Agnihotri, H. L. and Malik., S. N. *A Profile in Courage: A Biography of Chaudhri Chhotu Ram* (New Delhi, 1978).

Ahmad, I. (ed.), *Caste and Social Stratification among Muslims* Delhi, (1973).

Ahmad, Jamal-ud-Din, *Speeches and Writings of Mr Jinnah*, 2 vols. (Lahore, 1968).

Ahmad, S., 'Peasant Classes in Pakistan' in K. Gough and P. Sharma (eds.), *Imperialism and Revolution in South Asia* (New York, 1973).

Ahmad, W. (ed.), *Letters of Mian Fazl-i-Husain* (Lahore, 1976).

Ahluwalia, M. S., 'The Naqshbandis of Sirhind' in F. Singh (ed.), *Sirhind through the Ages* (Punjab University, 1972).

Ali, I., *Punjab Politics in the Decade before Partition* (Lahore, 1975).

Arberry, A. J., *The Koran Interpreted* (New York, 1955).

Barrier, N. G., *The Punjab Alienation of Land Bill of 1900* (Duke University, 1966).

Begg, W. D., *The Big Five of India in Sufism* (Ajmer, 1972).

Bhattacharya, R. K., 'The Concept of Ideology and Caste among Muslims of Rural West Bengal' in I. Ahmad (ed.), *Caste and Social Stratification among Muslims* (Delhi, 1973).

Bhatty, Z., 'Status and Power in a Muslim Dominated Village of Uttar Pradesh' in I. Ahmad (ed.), *Caste and Social Stratification among Muslims* (Delhi, 1973).

Burki, S. J., *Pakistan under Bhutto 1971–1977 (London, 1980).*

Chatterji, G. C., *The Punjab Past and Present* (Lahore, 1939).

Chopra, G. L., *Chiefs and Families of Note in the Punjab*, 2 vols. (Lahore, 1940).

Darling, M., *Rusticus Loquitor* (Lahore, 1929).

Eaton, R. M., *Sufis of Bijapur 1300–1700: Social Roles of Sufis in Medieval India* (Princeton, 1978).

Eglar, Z. S., *A Punjabi Village in Pakistan* (London, 1964).

Franda, M., *West Bengal and the Federalizing Process in India* (New Jersey, 1968).

Frankel, F. R., *India's Green Revolution: Economic Gains and Political Costs* (Princeton, 1971).

Gellner, E., *Saints of the Atlas* (London, 1969).

Gibb, H.A.R., 'An Interpretation of Muslim History', *Muslim World* 45, 11 (1955).

Gilmartin, D., 'Religious Leadership and the Pakistan Movement in the Punjab', *Modern Asian Studies.*, Vol. 13, No. 3 (1979).

Gopal, M., *Sir Chhotu Ram: A Political Biography* (New Delhi, 1977).

Gough, K. and Sharma, P., *Imperialism and Revolution in South Asia* (New York, 1973).

Haig, W. (ed.), *The Cambridge History of India*, Vol. 3, Turks and Afghans (Cambridge, 1928).

Hardy, P., *The Muslims of British India* (Cambridge, 1972).

Heeger, G. A., 'The Growth of the Congress Movement in the Punjab 1920–1949', *Journal of Asian Studies*, 32, 1 (1972).

Hodson, H. V., *The Great Divide* (London, 1969).

Husain, A., *Mian Fazl-i-Husain: A Political Biography* (London, 1946).

Husain, M. A., 'Agricutlure in the Punjab' in G. C. Chatterji, *The Punjab Past and Present* (Lahore, 1939).

Ikram, S. M., *Modern Muslim India and the Birth of Pakistan* (Lahore, 1977).

Isphani, M.A.H., *Quaid-e-Azam Jinnah as I Knew Him* (Karachi, 1966).

Jafri, S.Q.H. and Bukhari, S.A. (eds.), *Quaid-i-Asam's Correspondence with Punjab Muslim Leaders* (Lahore, 1977).

Jones, K. W., *Arya Dharm. Hindu Consciousness in 19th Century Punjab* (Berkeley, 1976).

Kessler, C. S., 'Islam, Society and Political Behaviour: Some Comparative Implications of the Malay Case', *British Journal of Sociology*, Vol. 23 (1972).

Khaliquzzaman, C., *Pathway to Pakistan* (Lahore, 1961).

Khan, Muin-ud-Din Ahmad, *History of the Fara'idi Move-*

ment in Bengal 1818–1906 (Karachi, 1965).
Latifi, A., *The Industrial Punjab* (London, 1911).
Lavan, S., *The Ahmadiyah Movement* (Delhi, 1974).
Low, D. A. (ed.), *Soundings in Modern South Asian History* (London, 1968).
Magsi, M.A.K., *Development of Local Self-Government in the Punjab 1919–32* (Lahore, 1973).
Malhotra, S. L., *Gandhi: Experiment with Communal Politics* (Chandigarh, 1975).
Mansergh, N. (ed.)., *The Transfer of Power 1942–1947*, Vols. 1, 4, 5 and 6 (London, 1970, 1973, 1974 and 1976).
Mehta, A. and Patwardhan, A., *The Communal Triangle in India* (Allahabad, 1941).
Milne, D., *A Brief Outline of the Agricultural Conditions in the Punjab* (Lahore, 1927).
Milson, M. (trans.), *Kitab Adab al-Muridin of Abu al-Najib al-Suhrawardi: A Sufi Rule for Novices* (Cambridge Mss., 1976).
Musgrave, P. J., 'Landlords and Lords of the Land: Estate management and social control in Uttar Pradesh 1860–1920', *Modern Asian Studies*, Vol. 3 (1972).
Narendranath, R., 'The Punjab Agrarian Laws and their Economic and Constitutional Bearings', *Modern Review*, 65 (1939).
Nizami, K. A., *The Life and Times of Shaikh Farid-U'd-Din Ganj-i-Shakar* (Aligarh, 1955).
Pemble, J., *The Raj, the Indian Mutiny and the Kingdom of Oudh* (Hassocks, 1977).
Philips, C. H. and Wainwright, M. D. (eds.), *The Partition of India* (London, 1970).
Qasimi, J., *Baba Fariduddin Masud Ganj-i-Shakar* (Lahore, 1971).
Reeves, P. D., 'Landlords and Party Politics in the UP 1934–7' in D. A. Low, *Soundings in Modern South Asian History* (London, 1968).
Rizvi, G., *Linlithgow and India* (London, 1978).
Robinson, F., *Separatism among Indian Muslims: The Politics*

of the United Province's Muslims 1860–1923 (Cambridge, 1974).

Rothermund, D. (ed.), *Islam in South Asia* (Wiesbaden, 1975).

Saini, B. S., *The Social and Economic History of the Punjab 1901–1939* (Delhi, 1975).

Salim, M., 'Shaykh Baba Al-Din Zakariya of Multan', *Journal of the Pakistan History Society*, XVII, 1 (1969).

Sayeed, K. B., *Pakistan: The Formative Phase 1875–1948* (London, 1968).

Scott, J. C., 'The Erosion of the Patron-Client Bond and Social Change in Rural South East Asia', *Journal of Asian Studies*, 32, 1 (1972).

Sen, S., *Muslim Politics in Bengal, 1937–1947* (New Delhi, 1976).

Siddiqi, M.D.A., 'Caste among the Muslims of Calcutta' in I. Ahmad (ed.), *Caste and Social Stratification among Muslims* (Delhi, 1973).

Singh, B. N., 'Punjab Canals' in G. C. Chatterji (ed.), *The Punjab Past and Present* (Lahore, 1939).

Trevaskis, H. K., *The Land of the Five Rivers* (Oxford, 1928).

Ullah, A., *The Cooperative Movement in the Punjab* (London, 1937).

Verma, D., 'Provincial Autonomy in the Punjab April 1937–October 1939', *Indian Journal of Political Science*, Vol. 1 (1939).

Washbrook, D., 'Country Politics: Madras 1880–1930', *Modern Asian Studies*, 7, 3 (1973).

Woodruff, P., *The Men Who Ruled India*, Vol. 2, *The Guardians* (London, 1971).

Zaheer, S., *Light on the League-Unionist Conflict* (Bombay, 1944).

Index